D1520016

# CONSUMING ANXIETIES

# CONSUMING ANXIETIES

*Consumer Protest, Gender, and*
*British Slavery, 1713–1833*

CHARLOTTE SUSSMAN

STANFORD UNIVERSITY PRESS

STANFORD, CALIFORNIA

2000

Stanford University Press
Stanford, California
© 2000 by the Board of Trustees of the
Leland Stanford Junior University

Printed in the United States of America

Library of Congress Cataloging-in-Publication Data

Sussman, Charlotte.
    Consuming anxieties : consumer protest, gender, and British slavery,
1713–1833/Charlotte Sussman.
        p.   cm.
    Includes bibliographical references and index.
    ISBN 0-8047-3103-9 (cloth : alk. paper)
        1. Consumption (Economics)—Great Britain—History. 2. Women abolitionists—
Great Britain—History. 3. Slavery—Great Britain—History. 4. Protest movements—
Great Britain—History.    I. Title.

HC260.C6 S873  2000
322.4'4'094109033—dc21                                                    00-022872

♾ This book is printed on acid-free, archival quality paper.
Original printing 2000
Last figure below indicates year of this printing:
09   08   07   06   05   04   03   02   01   00

Designed and typeset by Robert C. Ehle in 10/12.5 Electra,  with ITC Bodoni Display

# Acknowledgments

A great number of people have contributed generously to the writing of this book. My deepest debt of gratitude is to Laura Brown, whose intellectual example and support helped me see the project through from beginning to much-delayed end. I was lucky enough to take a graduate seminar with Donna Landry while she was a fellow at the Society for the Humanities at Cornell, and since then I have enjoyed the benefit of her critical acumen and invaluable advice. The guidance of Mary Jacobus and Harry Shaw was indispensable during the initial stages of the project.

Many friends and colleagues have read and commented on various sections of the manuscript. My heartfelt thanks to Srinivas Aravamudan, Mary Chapman, Laura Mandell, and Lisa Moore for helping me see the parameters and implications of the project anew, not once, but many times. It has been my good fortune to have so many generous and intellectually challenging colleagues at the University of Colorado, and I am grateful to Richard Halpern, John Stevenson, and Sue Zemka for their incisive comments on early and late drafts. The attention of Catherine Gallagher and the editorial board of *Representations* to an earlier version of Chapter 4 improved it immensely. I am grateful for permission to reprint the chapter here, as well as for permission to reprint Chapter 3, an earlier version of which appeared in *ELH*. Helen Tartar, Kristina Straub, and the anonymous readers for Stanford University Press pointed out to me the sometimes submerged outlines and endpoints of the project. Also, at Stanford University Press, I am grateful for the help of Mary Severance and Ruth Barzel. In the long process of research and writing, I have received all kinds of help, from Henry Abelove, Katherine Eggert, Markman Ellis, Margaret Ferguson,

Teresa Feroli, Rhonda Garelick, Jane Garrity, Charlotte Grant, Karen Jacobs, Sarah Peterson Pittock, Elizabeth Robertson, Jeffrey Robinson, David Simpson, Elizabeth White, and many others.

Research for this book was supported by fellowships from Cornell University and the University of Colorado, Boulder. I am grateful for all the assistance I received from librarians at Cornell, the Friends House Library in London, the John Rylands Library, and the Bristol University Library. I appreciate the generosity of Janet Sorensen and Marjorie Stone in sharing their unpublished work with me.

My grandmother, Lillian Sussman, always followed the progress of this book closely; I am deeply sorry she did not live to see it completed. Finally, my thanks to my family—Herbert, Elisabeth, and Lucas Sussman—for continually demonstrating the viability and pleasure of intellectual inquiry, and to Jeremy Green, without whose patience, generosity, and intelligence I would be lost.

C. S.

# Contents

# CONSUMING ANXIETIES

# Introduction

Look out poor Boston make a stand
Dont suffer any tea to land
For if it once gets footing here
Then farewell Liberty most dear.

—Alfred F. Young, "The Women of Boston:
'Persons of Consequence' in the Making of
the American Revolution, 1765–76"

The historical context of this passage is probably quite familiar; the rhyme belongs to the agitation against British imports that eventually led to one of the most dramatic consumer actions of the eighteenth century—the Boston Tea Party. This kind of anti-colonial strategy has a number of more recent counterparts: for instance, the refusal of Irish tenants to pay rent to Charles Cunningham Boycott—the event that gave the tactic its name—during the days of the Land League in the 1890s.[1] Perhaps even better known is the Gandhi-led Swadeshi movement, which used home industry to undermine British colonial power in India. And there are many more examples; indeed, boycotts are so commonplace these days, one hardly notices them. Yet, it seems important to ask why this mode of political protest has proved so influential over the past two hundred years, and, furthermore, why it might have been particularly useful in anti-colonial struggles. While the origins of both consumer culture and European colonialism are starting to be very well documented, the connections between them have barely begun to be explored.

This book examines the history of consumer protests against colonialism from 1713 to 1833—from the Treaty of Utrecht to the abolition of slavery in the British Caribbean. It argues that recognizing the impact of consumerism on perceptions of the colonial periphery during this period reveals the crucial role of commodity fetishism in colonialist ideology; conversely, acknowledging the effects of colonial and mercantile expansion on domestic consumer practices explains some of the contemporaneous anxiety surrounding colonial commodities. The feminizing of certain aspects of consumerism during the eighteenth century is an important, though frequently overlooked, aspect of the history of consumerist critiques of colonialism, and attention to gender illuminates the ways in which colonialism permeated not only the public sphere of politics and trade, but also the seemingly private realms of domesticity and sentiment. The book falls roughly into two parts. The first three chapters deal with the history of consumer protests against colonialism and imperialism, including uses of the tactic in Ireland early in the eighteenth century, and the midcentury anxiety over colonial products in English domestic spaces. The last three chapters concentrate on the role of commodity culture and consumer protest in the British debates over Caribbean slavery. Although its roots in earlier anti-colonial protests are not always recognized, antislavery activists inherited and expertly manipulated a set of tactics developed in previous contests.

Over the course of this period, however, consumerist critiques of colonialism generated not only material strategies, but also particular discursive constructions.[2] Indeed, in many cases, the symbolic manifestations of abstention movements in powerful rhetoric and resonant images were more culturally important than their immediate political effects. Furthermore, discussions of the moral impact of certain consumer practices in relation to colonial policy provided a framework in which questions about who should lay claim to sociopolitical agency could be negotiated. Many of these debates were carried out in print in what Jurgen Habermas has called the "public sphere." In these conflicts, matters once considered "private"—including the private business dealings of slave traders, plantation owners, and housewives—and those considered "political"—such as government policies on trade, navigation, and war—were transformed into public issues, about which any rational citizen might have an opinion.[3] During most of the eighteenth century, moreover, the division between political and literary material in the public sphere was quite fluid; thus, as is clear from the poem above, questions about the legitimacy of certain kinds of consumerism entered public discussion not divorced from the literary, but on a continuum with it. The juxtaposition of material we now consider to be "literary" and "political" throughout this book should make visible the continuities between the rhetoric and imagery found in eighteenth-century literature and in the language of consumer protest. In order to understand the centrality and power of these figures, it is necessary to bring the tools of literary analysis to bear on them, just as it is crucial to bring the methodologies of social history to bear on the same tropes, the better to understand the reasons for their repetition. Lynn Hunt has written that "the best interdisciplinary work produces its effects back in the various disciplines it crosses, rather than creating an altogether new and different interstitial space (such as cultural studies sometimes seems to imply)."[4] One thing revealed by moving outside the traditional subject matter of eighteenth-century literary studies is the social and political power granted to literature by other cultural fields during this era.

Rarely has a political movement been so conscious of the cultural power of literary methods and texts as the antislavery movement was. By this I mean not only that it consistently relied on rhetorical strategies borrowed from literary discourse, both sentimental and satirical, but also that activists counted on the motivational power of the stories and poems they distributed to awaken abolitionist energy. This faith in the power of rhetoric was evident from the beginning of the movement, nowhere more so than in the letter Ignatius Sancho, a former slave living in London, wrote to Lawrence Sterne in 1766:

> I think Sir, you will forgive, perhaps applaud me for zealously intreating you to give half an hours attention to slavery (as it is at this day undergone in the West Indies; that subject handled in your own manner, would ease the Yoke of many, perhaps occasion a reformation throughout our Islands—But should only *one* be the better for it—gracious God! what a feast! very sure I am, that Yorick is an epicurean in Charity—universally read & universally admired—you could not fail.[5]

Sterne responded to this appeal in *Tristram Shandy*, though perhaps not as overtly as Sancho might have hoped. Still, the exchange illuminates the regard with which abolitionists viewed the power of printed appeals, and suggests one of the reasons for that regard. The backbone of the antislavery movement was made up not of those fighting for governmental representation but of those by and large excluded from conventional political processes—women, religious dissenters, and slaves themselves. For these groups, the new cultural importance attached to print during the eighteenth century provided a welcome source of power and legitimacy for their social agenda. Yet, the fact that Sancho felt that he must turn to Sterne to make the antislavery message "universal" registers the degree to which access to the public sphere of print was not undifferentiated. Women, dissenters, and former slaves all faced particular obstacles in making their voices heard.[6]

To claim that the debates about the relation of consumer practice to colonial policy were carried out primarily in print is not, of course, to say that they functioned only at the level of description. On the contrary, the discursive formations governing racial and colonial relations have always been attended by material consequences. As Henry Louis Gates Jr. points out about race, which "pretends to be an objective term of classification, when in fact it is a dangerous trope": "the sense of difference defined in popular usages of the term 'race' has both described and *inscribed* differences of language, belief system, artistic tradition and gene pool."[7] In other words, while the use of the term "race" to describe cultural and ethnic difference may seem to be metaphorical, such figures have tended to be made concrete by social and political practices. As Gates notes, "scores of people are killed every day in the name of differences ascribed only to race."[8]

Needless to say, imperialism and racism can and have taken place independently of one another. In Britain, during the eighteenth century, however, the social and political practice that most violently determined the material consequences of racial definitions was also the most important colonial venture of the period—the use of slave labor from Africa in the sugar-producing colonies of the Caribbean. As a good part of this book is concerned with Britain's involvement with chattel slavery, it may be useful to sketch that history here. The War of Spanish Succession ended in 1713, and as part of its settlement at the Treaty of Utrecht, Britain procured from Spain the Asiento, the monopoly rights to the slave trade, for a period of thirty years. While Britain had used slave labor in the Caribbean since the early sixteenth century, this event marked the beginning of its greatest involvement in the slave trade; "annual shipments of slaves by the British probably tripled over the eighteenth century, rising from 12,000 to 14,000 before

1720 to 42,000 during the 1790s."[9] For a long time, this profitable practice caused British subjects very few moral qualms, but by the 1780s, Britons began to grow dissatisfied with the economic and moral structures that governed the West Indian Trade, and the first wave of agitation to abolish the slave trade and emancipate Britain's slaves began to swell.[10] Antislavery activists, however, were not immediately successful. Propositions to end Britain's involvement in the trade were defeated in parliamentary debates in 1791 and 1792, and despite promises to the contrary, the trade was not abolished until 1807. It took another thirty years for complete emancipation; West Indian slaves were granted their freedom in 1833, but many of them continued to be bonded in "apprenticeship" until 1838.

To write now about Britain's involvement with the slave trade is to stand on the shoulders of giants. Since the groundbreaking publication of Eric William's *Capitalism and Slavery* in 1944, most historians have agreed that Britain's withdrawal from the slave trade in the early nineteenth century was in some way a reaction to metropolitan changes in modes of production.[11] Williams himself argued that the roots of abolitionism were not in humanitarian ideals, but in motives of profit, and that the shift from mercantile to industrial capitalism provided the economic motor for social reform. One of the most prominent recent scholars of slavery, David Brion Davis, puts less emphasis on economic change as the primary catalyst for social change, but he also focuses on conditions of production, seeing Britain's growing distaste for slave labor as part of an ideology that legitimated the "free labor" of wage slavery.[12]

One of the most significant challenges to this account of British abolitionism in the past few years has been a consideration of the ways in which the antislavery movement was inflected by gender ideologies. In 1992, two substantial books appeared on women's involvement in the abolitionist movement in Britain, Moira Ferguson's *Subject to Others: British Women Writers and Colonial Slavery, 1670–1834*, and Clare Midgley's *Women Against Slavery: The British Campaigns, 1780–1870*. Both these works argue implicitly that the lives of white women living in Britain during the eighteenth century were to some degree structured by the dynamics of colonialism and race.[13] Ferguson's book focuses on women's writing about slavery and breaks new ground in the wealth of archival material it brings to bear on this long-neglected body of work. Her book also grapples with one of the central problems for feminist histories of white women's involvement in struggles over race. Feminist literary and social historians have often found themselves drawn to abolitionism as a social arena in which a link between sexual and racial oppression seems visible. Ferguson, for example, claims that "the discourse on slavery . . . introduced an uneven, but vaguely discernible profile of women united across class, race, and gender lines by common, though diversely configured oppressors."[14] Yet, she tempers such utopian images of female solidarity, acknowledging that while abolitionists helped end slavery, racism managed to survive that institution, its dynamics perhaps reinforced by the strategies of the antislavery movement. Thus, Ferguson concludes that "the historical intersection of a feminist impulse with anti-slavery agitation helped secure white British women's political self-empowerment. Concurrently, that intersection fundamentally, though unintentionally, damaged future race relations."[15]

Clare Midgley's work, while echoing Ferguson's conclusions, offers some productive ways of understanding this tension in white women's involvement in the antislavery movement. Most important, she ascribes a great deal of power to the category of class in determining the actions of British women active in the cause, most of whom were of the urban bourgeoisie. Midgley explains that because such women were "often supporters of missionary work to 'heathen' women and among poor women in Britain, and themselves the employers of working-class women as domestic servants, middle-class white women campaigners tended to view both working-class and black women as passive victims on whom they had the power to bestow benefits, rather than as equals and co-campaigners."[16] Seeing the allegiances of female antislavery activists as bisected by the bonds of class and sex helps explicate the contradiction between their identification with West Indian slave women, and their denial of alternative forms of agency or subjectivity to such women.

The growth of historical interest in women's involvement in the slavery debates may have been fostered by a more general reconsideration of women's social and literary history. Feminist accounts of the period 1740–1840 have been reconceptualized and reinvigorated recently by attention to the category of domesticity. Domestic ideology, according to Nancy Armstrong, posited that the private sphere of the household "recentered the scattered community at myriad points to form the nuclear family, a social organization with a mother rather than a father at its center."[17] In this dynamic, the woman who inhabited the leisured, private space of the home was granted jurisdiction over moral questions. This woman was likely to be white, middle class, religious, and sympathetic to abolitionist appeals. Indeed, in the debates over slavery, women were able to draw on the ideology of separate spheres to forge a new kind of political voice for themselves. At the same time, the increasing prominence of this social category in metropolitan Britain meant that the condition of the domestic sphere in Britain's colonies also came under increased scrutiny. For slaves and their owners alike, the brutality of slave culture was perceived as a threat to domestic happiness. How best to safeguard the domestic woman became an important issue in the debate over labor conditions in the slave colonies during the late eighteenth and early nineteenth centuries.

The category of domestic ideology certainly enables an understanding of the function of gender in arguments for and against slavery. It is necessary, however, to do more than simply extend the ideas of Armstrong and others into colonial settings. In order to account for the contradictions in women's involvement in the debates over slavery, we must pay particular attention to the tensions between domestic ideology and that which fell outside its organizational principles. Such scrutiny illuminates the ways in which this discourse precluded the representation of certain kinds of female lives and labor, and allows us to interrogate the cultural function of that exclusion. More specifically, a critical view of domestic ideology helps account for the representational fate of the labor done by female slaves in a discourse structured around a split between a feminized private space, and a masculine public sphere. Efforts by both white and black women to represent female slaves' manual labor, as well as their sexual exploitation, trouble that division profoundly. Thus, while this book relies on the explanatory power of the category of domesticity, the materials it treats also reveal the limitations of emphasizing the hegemonic nature of that discourse during this period.

To summarize, accounts of Britain's involvement in imperialism and slavery during the period from 1713 to 1838 have focused on the changing relation between metropolitan and colonial systems of labor. More recently, drawing on demonstrations of the centrality of domestic virtue to social organization during this period, feminist scholars have complicated that explanatory framework by emphasizing the significance of women's entrance into colonial politics. Similar efforts, however, have not been made to integrate a history of slavery with an equally important element of eighteenth-century British society—the rise of consumerism. This omission is surprising, since the formation of a consumer society has begun to be seen as one of the central developments of eighteenth-century British culture. In *The Birth of a Consumer Society: The Commercialization of Eighteenth-Century England*, Neil McKendrick, John Brewer, and J. H. Plumb influentially claimed that "there was a consumer revolution in eighteenth-century England. More men and women than ever before in human history enjoyed the experience of acquiring material possessions."[18] As incomes rose and prices dropped during the early part of the eighteenth century, a broader segment of society was able to purchase objects formerly the exclusive privilege of the upper classes. These commodities, items that made life more comfortable or fashionable, included: "ceramic tableware (perhaps Spode or Royal Derby) to replace pewter mugs and platters; metal knives and forks supplanting wooden implements; iron hobs and grates, cushioned chairs, Axminster and Wilton carpets, kitchen ranges, wallpaper, framed prints for . . . [the] walls, the latest delicate Sheraton furniture (no one wanted antiques) and brass ornaments."[19] An influx of raw materials from Britain's expanding trading empire also influenced this change in spending patterns; sugar, tea, chocolate, coffee, mahogany, and East Indian textiles became more widely available during this period as well. Yet, very few scholars of slavery and colonialism in the British Empire during the eighteenth century have paid much attention to concomitant changes in patterns of metropolitan consumption—nor have they considered the importance of such emergent practices to new forms of social critique, such as the abolitionist movement.

There are at least two significant exceptions to this neglect; Sidney Mintz's *Sweetness and Power: The Place of Sugar in Modern History* provides an intriguing account of the relation between the consumption of sugar—Britain's most important colonial product during this period—and the industrial revolution; and Tim Breen's article, "Baubles of Britain: The American and Consumer Revolutions of the Eighteenth Century" demonstrates the importance of commodity choice to the anti-colonial protests of the North American colonists in the 1760s. Yet, while both of these studies mention the part played by women in the development of consumer practices, neither gives gender ideologies the significance they deserve, considering the centrality of women both to struggles over colonialism and to the history of consumerism.[20] The relationship between femininity and consumption, however, can tell us a great deal about women's involvement in, and occasional resistance to, Britain's imperial expansion.

Investigations of this ideological nexus have already begun, preeminently in the work of Laura Brown, who concludes that "the female figure, through its simultaneous connections with commodification and trade on the one hand, and violence and difference on the other, plays a central role in the constitution of . . . mercantile capitalist ideology."[21] This set of beliefs about women's involvement in mercantile accumulation is perhaps best articulated in Gulliver's explanation of Britain's quite literal thirst for economic conquest: "this whole globe of earth must be three times gone round, before one of our better female yahoos could get her breakfast, or a cup to put it in."[22] The results of such ventures appear in domestic settings, such as Belinda's dressing table in *The Rape of the Lock*, where "Unnumber'd Treasures ope at once, and here / The various Off'rings of the World appear."[23] This female desire for and command of luxury was often coupled with sexual voracity, as it is in Smollett's later, and already somewhat archaic, depiction of the farcical Tabitha Bramble in his novel of 1771, *Humphry Clinker*.[24]

Brown, however, ends her analysis in 1730; an extension of this investigation of the relationship between women, commodification, and colonialism into the later eighteenth and early nineteenth centuries, however, must encompass two different discursive moments. These moments are an early eighteenth-century idea of feminine greed, such as Brown describes, which helped underwrite the imperial and mercantile expansion of the period, and a later investment of consumer practices with the morality and emotional energy of sentimentalism.

While the earlier period is characterized by a general celebration of colonial and imperial expansion, the later saw the defeat of British colonialism in the War of American Independence, and revolution elsewhere, particularly in France and Haiti. The increasing political importance of female compassion for the oppressed can be seen as related to the increased instability of colonial power. Felicity Nussbaum's illuminating discussion in *Torrid Zones* (1995) begins this investigation of the later part of the century by demonstrating the relationships between colonized women and their English counterparts in representations of sexuality, and particularly of maternity. More work remains to be done, however, on the nature of women's political agency during this period.

Changing perceptions of female acquisitiveness are already visible in Richardson's Pamela, who eschews greed, and instead combines morality and sentiment in her choice of possessions. Addressing the clothing she takes from her first mistress's estate, Pamela exclaims:

> come to my arms, my dear *third* parcel, the companion of my poverty, and the witness of my honesty; and may I never deserve the least rag that is contained in thee, when I forfeit a title to that innocence, that I hope will ever be the pride of my life! And then I am sure it will be my highest comfort at my death, when all the riches and pomps of the world will be worse than the vilest rags that can be worn by beggars! And so I hugged my *third* bundle.[25]

Pamela's clothing, like Belinda's toiletries, is granted a projected agency—it is a verbal subject, even explicitly personified. Yet, what distinguishes Pamela from Belinda is the former's belief that certain possessions can be both the "witnesses" of interior qualities, and the "companions" of virtuous actions. In some ways, this passage seems to be about renunciation and a pious asceticism. But Pamela here chooses *between* possessions, rather than simply refusing immoral goods. Thus, the passage implicitly comments on female consumer habits. Richardson's heroine emphasizes her own discrimination here. She has divided her clothing up according to its moral connotations, and chooses the *third* bundle only; her emotional investment in that choice is apparent in her happy embrace of the clothing. Of course, this episode does not concern the more conventional sites of female consumer activity, metropolitan shops and amusements, but it still suggests an important reconfiguration of representations of female consumption in the later eighteenth century.[26] Primarily, it works to disassociate feminine interest in possessions from the suspicion of luxury and greed, by proposing that women might have an interest in objects that, while emotional, is not licentious or acquisitive. Furthermore, it presents Pamela herself as a moral agent making the right choice. It was this ideal of female consumption, at once sentimental, moral, and discriminating, that critics of colonial production, particularly abolitionists, were able to put to political use.

A related development in cultural assumptions about feminine relations to commodities has to do with the growing concern over women's consumption of texts during the eighteenth century. Women's emotional investment in texts, particularly fictional narratives, increasingly was seen as immoral, anti-social, and prurient.[27] Indeed, much of the energy previously expended on critiques of feminine greed for luxury was absorbed into an ongoing critique of the perceived female longing for representation. The connection between anxiety over a feminine desire for exotic substances (like the female Yahoo's demand for tea) and a feminine need for stimulating novels is underlined by the frequent figuration of reading as eating. The *Ladies' Magazine* of 1812, for example, warns that "Books, merely entertaining, produce the same effect upon the mental faculties, which a luxurious diet does upon the corporeal frame: they render it incapable of relishing those pure instructive writings, which possess all the intrinsic qualities of wholesome, unseasoned food."[28] I would argue that this analogy marks cultural attitudes about reading as part of a more general discourse of consumerism. The writer's need to differentiate good reading from bad reading, just as "luxurious" food is differentiated from "wholesome" food, signals not a refusal of consumer culture, but rather the necessity for discrimination in all object choices, especially for women.

The historical scope of this book is marked off by two political events: the Treaty of Utrecht in 1713, which granted Britain monopoly rights to the trade in slaves, and the emancipation of Britain's slaves in the Caribbean in 1833. This historical framework highlights the effects of the category of slavery on thinking about commodities, particularly colonial commodities, during this period. But I would also like to put Britain's gradual endorsement of abolition in the context of a more general shift in its perceptions of the colonial periphery during the eighteenth century. In the earlier part of the century, the colonies were viewed as places where British power and influence would be acknowledged, and even desired. In 1713, for example, immediately after the signing of the Treaty of Utrecht, Pope wrote, in "Windsor Forest," that:

> The Times shall come, when free as Seas or Wind
> Unbounded Thames shall flow for all Mankind,
> Whole nations enter with each swelling Tyde,
> And Seas but join the regions they divide;
> Earth's distant ends our Glory shall behold,
> And the new World launch forth to seek the old.[29]

Pope's seas are English seas, indistinguishable from the Thames itself. In his view, trade will be both unifying and glorifying: the new world will "seek the old" on the old world's terms. By the end of the eighteenth century, however, the colonies began to be perceived as dangerous places, where British power might be resisted, and even thwarted; Pope's image of the Atlantic as cooperative with English imperialism became less persuasive. Instead, by 1773, the abolitionist Thomas Day was writing, in the voice of a "Dying Negro" who throws himself into the Thames:

> And may these fiends, who now exulting view
> The horrors of my fortune, feel them too!
> Be theirs the torment of a ling'ring fate,
> Slow as thy justice, dreadful as my hate,
> Condemned to grasp the riven plank in vain
> And chac'd by all the monsters of the main,
> And while they spread their sinking arms to thee,
> Then let their fainting souls remember me![30]

Here, the ocean is allied with the violent vengeance of the slave, both a colonial laborer and a valuable commodity. In what may be a limit case for the anxiety caused by the "tides of luxury," the sea literally rises to destroy the slave traders who have profited by it. This poem suggests that the Atlantic, which carries luxury items to Britain, is also the point at which the balance might tilt in favor of the colonized. If Pope's

Atlantic is merely an extension of the Thames, then Day's Thames is an extension of the Atlantic, an intrusion into the heart of England itself.

This attitudinal shift coincided with a decline in the glorification of indiscriminate accumulation, and with an increasing fear that Britain's consumption of colonial goods was compromising its self-sufficiency; as the century wore on, the riches of the New World were increasingly perceived as less an accessible cornucopia than a dangerous addiction. The turning point in this trajectory was probably marked by the Seven Years' War. This conflict, fought between 1756 and 1763, was unique among eighteenth-century wars in that it did not disrupt colonial trade, but instead actually expanded it, as Britain captured Quebec, Martinique, and Havana, among other New World territories. Yet, this midcentury imperial expansion finally worked to demonstrate the limits of Britain's fiscal control of its colonies, intimating a shift from an empire based on economic domination to one held or lost by military force. The North American tax policies of the 1760s that led to the American Revolution were a direct result of Britain's need to make the colonies pay for the war that had been fought to defend them. Paradoxically, then, the very wealth that streamed into British metropolitan centers after the war became a sign of Britain's dependence on her colonial subjects; in order to attain it, the nation tacitly had to admit its reliance on its Atlantic colonies for revenue. As John Brewer suggests, "the hubris of the Seven Years' War had its nemesis in the American War of Independence."[31] Or, as Linda Colley puts it: "from [1763] until the American Revolution and beyond, the British were in the grip of collective agoraphobia, captivated by, but also adrift and at odds in a vast empire abroad."[32] In this context, Britain's growing uneasiness about slavery after the war can be seen as partly motivated by a discomfort over its dependence on the luxurious products of slave labor, along with the less visible financial benefits of its Caribbean holdings.

The effects of mercantile and colonial expansion on domestic consumer practices, and vice versa, can best be read through consumer reactions to newly available commodities from the colonial periphery. Often, even at times when accumulation and expansion were being glorified, those reactions were characterized by a nebulous anxiety, and by a suspicion that such objects retained traces of the violence with which they were appropriated from foreign locations, or produced by captive labor. This discomfort was both an anxiety about consumption, and a consuming anxiety, since the rhetoric surrounding it tended to warn that in taking in colonial objects, consumers were destroying something within themselves. To combat such self-destruction, consumers were urged to exercise extreme discrimination in choosing commodities, or even to refuse the most suspicious items. Abstention movements—the refusal to consume particular commodities on moral or political grounds—thus prove to be important intersections of the history of colonialism and the history of consumerism.

The anxiety produced by colonial commodities in metropolitan settings, however, was not neutralized entirely by the rationalist dynamics of commodification. On the contrary, the emphasis abstention movements placed on the agency of individual consumers seems to have had an analogical double in images of involuntary somatic responses to commodities by individual bodies. Often, this affect was produced in relation to the suggestion of cannibalism, or the related horror of consuming taboo parts of or fluids from the human body. Representations of cannibalism, an ancient form of terror and a method for reinforcing cultural difference, show up with remarkable frequency during the period covered by this book, in Swift, Smollett, and the abolitionist campaigns against slave-grown sugar.[33] Accusations of cannibalism were directed by slave owners at slaves and by slaves at slave owners.[34] Earlier, allegations of cannibalism had been leveled at the native Irish by invading England armies in the sixteenth century, but perhaps the most iconic image of cannibalism in the colonial arena for the eighteenth century appears in Defoe's *Robinson Crusoe*. When Crusoe sees "the shore spread with Skulls, Hands, Feet, and other Bones of humane Bodies," and realizes he has found the place where "the Savage Wretches had sat down to their inhumane Feasting upon the Bodies of their Fellow Creatures," he relates that: "I turn'd away my Face from the horrid Spectacle; my Stomach grew sick, and I was just at the Point of Fainting, when Nature discharg'd the Disorder from my Stomach; and having vomited with uncommon Violence, I was a little relieved" (164–65). Peter Hulme has demonstrated that this act "finally allows Crusoe clearly to distinguish himself from others. . . . [T]he vomiting symbolically voids him, producing that impossible 'pure' body, alimentarily chaste."[35] Yet, if we imagine the scene of cannibalism as the limit case of "improper" consumption, Crusoe's extreme involuntary gesture of disgust can also be read as his refusal to engage in such consumer practices.

The eighteenth-century relationship between colonialism and consumerism made images of the dismembering and ingestion of foreign bodies especially resonant. Consumer protests against colonial goods emphasized the direct connection between colonial producers and domestic consumers in their quest to convince the public of their efficacy. Yet, the rhetoric surrounding these movements often exceeded their rationalist claims, and brought them close to invoking the taboo, gothic horrors of cannibalism. Their representations of the intimate, almost physical, relationship between producer and consumer were characterized by a supererogatory negative affect, which at times seemed to work against the explicit political intention of such discourse. Frequently, such discussions of the effects of non-European foodstuffs focused on the dangerous repercussions their ingestion would have on individual bodies. Although usually less literal-minded than Defoe, the rhetoric of eighteenth-century abstention movements also advocated a kind of "alimentary chastity." This tendency to rely on the generation of negative affect around both the producers and the consumers of suspicious goods presages a crucial ambiguity in the function of these tropes in the antislavery movement.

A characteristic deployment of this kind of disgust for abolitionist ends takes place in this anonymous poem, published in the *Scots Magazine* in 1788:

> O'er the far beach the mournful murmurs run
> And join the rude yell of the tumbling tide,
> As faint they ply their labours in the sun
> To feed the luxury of British pride!
> . . .
> Are drops of blood the horrible manure
> That fills with luscious juice the teeming cane?
> And must our fellow creatures thus endure,
> For vile traffic the indignity of pain?

Yes, their keen sorrows are the sweets we blend
With the green bev'rage of our morning meal,
The while to love *meek mercy* WE pretend,
Or for fictitious ills affect to feel.

(199)

This poem relies on the structure of metonymy to depict the relationship between the suffering slave and the British consumer. The laboring slaves are represented by their sad emanations—their "mournful murmurs run" and their "keen sorrows" are blended. This rhetorical disassociation of sounds from laboring bodies can be read as signaling the commodified nature of the relationship between metropolitan consumer and colonial producer; the British drinker of sugared tea never sees the slaves, but only consumes the alienated products of their labor. The poem reveals that such commodities are really emblems of unimaginable suffering, but the metonymical structure remains intact. The complex economic system that facilitates the British consumer's enjoyment of luxuries produced in the farthest reaches of the empire is obscured by the seeming independence of individual sights, sounds, and tastes.[36]

The drops of blood that fertilize the sugarcane might also be read as metonymical—they stand in for the whole brutalized body of the slave. They may even be metaphorical, an image of generalized suffering. Yet, the logic of the poem, which traces the relationship between production and consumption, from blood to cane to sugared tea, seems to literalize the image. That is, it suggests that in drinking tea with sugar produced by slave labor, British consumers may actually be drinking blood. Disgust for a product so indissociable from the bodily fluids of the slave underwrites the mercy and sympathy an ethical consumer is supposed to feel for captive laborers. This rhetoric, which seeks to rejoin the commodity with the body that produced it, functions most overtly as a critique of certain dynamics of the international market. The negative affect it generates is supposed to disrupt the objectification of commodity relations by reminding the consumer of the misery they cause. Yet, there is a way in which this kind of rhetoric also works in concert with a racist discourse that dehumanizes cultural others. In the poem above, and in many similar representations of colonial suffering, slaves are not represented as whole bodies with any kind of agency.

Despite the poem's assurance that slaves are our "fellow creatures," the slaves themselves are seen as a collection of bodily fluids and incoherent sounds. Even as the consumer is granted new moral agency in the realm of market relations by the discourse of abstention movements, the slave is rendered inhuman, a bundle of involuntary bodily functions.

Such representations of the relationship between British subjects and the inhabitants of the colonial periphery would not have been possible without a particular idea of the power of the consumer, which turned the international marketplace into a direct relation between individuals. Yet, there is a certain ambiguity in these images, centering on the nature of the negative affect on which they tend to rely to make their political points. The significance of this affect, whether it is registered as disgust or as sentiment, is hard to pin down. One way of reading it is as the remainder of a process that sought to contain the military and economic violence of colonial expansion in the seeming neutrality of commodity relations. In this interpretation, the eruption of supererogatory affect in representations of colonial objects, such as sugar, is an emblem of the irrepressibility of the violence of imperial expansion. Another reading, however, would see such affect as the supplement of objectification, working in concert with a policy of colonial expansion to dehumanize and "other" non-European peoples. In this second interpretation, colonial subjects are stranded between two poles of British perception—seen either as objects, or as generators of excessive emotion—never perceived as agents or subjects in their own right.

It will become apparent that this ambiguity, or oscillation, between a utopian moment of critique, and a reactionary moment of racist revulsion, persists even in the most vehement critiques of colonialism. Nevertheless, my tendency is to read the characteristic rhetorical technique of this discourse, a moment of literalization when the bodies of both producers and consumers are physically connected with a commodity, as a moment when the possibility of critique is adumbrated. To interpret texts in this way is to do so from a particular political vantage point, one that affirms the possibility of disruption and change in a seemingly hegemonic system. Paradoxically, it involves reading moments of uncontrollable affect not as monuments to the crushing power of a racist ideology, but as places where the balance of colonial power is revealed to be unstable. At the very least, I would argue, the moment when figures become literal, as in the poem above, registers the limits of the discourse that organized representations of the colonial periphery.

The first chapter of this book examines the place of "boycotts" in eighteenth-century consumer culture. It begins by providing an overview of the construction of an idea of consumer rights and the use of that concept in anti-colonial movements during the eighteenth century. In particular, it focuses on the growth of a discourse emphasizing the consumer's right to abstain from immoral products. The chapter argues that this growth in the agency and power of individual consumers was part of a shift from mercantile capitalism to free-market capitalism in Britain during the eighteenth century. This ideological development elevated individual consumers from passive participants in a mutually beneficial network of international trade to the arbiters of the moral and economic ramifications of that network. Exploring the negative manifestation of "consumer rights"—the deployment of the individual's right to abstain from immoral products—the chapter proposes that colonial luxury goods, such as tea and sugar, were among the first commodities to be the objects of such movements. Crucially, the mechanisms for socioeconomic change promised by such campaigns were not dependent on governmental structures, and therefore were open to participants who were not allowed to vote or run for office, such as women, colonial subjects, and religious dissenters. It is important to note, however, that despite their progressive ideals and humanitarian aims, abstention movements remained inside the structure of commodification. That is, they imagined the relation between domestic consumption and colonial production to be reducible to a relation between middle-class metropolitan consumers and luxury items. Thus, while we should acknowledge the anti-colonial politics of these movements, it would be a mistake to see them as anti-capitalist; their participants believed in free trade and relied on the dynamics of the market to rectify moral wrongs.

The second chapter concentrates on Jonathan Swift, an early and influential writer of and on consumer protests against colonialism. It argues that Swift's writings of the 1720s, from *Gulliver's Travels* to *The Drapier's Letters* to "A Modest Proposal," persistently return to the paradoxes and inequities of quantifying the value of goods and people in tense, intercultural settings. The chapter begins by discussing the profitability of Gulliver's adventures, his conversion of his exotic experiences into visible, exchangeable objects, like the Lilliputian sheep. It then turns to *The Drapier's Letters*—Swift's anonymous appeals to the Irish to boycott a new coin minted in England—as an early example of consumer protest. Nicholas Canny has argued that England "tested" some of its colonial policies in Ireland in the sixteenth century, before turning to the colonization of the Americas. In the same way, new tactics of anti-colonial protest may have appeared first in England's "internal colony" during the eighteenth century, then in relation to the Americas. The chapter argues that Swift's representations of the native Irish in his political writings of the late 1720s also engage with another important aspect of eighteenth-century colonialism: the effects of a growing trade in commodified bodies on British attitudes toward the colonies.

Chapter 3 explores the new uneasiness about colonial wealth and commodities caused by the expansion of Britain's trading empire after the Seven Years' War, concentrating on its manifestations in Smollett's novel, *Humphry Clinker*, published in 1771. It argues that the novel imagines British bodies to be under attack by the forces of mercantile accumulation, forces materialized in the catachrestic "tide of luxury." The novel reacts to this anxiety by producing fantasies of English economic and physical self-sufficiency—images of consumers able to abstain from purchasing commodities that disturb the social order.

Chapters 4, 5, and 6 focus on the role of consumerism in the abolitionist struggle to end slavery in the British Caribbean. Chapter 4 turns to the rhetoric that the abolitionist campaign to boycott slave-grown sugar directed at sympathetic female consumers. Like Smollett's novel, this political literature represents colonial commodities as a threat to English social life, figuring slave-grown sugar as a moral threat to British values, and, implicitly, as a physical threat to British consuming bodies. In this case, however, the texts depict female sensitivity to faraway scenes of colonial suffering as a bulwark against this danger. By combining an insistence on women's control of consumption for the home with a belief in feminine moral authority, these texts map out the role female domestic virtue might play in deciding the nature of

Britain's involvement with Caribbean slavery. This chapter also argues that the emphasis this movement places on female sensibility marks a new relationship between consumer culture and colonial ideology; abolitionist writings suggest that the relationship between Britain and her Caribbean colonies should no longer be organized around the consumption of colonial products, but rather around the sentimental consumption of texts depicting colonial suffering.

Chapter 5 continues this analysis of the relations between femininity, colonial ideology, and textual consumption. It addresses the ways in which ladies' antislavery societies promulgated particular kinds of reading communities and forms of textual consumption in order to realign sentimental reading with political responsibility.[37] These groups reimagined women's involvement in politics by connecting an increasingly naturalized idea of feminine susceptibility to fiction with the new importance of literacy and textual consumption to political practice. They proposed that reading about scenes of suffering would produce emotions that would lead directly to political action. At the same time, however, that these groups worked to make feminized sentimental affect politically useful, they also made the socially constructed nature of certain reading practices and forms of consumption part of a set of "natural" responses among educated subjects. The textualized and commodified nature of these scenes of suffering, even the narrative conventions they borrow from sentimental fiction, are made invisible by the abolitionist insistence on the inevitability and moral virtue of women's sympathetic identification with texts.

I conclude Chapter 5 by examining the work of an Afro-Caribbean woman writer, who used the growing importance of textuality to both moral and political debate to represent herself. Despite the ways in which the sentimental discourse of race relations codified the difference between white and black women, the political methods of ladies' antislavery societies made technologies of representation available to, and acceptable from, Afro-Caribbean women, particularly as the nineteenth century progressed. The autobiography of Mary Prince, which was transcribed, disseminated, and defended by ladies' antislavery societies, illustrates the complex mediation of Afro-Caribbean self-presentation both by codes of femininity and by the dynamics of textual consumption.

In Chapter 6 I discuss the importance of a racialized sexuality in the debates about the viability of slave economies at the turn of the eighteenth century. Reading sentimental novels by Charlotte Smith and Sophia Lee, along with political texts, I argue that sentimentality and domestic ideology organized English consumption of images of the Caribbean during this period, just as a discourse of commodification had done in earlier decades. The shift between these two representational strategies illustrates a historical change in British perceptions of the colonial periphery; the suspicion that the non-European world is inhabited by desirable and potentially dangerous bodies replaces a sense that the colonies were an almost uninhabited arena for the accumulation of wealth. Like Chapter 5, this chapter is concerned with the problem of accounting for female labor within an ideology that positioned women as consumers.

Finally, my Conclusion assesses the legacies of consumerist critiques of colonialism and of the abolitionist movement in which they flourished. I take note of the persistence of a nationalistic, morally careful, sentimental consumer—a figure first imagined in the early eighteenth century—in contemporary culture. I also examine the challenge posed by the concept of race to the ideals of sentimental philanthropy. After the emancipation of slaves in the British colonies in 1838, appeals to a universal sensibility, mutual emotions discovered in sympathy and tears across vast distances, began to disappear from British conceptions of cultural difference, to be replaced by a more essentialist and "scientific" understanding of race; the formulations of sentimental abolitionism—in their emphasis on the body's natural reactions to moral dilemmas—may have held the seeds of this development. The book ends with a consideration of Elizabeth Barrett Browning's poem of 1848, "The Runaway Slave at Pilgrim's Point," as a critique of sentimentalism, and a racialization of the discourse of antislavery.

Chapter 1

# Colonialism and the Politics
# of Consumerism

> As soon as any man finds a right reason, not before known,
> against continuing to purchase anything, or deal with anybody,
> he has an unquestionable right to desist immediately from
> buying such a thing, or from dealing with such a person: and
> to restrict this right would be to cut the sinews of all free and
> vigorous enterprize. Commerce always languishes in propor-
> tion as this fundamental right is invaded.
>
> —"On sophistical arguments against a conscientious disuse of sugar
> produced by slave labour."

With such rhetoric, the abolitionist campaign to abstain from consuming slave-grown sugar urged its sympathizers to exercise their power as
consumers in the service of overthrowing Caribbean slavery. The language of this argument might seem hyperbolic to twentieth-century
readers: why would a prospective buyer of sugar need to be told so
vehemently that he or she has a right not to purchase that item? In an
era of political boycotts on all levels, from international trade embargoes to word-of-mouth campaigns, the idea of combining a political
ethos with consumerism may seem commonsensical. But the self-
evident quality of consumer rights, and the abolitionists' universalizing
assignation of such rights to "any man," masks their innovative status in
eighteenth-century Britain.

During the eighteenth century, British economic theory gradually
assigned more and more importance to the role of the consumer in economic development. This move toward privileging demand over supply
as the agent of economic growth may have culminated in *The Wealth
of Nations*, published in 1776, in which Adam Smith argues that:

> Consumption is the sole end and purpose of all production and the inter-
> est of the producer ought to be attended to only so far as it may be neces-
> sary for promoting that of the consumer. This maxim is so perfectly self-

evident that it would be absurd to attempt to prove it. But in the mercantile system, the interest of the consumer is almost consistently sacrificed
to that of the producer; and it seems to consider production and not consumption, as the ultimate end and object of all industry and commerce.[1]

Smith's account associates the "interests" of the producer with the
"absurdity" of mercantile systems, and the privileges of the consumer
with the dynamic forces of "industry and commerce." Necessarily, an
intense interest in the consumer accompanied this privileging of consumption over production.[2]

This chapter investigates the intersection between the development
of an idea of consumer rights and the growing political importance of
such rights in the struggles over Britain's colonial policies during the
eighteenth century. In contrast with most accounts of Britain's consumer revolution, it focuses on the negative manifestation of those
rights: on the consumer's choice not to purchase or consume certain
newly available commodities. Such abstention movements need to be
understood in the context of the history of colonialism, as well as in the
context of the history of consumerism, since they often centered on
goods that were taken as exemplary of the tensions of the international
market, such as tea or sugar. The dangers and inequities of the ever-
more-tightly meshed dynamics of that market may have been seen
from the perspective of Britain's colonized subjects—as was the case
with those in Ireland, or the abstention movements that preceded the
American Revolution—or from that of concerned British citizens—as
was the case with the movement to abstain from using slave-grown
sugar. In either case, these behaviors illustrate a discomfort with mercantilist imperialism, and seek to replace a market governed by tariffs
and monopolies with one driven by the demands of individual consumers. Furthermore, they represent a mechanism for socioeconomic
change that functioned outside the structures of British government,
since consumers could participate in such movements even if they
were denied the right to sit in parliament, or vote, or sign parliamentary
petitions. For this reason, abstention movements provided a political
forum open to women, to colonized subjects, and to religious
dissenters.

At the same time, however, abstention movements hold a paradoxical place in the history of emancipation that such groups helped to

bring about. Generally speaking, these campaigns combine an explicitly moralizing and humanitarian rhetoric with an implicit argument for the reconsolidation of an insular and self-sufficient national identity. This latter characteristic is most apparent in their tendency to motivate abstention by attaching supererogatory negative affect to commodities themselves, and, by extension, to the conditions in which such immoral items were produced, and even to the laborers who produced them. According to the logic of such rhetoric, by refusing suspicious products, consumers were helping to keep their own culture pure of disgusting items, as well as of disgusting peoples and practices. A hint of biological racism emerges in the way that the distaste campaigners sought to generate around suspect foreign goods often derived from those campaigners' negative characterizations of the biological attributes of the cultural others who produced them. These early consumer boycotts not only articulate the rationalist claims of classical economics but also presage a racialized account of the difference between colonial producers and domestic consumers. This contradiction makes these actions an ideal place to examine the limits of a politics predicated on commodity capitalism.

## EMULATION

The standard account of the growth of consumerism in eighteenth-century Britain has come to be that put forward by Neil McKendrick, John Brewer, and J. H. Plumb in *The Birth of a Consumer Society: The Commercialization of Eighteenth-Century England*. In the introduction to that book, McKendrick argues that "there was a consumer revolution in the eighteenth century. More men and women than ever before in human history enjoyed the experience of acquiring material possessions."[3] This revolution was made possible by the nature of the English class structure, in which "there was a constant striving to clamber from one rank to the next, and where possessions . . . both symbolized and signalled each step in the social promotion."[4] In other words, changes in patterns of consumption, and in the commodities consumed, could both register and produce the permeability of class barriers in eighteenth-century England. McKendrick argues that "spurred on by social emulation and class competition, men and women surrendered eagerly to the pursuit of novelty, the hypnotic effect of fashion, and the

CHARTA" to consume whatever food they please, even a luxury from "so remote a country as China." Their consumer choices become the literal cause of their inability to perform the duties exacted from them. The influx of foreign foodstuffs into England creates certain patterns of consumption that are destroying English culture by breaking down the division of labor.

Thus far, Hanway's text appears to be primarily a reaction to the changes in English class structure produced by a kind of emulative consumerism. Yet, restricting Hanway's "Essay" to the context of England's shifting class relations necessitates leaving out important aspects of its argument. Hanway sees the breakdown of differences between classes in direct relation to the disintegration of Britain's coherence as a nation. He points out that tea drinkers will no longer be able to answer the needs of their nation: "He who should be able to drive three Frenchmen before him, or she who might be a breeder of such a race of men, are to be seen sipping their tea."[10] Hanway here makes the effects of tea drinking physical rather than attitudinal; it renders the laboring classes incapable of fighting and reproducing.

Indeed, Hanway often seems to corporealize what might be interpreted as an economic argument against the desire of the laboring classes to emulate their betters. He figures tea drinking as an "infection" and a "disease"—something that marks itself directly and internally on the body itself. It is as something that alters physical characteristics that Hanway thinks tea drinking will be the agent of a growing lack of differentiation between England and what he believes to be inferior nations:

> [Tea drinking] has prevailed indeed over a great part of the world; but the most effeminate people on the face of the whole earth, whose example we, as a WISE, ACTIVE, and WARLIKE nation, would least desire to imitate, are the greatest sippers, I mean the Chinese, among whom the first ranks of the people have adopted it as a kind of principle, that it is below their dignity to perform any manly labour, or indeed any labour at all: and yet, with regard to this custom of sipping tea, we seem to act more wantonly and absurdly than the Chinese themselves.[11]

Consuming the food of another culture somehow transforms the English into that culture. From being "active and warlike," the English may become as "effeminate" as the Chinese in "wantonly" drinking their tea. Hanway implies that these new consumer practices threaten a certain definition of masculinity. This threat takes place on two fronts; tea drinking both makes men passive rather than active and imbues them with an excess of sexual energy or wantonness.[12] Yet, Hanway combines an orientalist feminization of the East with a concern about labor relations; "manly labour" may cease altogether as a result of the influence of Chinese produce. In his figuration of the damage done to British bodies by foreign products, the problem of national identity intersects with problems of productivity and class relations.

Hanway thus describes the dangers posed by newly available goods as an issue of appetite, urging that "if we do not become more moderate in our consumption of [sugar] and indeed of many other articles, we shall find ourselves grown poor, and the cause of the decline of our wealth will be very difficult to account for in any other way than that we have *devoured it*."[13] In this formulation, the spoils of mercantile accumulation—the results of England's far-reaching trade network—provoke a kind of auto-cannibalism, in which the body consumes itself in consuming foreign commodities. Eating these foreign substances, English society eats itself; Hanway claims that "we enervate our bodies by consuming so much tea and sugar, and SIP OUT OUR VITALS in every sense."[14] The phrase "in every sense" reveals the cultural work that Hanway's text carries out in describing the evils of tea drinking. By metaphorically conflating physical ingestion with economic activities, he allows one to substitute for the other; the changing patterns of consumerism brought about by the expansion of international trade are explained as a problem of digestibility. Rather than bettering their social status by means of their new purchasing power, the laboring classes harm their own bodies by imbibing unhealthy liquids, just as their masters and mistresses do. At the same time, they injure the British nation as a whole. The "enervation" produced by tea and sugar depletes the "manly labour" and productivity necessary to Britain's strength and coherence.

As the interlocking of domestic and international concerns in Hanway's "Essay on Tea" makes clear, an account of changing consumer practices in eighteenth-century England must take into consideration not only changing definitions of social class in England itself but also the relationship between the growing British economy and

mercantile and colonial expansion. This network is particularly apparent in responses to items like tea and sugar, transported back to
England from the periphery of the British trading empire. McKendrick
lists among the objects that produced the "consumer revolution"
household goods, such as Wedgewood's crockery, along with fashionable clothing in the form of "hats and gloves, and belts, and wigs, and
shoes and dresses."[15] But Britain's intake of colonial foodstuffs increased as well, changing chocolate, tobacco, coffee, and especially tea
and sugar from luxury goods to objects of mass consumption by 1800.
Hanway's concern over changing patterns of consumption of these articles is not misplaced. The consumption of tea "rose from twenty thousand pounds in 1700 to over one million pounds in 1721, nearly six million pounds in 1768 and nearly eleven million pounds in 1785."[16]
Carole Shammas claims that "probably no area of consumption
changed as much over the course of the early modern period as that of
food."[17]

Tea consumption and sugar consumption were related almost inextricably in eighteenth-century England. K. N. Chaudhuri notes that
"the relationship between the two products was so close that a pamphlet printed in 1744, at the request of the tea dealers, attempted to estimate the total English consumption of tea from the known consumption of sugar."[18] The two commodities also shared some conditions of
production; both were objects of mercantile trade, benefited from pref-
erential trade duties, and were controlled by monopolies—the East
India Company and the West India Company, respectively. Yet, British
importation of these products also differed in several respects. Tea
grown in the British colonial territory of Assam was not auctioned in
London until 1839; throughout the eighteenth century, it was imported
into Britain from China.[19] Thus, while the tea trade illustrates the
expansion of mercantilism during the period, it did not rely on the
direct exploitation of colonial labor. Sugar production, however,
depended on the use of slave labor transported from Africa to the
Caribbean; it involved direct British supervision of the colonized territories of the West Indies.

The combination of tea and sugar importation, however, changed
the nature of British consumption practices irrevocably. In *Sweetness
and Power: The Place of Sugar in Modern History*, Sidney Mintz argues

that these twinned commodities reveal "the intimacy of the links between colony and metropolis fashioned by capital. So vital had tea and sugar become in the daily lives of people that the maintenance of their supply [became] a political, as well as an economic, matter."[20] He claims that "during the period 1750–1850 every English person, no matter how isolated or how poor, and without regard to age or sex, learned about sugar. . . . [A] rarity in 1650, a luxury in 1750, sugar had been transformed into a virtual necessity by 1850."[21] As workers' wages rose, the practice of consuming such articles spread throughout the British class structure, but the concept of emulative consumption does not fully explain the new importance of these items to the laboring classes.[22] Shammas notes that "if there is any dietary change that can be documented as occurring in the eighteenth and nineteenth centuries, it is the increasing reliance on appetite appeasers such as tobacco, caffeine drinks and sugar."[23] She argues that as grain prices rose in the second half of the eighteenth century, workers consumed more tea and sugar products because of the cheap energy they provided, and the way they suppressed hunger for more sustaining nutriments.[24] Thus, the new availability of these luxury goods may have stimulated both consumption, as a wider group of people were able to purchase such comforts, and industrial production, as the working classes slowed their intake of beer and ale, which were more nutritious than sugared tea, but had been less conducive to regulated, supervised labor. Mintz claims bluntly "that sugar, and other drug foods, by provisioning, sating — and indeed, drugging — farm and factory workers, sharply reduced the overall cost of creating and reproducing the metropolitan proletariat."[25]

Tea and sugar consumption, therefore, played a contradictory role in the lives of new industrial or proto-industrial laborers. On the one hand, their increased consumption of tea and sugar demonstrated the new accessibility of luxury goods and evidenced a new degree of purchasing power. On the other hand, the increase was part of the decline in nutritional values occasioned by the shift from agricultural to industrial labor, as workers gave up the time-consuming preparation of nutritious oat porridge and vegetable stock in favor of the prepared foods made possible by sugar. Thus, Mintz can argue, against McKendrick's emphasis on the importance of social emulation in the consumption of tea, that we need to attend to the specific cultural and nutritional functions of tea drinking for the laboring classes—notice "that the sweet-ened tea was hot, stimulating and calorie-rich; that hard work for wages under difficult conditions typified the circumstances under which tea came to be drunk; that tea had the power to make a cold meal seem like a hot one."[26] The consumption of tea, sugar, and other formerly luxurious colonial foodstuffs was not an arbitrary locus for the cultural anxiety surrounding mercantile expansion. Such anxiety illustrates that the problems of imperialism could not be confined to the colonial arena; indeed, they were inextricably linked to the changing class struc-ture of England itself, and to the uncertain nature and power of the emerging industrial workforce.

### CONSUMERISM AND ANTI-COLONIAL NATIONALISM

Evidence of the imbrication of colonialism and consumerism can be found in other arenas as well. Conflicts over the proper consumption of certain commodities took place not only between different social classes in England itself, but also between different segments of the heterogeneous British Empire. Colonial consumers often criticized the emulative consumption of English commodities on nationalist grounds. Some of the earliest campaigns of this kind occurred in Ireland. Swift, for example, in "A Proposal that all the Ladies and Women of Ireland should appear constantly in Irish Manufactures" (1729) argues that Ireland's economic distress can be alleviated, and its national pride restored, if its consumers are willing to refuse English products, and to exercise discretion in their purchasing habits. He claims that he has never "discoursed any reasonable man upon this subject, who did not allow that there was no remedy left us, but to lessen the importation of all unnecessary commodities, as much as it was possible."[27] What his country lacks, according to Swift, is a pattern of purchasing goods that would consolidate the Irish as a community. The success of such practices, he suggests, will only come about through collective action:

> I believe no man is so weak, as to hope or expect that such a reformation can be brought about by a law. But a thorough, hearty and unanimous vote, in both Houses of Parliament, might perhaps answer as well: Every Senator, noble or plebeian, giving his honour, that neither himself, nor any of his family would, in their dress or furniture of their houses, make use of

anything except what was the growth and manufacture of this kingdom; and that they would use the utmost of their power, influence and credit, to prevail on their tenants, dependents and friends to follow their example.[28]

This is an early formulation of what we might call consumer power: the ability of a consumer to choose among commodities according to certain beliefs, and thus to influence social conditions by manipulating economic markets. While this effort in some sense escapes government control, it is not, in Swift's formulation, a form of political agency equally available to a broad spectrum of individuals. Rather, it is the domain of wealthy men, who will enforce it through a combination of "power, influence and credit." Commodity choice may not be the province of law, but, in place of legal injunctions, political representatives should undertake to "prevail" on those under their nominal control—their families, dependents, and tenants—to refuse English goods.

This linking of an anti-colonialist nationalist politics with a particular practice of consumption, albeit for a limited section of the population, was put to perhaps its most successful use by rebellious North American colonists in the 1760s. Tim Breen has charted how the North American consumer boycotts created a national unity of sentiment; he argues that "Americans discovered political ideology through a discussion of the meanings of goods, through observances of non-consumption that forced ordinary men and women to declare exactly where they stood on the great constitutional issues of the day."[29] The North American colonists found that an ethics of consumption could carry an emerging discourse of national identity. The choices they made about consumer goods became the language in which the colonists could argue against England's political oppression.

These anti-colonial protests centered on the newly available luxury foodstuffs, such as tea, with which Hanway is also concerned. The connection is not coincidental, since the North American protests were a reaction to the interdependence of colonial and domestic economies to which Hanway also responds. Tea did not merely symbolize this relationship; its consumption was the instrument by which England hoped to make the American colonies contribute to the mercantile empire of which they were a part. The new taxes of the 1760s were part of a plan to make the colonies pay for Britain's enormous expenditure during the Seven Years' War, which had been fought, in part, to pro-

tect and increase British colonial holdings. In 1773, in an effort to help
the East India Company perpetuate its monopoly on the sale of tea and
sell 17 million surplus pounds of tea stored in England, the British government passed the Tea Act of 1773, which taxed tea consumption in
North America. Breen argues that "by transforming this ubiquitous element of daily life into a symbol of political oppression, parliament
inadvertently boosted the growth of national consciousness."[30] The
Boston Tea Party and the related boycotts provide a kind of counter
example to Hanway's fearful scenarios of lower-class consumption of
tea. Here, consumer choice is deployed not to transform the laboring
classes into imitations of their employers through an increased consumption of tea, but rather to differentiate and liberate the North
American colonists from their English rulers.

Yet, the tea boycotters also shared some of Hanway's assumptions
about the roots of consumer behavior in the domestic sphere. The
activities of the North American colonists emphasized the power that
women had over their own consumption practices and over those of
others. Breen claims that these boycotts gave women an important kind
of political agency, as "mothers and daughters monitored the ideological commitment of the family."[31] The domestic sphere symbolized
"self-sufficiency which had in fact never existed, but which in this
political crisis seemed the best strategy for preserving liberty."[32] The
regulation of consumption within the home, overseen by feminine
eyes, became the locus of national purity, as evidenced in this anonymous poem of the 1770s, entitled "A Lady's Adieu to Her Tea-Table":

> No more shall my teapot so generous be
> In filling the cups with this pernicious tea,
> For I'll fill it with water and drink out the same
> Before I'll lose LIBERTY, that dearest name.
> Because I am taught (and believe it is fact)
> That our ruin is aimed at in the late act
> Of imposing a duty on all foreign teas
> Which detestable stuff we can quit when we please.
> LIBERTY'S the Goddess that I do adore,
> And I'll maintain her right until my last hour
> Before she shall part I will die in the cause
> For I'll never be governed by tyranny's laws.[33]

Here the Goddess of Liberty is associated with consumers' right to "quit when [they] please"; in contrast, "tyranny's laws" are aligned with the artificial regulation of consumption. The focus of this contest between liberty and tyranny is the "Lady's Tea-Table," a space imagined as exemplary of a new national identity. The Lady speaks for a group who can "quit when we please"—an action that undermines the distant political processes to which the American colonists objected. Yet, while a politics underwritten by consumption practices seems to presume a consumer identified more by political beliefs than by social status, the freedom of that consumer's actions nevertheless is predicated on a certain class position. For Swift, the position from which nationalist action is best carried out is that of land-owning men; for the author of this poem, that position is filled by a middle-class woman whose leisure frees her from the pressures of the market and allows her to contemplate an ethics of consumption. In either case, the universalizing "we" of national identity is more demarcated than it may appear at first.

## CONSUMERISM AND ETHICS

Yet, despite the fact that the political efficacy of nonconsumption practices may have been limited to the middle classes, for whom items like tea and sugar were a luxury rather than a necessity of working life, the universalizing rhetoric of consumerism, which insists that "we" all have the power to chose what we consume, carried great cultural force. In *The Romantic Ethic and the Spirit of Modern Consumption*, the sociologist Colin Campbell tries to trace the genealogy of this discourse, which links individual identity and agency to feelings about consumer choice. Against McKendrick's emphasis on emulation, he argues that "no good reason is given [by McKendrick] to explain why people should have become more actively emulative [during the eighteenth century]. . . . It may well be that if demand was the key to the Industrial Revolution, then fashion was the key to that demand, but as yet no adequate explanation for either the origin or functioning of that phenomenon [i.e., fashion] has been offered."[34] Looking for such an explanation, Campbell traces the process by which commodities were invested with the individualized fantasies of consumers. To find the source of such projected affect, he investigates the growing value of individual emotions from a Calvinist protestantism, through an eighteenth-century sentimentality, to a romantic concern for individualized daydreams and fantasies. If sentimentalism forged "an emotionalist deistic ethic in which the good man or woman revealed their virtue — in the form of a profound sensibility to the plight of others — through a display of frequent and profound emotions," then romanticism contributed the "longing to experience in reality those pleasures created and enjoyed in imagination" to "the spirit of modern consumption."[35] Emphasizing the way that "the modern consumer will desire a novel rather than a familiar product because this enables him to believe that its acquisition and use can supply experiences which he has not so far encountered in reality" allows Campbell to "direct attention to the character of consumption as a voluntaristic, self-directed and creative process in which cultural ideals are necessarily implicated."[36] Most important for my own argument, Campbell argues that we cannot account for the "consumer revolution" of the eighteenth century without understanding its relation to the historically specific development of an ethics of emotionalism.

Furthermore, an understanding of eighteenth-century consumerism that sees it in relation to an ethics rooted in Protestant ideals of self-realization helps explain rhetoric like John Wesley's criticism of tea consumption. Wesley opposes tea not for the nationalist reasons espoused by the North American colonists, nor for the socially conservative reasons advanced by Hanway, but out of a concern for the relation between the body of the consumer and his or her religious duty. In his "Letter to a Friend, Concerning Tea," a pamphlet published in 1758, Wesley puts forward a number of reasons why his followers should not indulge in this luxury. The money spent on tea, he notes, could be better spent on charity. Also, the addictive qualities of tea "have too much Hold on the Hearts of them that use it. That (to use a scriptural phrase) they are *under the power* of this Trifle."[37] Finally, however, Wesley appeals to his followers' duty to God. "For how few understand, *Whatever ye eat or drink, or whatever ye do, do all to the Glory of God?* And how glad ought you to be, of a fair occasion to observe, though the Kingdom of God does not consist in *Meats and Drinks*, yet without exact Temperance in these, we cannot have either *Righteousness, or Peace or Joy in the HOLY GHOST?*"[38]

The connections Wesley draws in this pamphlet between the economic problem of spending on luxuries, like tea, and a spiritual commitment to worship God with one's body suggest an ethical dimension
to consumerism. Furthermore, the practice of such ethics is linked to
an affective response—the abstainer from tea will feel "Peace [and] Joy
in the HOLY GHOST." Like Hanway, Wesley proposes that individual
bodies are at risk from the widespread consumption of tea, but he sees
that risk as a danger to the individual's relationship to God, rather than
as a danger to worldly social categories. In other words, Wesley is advis-
ing his followers here to scrutinize their consumer choices in the same
introspective and self-critical way they would evaluate any moral
action, and to expect similar feelings of well-being to result from the
right choice as would result from other proper forms of worship.

This drive to formulate an ethics of consumption also prompted the
first campaigns to abstain from consuming slave-grown sugar. These
took place among the Quakers of North America, around the same
time as the anti-consumption campaigns described by Breen were
being waged. According to a study of this movement by Ruth Kettring
Nuermberger, the "earliest abstainer from slave products . . . to impress
the idea upon his fellow Quakers" was the tailor John Woolman.[39] In
1769, Woolman recorded in his journal his reasons for abstaining:

> [T]he oppression of the Slaves which I have seen . . . hath from time to
> time livingly revived on my mind, and under this exercise I for some years
> declined to gratify my palate with those sugars. . . . I do not censure my
> Brethren in these things, but believe . . . the trading in or frequent use of
> any produce known to be raised by the Labours of those who are under
> such lamentable oppression, hath appeared to be a subject which may yet
> more require the Serious consideration of the humble followers of
> Christ.[40]

According to Nuermberger, "Woolman joined the use of slave labor
goods with the Quaker testimony against war by arguing that the
seizure of slaves on the African coast was really an act of war. This
made slaves prize goods, against the acceptance of which the Quakers
had testified for years."[41] In this passage, however, Woolman characterizes the issue of consumer practices as a topic for "Serious consideration" rather than censure; he makes consumer choice a matter for self-
examination, closely related to the individual consumer's spiritual

status as a follower of Christ. Furthermore, he attributes his abstention to sentiment; he "declines" to avoid having the suffering of slaves "livingly revived on [his] mind."

This linking of emotionalism and ethics in thinking about consumerism certainly influenced the English campaign to abstain from slave-grown sugar. Like these earlier Quaker and Methodist activities, it emphasized the spiritual and moral responsibility of the individual consumer. As an early nineteenth-century antislavery pamphlet proclaims:

> It is the duty of the people of England to put an end to West India slavery, if they can, in a peaceable and lawful manner—They can to a certainty, so put an end to it, by the rejection of that produce, which forms the chief support and encouragement of slavery, and to abstain from using such produce is therefore their bounden duty. But that, which is the duty of the people of England *collectively*, must, of necessity, be the duty of everyone amongst them *individually*; because it is of individuals that the whole collective number is composed. Every individual may then say, to abstain from the produce in question, is therefore, plainly *my* duty; and whether others will unite with me in it, or not, I am resolved, for one, to maintain on this point, a conscience void of offense towards God and towards men.[42]

This passage urges the consumer to give up slave-grown produce, not for nationalist reasons, nor to protect the social hierarchy of England, but rather as part of a disinterested moral and spiritual commitment to the welfare of the slave. While such a choice may be part of a collective action, it is presented primarily as the ethical responsibility of the individual consumer, examining his or her conscience to arrive at the nature of his or her duty.

In the last two decades of the eighteenth century, and well into the nineteenth, abolitionists asked British consumers to abstain from consuming sugar grown in the West Indies as a method of undermining the slave economies that produced that sugar. Unlike the nonconsumption practices of the North American colonists, which contributed to a successful anti-colonial revolution, the campaign against slave-grown sugar seems to have had only a minor impact on the political process of emancipating British slaves.[43] The campaign had the misfortune to coincide with the Haitian Revolution of 1791, which deprived France of its largest sugar producer, and thus provided a new market for English sugar on the Continent. The resulting shortage even forced sugar prices up, and, as Seymour Drescher says, "the consumers of Europe easily cancelled out the abstainers of Britain."[44]

Drescher, however, agrees with the abolitionist Thomas Clarkson's estimate that three hundred thousand families were involved at the height of the campaign.[45] And internal evidence from the pamphlets themselves makes it clear that sugar abstention was a noteworthy phenomenon. In December 1791, the *Northampton Mercury* noted that "forswearing the use of rum and sugar seems to be the *rage*. In imitation of the inhabitants of Norwich, Yarmouth, Cambridge, etc., those of Truro, Falmouth and other towns in Cornwall have agreed not to use those articles until an abolition of the slave trade takes place."[46] A pamphlet entitled "An address to her Royal Highness the Duchess of York, against the use of sugar" enthusiastically declares:

> We were agreeably surprised when we found that this scheme was no sooner divulged abroad, than great numbers most cheerfully came in on it. Never, in so short a time, did a practice so novel, and which required a degree of self-denial, spread so rapidly. Six months, I believe I may say five, have not yet expired, since the public was required to lay aside the use of sugar; and yet, in the kingdom at large, the number of those who have complied with the proposal is reckoned considerably to exceed one hundred thousand.[47]

If this account is perhaps exaggerated, considerable interest in the issue can nevertheless be documented. William Fox's pamphlet, "An address to the people of Great Britain, on the utility of refraining from the use of West India Sugar and Rum" was "easily the most successful of abolitionist tracts," and went into "25 editions in London alone — 50,000 copies printed in about four months" along with "unauthorized editions in Birmingham, Manchester, Leeds, Sheffield, Sunderland, Hull, Dublin and Boston, Massachusetts."[48] The "sugar interest" of West Indian planters certainly took note; the author of "Strictures on an Address to the People of Great Britain, on the propriety of abstaining from West India sugar and rum" speaks with alarm of "the rapid and extraordinary manner in which [Fox's pamphlet] has been circulated in all parts of the kingdom."[49] And the author of "A vindication of the use of sugar and other products of the West India islands" bemoans "the disuse of sugar, which has lately become so general" and is forced to admit the "effect of [Fox's] publication has had on the practice of a great number of people . . . the persuasive eloquence of the author must be indeed considerable to have made so many converts to his system as he appears to have done."[50] It is safe to say, therefore, that both sugar producers and sugar consumers were concerned with the debate, concerned enough to write pamphlets, read them, and perhaps abstain in an organized way from consuming slave-grown sugar. The emphasis this movement placed on the power of individual consumers to manipulate an international market illustrates that it, along with the North American tea boycotts, can be seen both as a form of resistance to mercantilism, and as an attempt to formulate an ethic of consumption. It presented an ideal of a discriminating consumer who would create a self-sufficient domestic space.

The campaign explicitly opposed itself to pro-slavery mercantilists, who presented detailed descriptions of an interdependent world of colonial trade. For example, Benjamin Mosely (1742–1819), onetime surgeon general of Jamaica, argues that: "At home the merchant, from the transatlantic operation, supports legions of manufactures. With pointed finger on the globe, he follows the course of Phoebus with anxious care, through the heavenly signs propitious to his views; collects his rays from equatorial climes; diffuses their genial warmth over the frigid regions of the earth, and makes the industrious world one great family."[51]

In this description, a paternal, almost godlike, "merchant" rules the "family" of mercantile trade. It is he who regulates all these systems of production, organizing them into an international system. William Innes, author of "The Slave Trade Indispensable?," also presents an image of the family as intertwined with international trade. If the slave trade is abolished, he argues: "The Manufactures, Ship-builders, etc. will be materially affected . . . as there is not in Britain a manufacturing Town, which does not furnish articles to the islands. Shall these industries, workmen and their families, starve? Shall shipbuilding cease? How are the thousands in that Branch to be employed? Are they, with their *wives* and *infants* to be left naked and hungry?"[52]

Innes describes the British family not as self-sufficient, nor even as self-regulating, but rather as dependent on the organizing principles of international trade for its very survival.[53] These descriptions of the benefits of colonial trade to the British economy view consumption as just one aspect of a regulated mercantile economy; they were written to protect a trade bolstered by subsidies and trade tariffs. As another pamphlet observes, "the produce of sugar cane having been for so long received among our domestic necessaries, many thousands wholly, and many thousands in part, depend on its consumption for a livelihood."[54] For mercantilist writers, continued production had priority, and consumption had to be sustained and regulated in order to support the continuation of this system.

To combat these images, the abolitionist pamphlets calling for abstention from consuming slave-grown sugar reimagined the relations between production and consumption that held international trade together as a chain with which the British consumer imprisoned the West Indian slave. They hoped to persuade their readers that

> The DUTY of *abstaining* from the Consumption of West Indian Produce arises from the CONNECTION which subsists between the *Consumer* of that Produce and the *Means* by which it is cultivated. That connection, Sir, is more close and direct than some persons may be willing to admit. The consumer of the West India Produce, may be considered as the *Master-Spring* that gives motion and effect to the whole Machine of Cruelties. . . .
>
> [The slave trade] is a chain of wretchedness, every link of which is stained with blood! and it involves with equal criminality THE AFRICAN TRADER—THE WEST INDIA SLAVE HOLDER—AND THE BRITISH CONSUMER![55]

Such texts were eager to drive home to British buyers of sugar the closeness and directness of the connection between consumption and production. These pamphlets challenge the terms of the mercantilist arguments for the slave trade, as this dialogue makes clear:

> CUSHOO [a West Indian slave]: You pay for de kidnap and murder of poor Negro.
> MR. ENGLISH: How? I don't understand you.
> C: O me so make you understand, Massa—You pay the Grocer—
> E: Yes, or he wou'd not thank me for my custom.
> C: De Grocer pay de Merchant—de Merchant de sugar planter—him pay de Slave Captain—de Slave Captain pay de Panyarer, de Cabosher or de Black King.
> E: By this round-a-bout way you make us all thieves and murderers.
> C: No round-a-bout Massa, it come home straight line.[56]

Such texts give pride of place to a consumer who is the "master spring" of international trade, rather than to a merchant omnipotently survey-ing the globe and justly apportioning world resources: "The slave-dealer, the slave-holder, and the slave-driver are virtually the agents of the consumer, and may be considered as employed and hired by him to procure the commodity. For, by holding out the temptation, he is the original cause, the first mover in the horrid process."[57]

In this way, abolitionist rhetoric placed the consumer at the head of a chain of actions, in the place mercantilists would have expected to find the merchant, or the plantation owner; here, such people simply become "the agents" of the consumer. The consumer precedes the slave trader or the plantation owner in this chain because he or she holds out the original temptation for sugar production. Abolitionists locate the causes of slavery in the potentially indiscriminate nature of consumer desires. Only the imposition of an ethical framework onto consumer activity can work to free the Caribbean slaves.

In an article entitled "Capitalism and the Humanitarian Sensibility," Thomas Haskell argues that the source of such an ethical framework can be related to the workings of the market itself. Like Campbell, Haskell points out that for early industrial capitalism in the last part of the eighteenth century, the market was seen as a source of cultural amelioration and individual self-realization. He suggests that we look at the market "as the abolitionists and their generation often did: as an agent of social discipline or of education and character modification."[58] In this context, Haskell argues, we can see that the lessons taught by free-market capitalism had a corollary in ethical decision making; "at the most obvious level, the new stress on promise keeping contributed to the emergence of the humanitarian sensibility by encouraging new levels of scrupulosity in the fulfillment of ethical maxims."[59] Haskell does not argue that market relations produced the humanitarianism necessary for the abolitionist campaigns; rather, he points out that the same ways of thinking about the world produced both behaviors. He claims that humanitarianism and capitalism are linked by "bonds cre-ated not from class interest but by the subtle isomorphisms and homologies that arise from a cognitive structure common to economic affairs, judgements of moral responsibility, and much else."[60] Haskell's explanation of the rise of an ethics of consumption in the late eigh-teenth century differs from Campbell's in its emphasis on the activities of trade rather than on those of consumption, but he shares with Campbell the idea that during this period, market relations, rather than becoming divorced from ethical behavior, were seen as being closely related to the moral status of the individual.

Although Haskell discusses John Woolman, the early abstainer from slave-grown products, he records Woolman's opposition to slaveholding rather than to slave produce. He notes, that "from Woolman's perspective, the slaveholder's conduct was not immoral as long as he failed to see 'the relation of one thing to another and the necessary tendency of each.' To persist after being convinced of these causal connections was another matter, and, of course, convincing slaveholders that their conduct had more distant consequences than they recognized was Woolman's life work."[61] Here, Woolman propounds the same kind of causal links between consumption and production that were instrumental in the British campaign to abstain from the consumption of slave-grown sugar. Thus, despite Haskell's apparent lack of interest in abstention movements, his arguments illuminate the importance such campaigns placed on explaining the chains of actions that linked consumers to the violence committed in extracting value from slave labor. Furthermore, they make clear that such anti-consumption campaigns were not opposed to market relationships, or even to international trade, despite their invective against certain consumer practices. British abolitionists were generally in favor of free trade—which they felt would favor sugar produced by free labor in the East Indies—and only opposed to the monopolies, regulated trade, and high tariffs associated with mercantilism—which they believed would make the brutal structure of colonial slavery possible.[62]

Indeed, while it might seem that a campaign opposed to the indiscriminate consumption of newly available commodities might also protest the more general spread of capitalist social relations during this period, the reverse is probably more accurate.[63] The movement to abstain from consuming slave-grown sugar actually depended on a commodified relationship between colonial production and domestic consumption for its claim to efficacy. Only as consumers, a category of economic agent given new preeminence in the free-market capitalism of the later eighteenth century, could these campaigners proclaim their political power. Whereas mercantile arguments for the slave-powered sugar industry envisioned English producers of ships and clothes as dependent parts of a commercial system, abolitionist texts urging abstention from the consumption of sugar represented those same inhabitants of England as powerful individuals who controlled the conditions of production in other parts of the world. Instead of a network of mutually dependent producers, they described the power the purchaser of groceries in England wielded over the suffering producer of those groceries in the sugar islands. The nonconsumption argument thus switched the terms of mercantilists, who argued that sugar consumption was necessary because it supported the interests both of sugar producers and of the English producers of supplies for the colonies. Sugar production, they countered, was only carried out in the interests of sugar consumers. English subjects who were once the dependent producers of goods for the colonies become independent consumers of goods from the colonies. At their most vehement, abolitionists proclaimed that "every person who habitually consumes one article of West Indian produce is guilty of the crime of murder—everyone who does it, when convinced that what has been said [about slavery] is true, is deliberately guilty, and rendered more criminal by it being preceded by every species of cruelty and torture which inventive barbarity can devise."[64]

But if these pamphlets were primarily organized around berating the consumer for his or her immoral purchases, they also presented a powerful vision of the consumer's political and moral agency. Antislavery writers worked hard to convince their readers that consumption involved choice, or, more strongly, involved the "fundamental right" to be able to choose.[65] They had to assure consumers that "there exists no law by which they are obliged to use the Produce of the West India Islands—they have only to lay a restraint upon themselves, individually, to abstain from the consumption of that produce, and the end must eventually be accomplished."[66] By reimagining consumption as a fundamental right, rather than as an obligation, and by transforming international interdependence into individual choice (in the negative formulation of "restraint"), they helped create a new form of political agency—consumer power. As William Fox says, "The laws of our country may indeed prohibit us the sugar cane, unless we receive it through the medium of slavery. They may hold it to our lips, steeped in the blood of our fellow-creatures; but they cannot compel us to accept the loathsome portion."[67]

If "the laws" of England had conspired for years to make British consumers the passive "partakers of this drug," "a luxury which habit alone has rendered of importance," then consumers could resist those laws by resisting their own habits.[68] An empowered consumer was not merely one with the ability to choose, but was potentially heroic, resisting his "forced feeding" by mercantile traders, and overcoming his sugar addiction. Such heroism was founded on the conviction that consumer choice had an ethical dimension.

Furthermore, by proclaiming the moral or ethical nature of such choices, anti-consumption campaigns extended a form of political power to some individuals who were otherwise denied such agency. By choosing to refuse certain of the fruits of mercantilism, like sugar or tea, female or dissenting British consumers could protest Britain's imperial expansion into colonial markets. Conversely, the colonized subjects of Ireland or North America could use nonconsumption practices to challenge their subordination within a mercantile system. There is a way, then, in which these practices extended political agency to those outside the political franchise, such as women, colonial subjects, and religious dissenters. Such agency, however, was predicated on the luxury of choice, a negative correlative of bourgeois privilege, which was probably unavailable to the laboring poor. This form of political action was also associated with a certain form of capitalist ideology—one that celebrated the individual's power over the complex dynamics of international markets.

## COLONIAL PRODUCTION, DOMESTIC CONSUMPTION

The reactions to tea and sugar that I have been describing need to be seen in the context of what McKendrick calls the consumer revolution of eighteenth-century England. As he points out, it was during this period that a large number of British subjects first began to see themselves as capable of choosing between a multitude of newly available luxury goods, and to see the choices they made as potentially redefining their socioeconomic status. Only in a culture that focused so much of its energy and anxiety on the activities of consumers could such choices become important social signifiers, carrying political or moral weight. Yet, the motivations for these actions cannot be fully explained by McKendrick's analysis; he explores the forces that made people choose to purchase new commodities, while the episodes I have been describing revolve around the reasons that some of those people refused to buy certain items at certain times. Such actions were still predicated on the concept, new to the eighteenth century, of the consumer as an important economic agent, but in these cases, the consumer uses, or is urged to use, the negative aspect of his or her power of choice—abstention.

All of the attitudes toward tea and sugar consumption that I have described—those of Hanway, Wesley, the American colonists, and the British Abolitionists—in some way contradict the theory that social emulation was the primary motivation for consumer behavior during this period. While some aspects of Hanway's criticism of the spread of tea consumption to the laboring classes can be explained as his response to the breaching of class hierarchies by social emulation, other aspects need to be understood in terms of the way consumer habits helped form national identities irreducible to simple class identities during this period. In North America, such practices were used as anti-colonial interventions, and gave consumer habits an explicitly political significance. The British abolitionists who abstained from slave-grown sugar also hoped to use consumer choice as a political tool, but in doing so they drew not so much upon a nationalist rhetoric as on the concept that consumer choices had a moral or spiritual dimension, as some Methodists and Quakers believed. Despite the fact that hindsight reveals their circumscription by certain class distinctions, all of these reactions to the presence of the newly available luxury commodities of tea and sugar imagined consumer behavior to be motivated by something other than social emulation, and connections among consumers to be irreducible to class allegiance.

These responses—disparate as they may be—reveal that consumer behavior in England cannot be separated from the more complicated structures of the British Empire as a whole. The attitudes and activities surrounding tea and sugar in the second half of the eighteenth century suggest that the consumer revolution in England helped shape attitudes toward Britain's colonial empire during this period; the newly discovered power of the consumer produced innovative political contributions to two of the most important events of the day—the American Revolution and the abolition of the slave trade. For this reason, attention to attitudes toward consumerism during this period alters our idea of the relationship between capitalism and colonialism, particularly with regard to the antislavery movement. Since the publication of Eric Williams's *Capitalism and Slavery* in 1945, the relation between the British abolitionists of the late eighteenth century and the development of free-market industrial capitalism in Britain has come under intense scrutiny by historians. Most of these investigations, however, have centered fruitfully on the connection between British attitudes toward slavery and changing ideas about production during the industrial revolution. Williams himself argues that the development of industrial capitalism in Britain after the American Revolution destroyed slavery, not because of any humanitarian interest, but because the monopolies that supported Caribbean slavery obstructed the growth of international free trade; he argues that after 1783, "every important vested interest—the cotton manufacturers, the ship owners, the sugar refiners; every important industrial and commercial town— London, Manchester, Liverpool, Birmingham, Sheffield, the West Riding of Yorkshire, joined in the attack on West Indian Slavery and West Indian monopoly."[69] Here, the "vested interests" who attacked slavery are those who controlled the means of production in England—the owners of factories and refineries. Although a number of the statistics Williams uses to support his theories have been disproved, his sense that the economic and humanitarian developments of the late eighteenth century must somehow be related has been enormously influential.

Focusing on the ideological rather than on the economic aspect of that relationship, David Brion Davis also investigates changing attitudes toward production during the period. He argues that "while English society increasingly condemned the institution of slavery, it approved experiments in labor discipline which appear to gravitate toward the plantation model. . . . If British abolitionists could express horror over the iron chains of the slave trade, their acts of selectivity and definition helped to strengthen the invisible chains forged at home."[70] In Davis's line of reasoning, the similarity between industrial laborers and slaves was so unmistakable that it had to be mystified by the deflection of social outrage onto the physical brutality of slavery in order to secure the labor force necessary to fuel the industrial revolution. For Seymour Drescher, too, that moment of identification motivated the involvement of British workers in antislavery campaigns. The new industrial laborers of Manchester supported abolition because "Manchester was a town uprooted. No other agglomeration could have been so collectively and effectively moved by [the abolitionist Thomas] Clarkson's focus on the peculiar terrors of the slave trade: loss of kin, hearth and community. To be part of a lonely crowd, of a community of the uprooted, even by choice, was to feel the appeal on behalf of those uprooted by violence and forever."[71] Drescher relies on the idea that such workers recognized the correspondence between their own labor conditions and those of Caribbean slaves to explain their fervent antislavery sentiment. In all these accounts, changing attitudes toward labor power are seen as central to the development of opposition to Caribbean slavery.

In his thorough examination of popular support for abolition, however, Drescher also discusses the campaign to abstain from the use of slave-grown sugar. He notes that "it was . . . closely related to the new sense of consumer power" and that "it made the abolitionist elite uncomfortable because it was launched not merely as a symbolic means of pollution avoidance, but as an instrument of economic power."[72] In other words, the abstention movement revealed the connections between abolitionism, consumerism, class mobility, and sentiment. It illuminates an aspect of colonialist ideology during this period that has remained largely unexplored: the role played by commodity fetishism in structuring the relationship between metropolitan and colonial subjects. Marx reminds us that:

> The mystery of the commodity form is simply this, that it mirrors for men the social character of their own labour, mirrors it as an objective character attaching to the labour products themselves, mirrors it as a natural property of the things. Consequently the social relation of the producers to the sum total of their own labour presents itself to them as a social relation, not between themselves, but between the products of their labour.

Thanks to this transference of qualities, the labour products become commodities, transcendental or social things which are at the same time perceptible by our senses.[73]

The source of the political energy harnessed by the campaign to abstain from the consumption of slave-grown sugar was not a desire to undermine the ways in which the social life of late eighteenth-century England was already structured by commodity relations. On the contrary, its strategy depended upon imagining that the consumer's relationship to colonial foodstuffs, a relationship to commodities, could substitute for the complicated social relation between British laborers and colonial laborers. Such fetishization of tea or sugar suggests that altering the conditions of consumption will alter the conditions of production in the colonial world. Yet, while this assumption might hold true in a world of transparent relations between consumption and production, its effects elsewhere are limited because it obscures the complex and mediated relations between the colonial arena and domestic space. Attention to these nonconsumption practices uncovers the power of the new forms of political agency that arose with free-market capitalism. Yet, it also reveals the way such mechanisms for social change were limited by their inscription within the structures of a consumerist, capitalist society.

## Chapter 2

# From Curiosity to Commodity

## *Swift's Writings of the 1720s*

When Jonathan Swift made his first anonymous foray into Irish politics in 1720, he elected to frame his critique in the language of consumer culture. In "A Proposal for the Universal Use of Irish Manufacture" he urges the Irish to refuse the English goods forced upon them by mercantile policy and fashion, and to buy locally made items instead; "let a firm Resolution be taken," he proposes, "by *Male* and *Female*, never to appear in one single *Shred* that comes from England."[1] Ironically, Swift, despite his generally conservative stance, reveals himself here as one of the first, and most articulate, voices in the history of consumerist criticism of English colonialism. To understand what led Swift to adopt such strategies, we need to look not only to the history of consumerism outlined in the previous chapter, but also to the history of England's colonial policies in Ireland.

During the reign of Elizabeth I, England began to step up its involvement with Irish affairs. In the last third of the sixteenth century, its military presence on the island grew in response to rebellions in Munster and Ulster. At the beginning of the seventeenth century, the O Neil and O Donnell lands in Ulster were appropriated and reorganized as "plantations" under direct English control.[2] Despite a great deal of resistance, organized and otherwise, English hegemony in terms of language, land use, and religion gradually strengthened for the next two centuries. This process can be read as one of England's first experiments in colonial rule. Nicholas Canny has shown that the conquest and colonization of Ireland ran parallel to England's first intrusions into North America, and that "the Elizabethan conquest of

Ireland should therefore be viewed in the larger context of European expansion."[3] During the late seventeenth and early eighteenth centuries, Ireland continued to suffer under English colonial rule—but now in economic rather than military form. It was one of the first colonies to feel the strength of English mercantilist policies during the early eighteenth century—restrictions on trade were more severe in Ireland at this time than they were in the American colonies, for instance. These strategies eventually worked to constrain not only the Catholic natives of Ireland but also settlers of English descent. Consequently, it is in Ireland, most famously in Jonathan Swift's *The Drapier's Letters*, that some of the first economic protests against English colonialism occur.

Edward Said has argued that Swift occupied the unusual position of being both a traditional intellectual, by virtue of his position in the church, and an organic intellectual, by virtue of his advocacy for Ireland.[4] Swift's "organicity," of course, is made questionable by the fragmentation of "Irish" identity during the period, and by his own late and ambivalent conversion to Irish advocacy. Nevertheless, his engagement with the injustices of England's economic policies toward Ireland also gave him a particular purchase on the complexities of international mercantilism. Indeed, Swift's critique of the global context of colonial production during this period is remarkable. This chapter focuses on Swift's writing of the 1720s, a decade that saw the publication of both *Gulliver's Travels* and *The Drapier's Letters*, along with numerous other political tracts about Ireland, including a "A Modest Proposal." These texts make up an extraordinarily rich body of work and take on a number of rhetorical, psychological, and cultural debates, both topical and timeless. This decade, however, also saw Swift's growing involvement in issues of trade and colonial policy, and his increasing pessimism about the changes an individual, as either writer or political activist, could bring about in such a world.[5] His writings of the 1720s consistently come back to the paradoxes and inequities of quantifying the value of goods and people in tense, intercultural settings: the problem, that is to say, of the relationship between colonial production and metropolitan consumption.

In the last chapter of *Gulliver's Travels*, the protagonist delivers one of the most pointed and all-encompassing critiques of colonialism to be found in early eighteenth-century literature.[6]

> [A] crew of pirates are driven by a storm they know not wither, at length a boy discovers land from a topmast, they go on shore to rob and plunder, they see a harmless people, are entertained with kindness, they give the country a new name, they take formal possession of it for the king, they set up a rotten plank or a stone for a memorial, they murder two or three dozen of the natives, bring away a couple more by force for a sample, return home, and get their pardon. Here commences a new dominion acquired by *divine right*. Ships are sent with the first opportunity, the natives are driven out or destroyed, their princes tortured to discover their gold, a free license given to all acts of inhumanity and lust, the earth reeking with the blood of its inhabitants: and this execrable crew of butchers employed in so pious an expedition, is a modern colony sent to convert and civilize an idolatrous and barbarous people.[6]

Gulliver's indictment of imperial conquest is remarkably encyclopedic and generalized, moving from the reinscription of place names, to a kind of haphazard genocide, to the eventual justification of colonialism and the erasure of historical violence. But it appears somewhat incongruously in Swift's narrative. Gulliver has seen almost nothing like it in his travels, and it is embedded in several layers of satiric disavowal.[7] Gulliver prefaces the passage by explaining the impossibility of carrying out such a conquest in the lands he has visited (236); not only will they be difficult to conquer, but they also offer none of the traditional motivations for colonization—"gold, silver, sugar or tobacco" (237). Afterwards, he assures the reader that "this description . . . doth by no means affect the British nation," which plants its colonies with "wisdom, care and justice" (237).

Yet, at least one of the activities described has important, though somewhat muted, resonances for *Gulliver's Travels*: the very first motivation that Gulliver ascribes to maritime adventurers—their desire to rob and plunder. The difficulties of this project are immediately apparent. The adventurers must at first make do with taking away a couple of inhabitants as "a sample," and then only find the gold they are looking for by torturing the local princes. In fact, it is difficult to tell how exactly such ventures become profitable: are the natives merely curiosities, a "sample" of the value of a colonized labor force, or are they proof of the colony's existence? Will the profit of the venture ultimately be derived from the people, or the gold? What will govern the way value is assigned to these different resources in the intercultural strife and confusion of the colonial setting?

Lemuel Gulliver himself sets off with no intention of being a profiteer or imperialist. Trade does provide the general motivation for his travels, of course: he ends up in Lilliput after a "very prosperous" voyage to the South Sea, in Brobdingnag while "bound for Surat," in Laputa while on course for the East Indies, and in Houyhnhnmland after being captain of "a stout merchantman" hoping to "trade with the Indians in the South Sea" (16, 67, 123, 180). And, like the accidental imperialists he later describes, his shipwrecks result in some unlikely opportunities for making money. The first two books of *Gulliver's Travels* end with surprising evidence of the marketability of Gulliver's experiences; they conclude with the conversion of the strange cultural practices in which Gulliver has participated among the Lilliputians and the Brobdingnagians into visible and profitable objects. He eventually sells the miniature sheep he has brought back from Lilliput for six hundred pounds, and the "rarities" he recovers from Brobdingnag secure his voyage home. These images of the entrance of seemingly incidental non-European objects into a network of commodified exchange provide a kind of closure for the first two books of the narrative; they stabilize the complex interactions between Gulliver and the societies he visits by assigning market values to his experience. In the Fourth Voyage, these questions only escalate, as Gulliver learns to treat the bodies of the yahoos as the raw material of international travel. The first half of this chapter examines these issues of value and profit in the fantastical settings of *Gulliver's Travels*.

Still, the description of conquest and subjugation quoted above has little direct bearing on the scenes of *Gulliver's Travels*. Instead, it begs the question of what territories it does refer to, if not Lilliput, Brobdingnag, Laputa, or Houyhnhnmland. At least one critic has argued that Swift had Ireland in mind when he wrote the passage.[8] And, indeed, Ireland did suffer most of the cited abuses in the century before Swift wrote *Gulliver's Travels*. It had been settled and resettled by economic adventurers and mercenaries paid in land for their service to the English crown.[9] Gaelic names were being systematically replaced by English ones in compliance with the Act of Explanation of 1665.[10] Irish natives had been repeatedly massacred in the name of various versions of divine right.[11] During the seventeenth and eighteenth centuries, England gradually disempowered the Catholic population of Ireland, taking away both land and the right to hold office through the penal code.[12] Swift's position on many of these consequences of Ireland's colonial status is difficult to discern, although he certainly favored the restrictions on Catholics and Dissenters. It is clear, however, that he grew increasingly outraged by what he saw as the systematic extraction of Ireland's wealth by England's oppressive mercantile regulations.[13] Throughout the 1720s, both before and after the composition of *Gulliver's Travels*, Swift was outspoken on this issue.

Swift began parts of *Gulliver's Travels* in 1721, or even earlier, and probably had completed most of the First, Second, and Fourth Voyages by 1724. He might have finished the entire narrative that year, but, as Irvin Ehrenpreis says, "the *Drapier's Letters* came between."[14] In 1724 and 1725, Swift was busy composing, publishing, and avoiding prosecution for his most successful intervention into Irish politics, his campaign against the introduction of Wood's halfpence into the Irish economy. In these pamphlets, and in his other writings on Ireland in the second half of the decade, Swift moves away from the exploratory, suggestive investigation of value found in most of *Gulliver's Travels* and begins to take up the question of how Ireland's economic subjugation by England might be resisted. Among the modes of resistance he propounds most vehemently is the refusal, or boycott, of both English money and English goods, a strategy that breaks important ground in the history of consumerist critiques of colonialism. The second half of this chapter, then, outlines the history of Swift's advocacy of home consumption, from the bourgeois optimism of *The Drapier's Letters*, to the distopic vision of colonial degradation in "A Modest Proposal." As F. P. Lock reminds us, Gulliver's "protest against imperialism and colonialism goes well beyond the Anglo-Irish situation," but its composition during Swift's greatest involvement in Irish politics seems to imply that his condemnation of the more far-flung aspects of colonialism cannot be dissociated from his more local concerns.[15] At the same time, reading *Gulliver's Travels* in the context of Swift's writings on Ireland reveals the links between the condition of the Irish and the international range of England's mercantilist empire.

When Gulliver's first two voyages have been taken as topical satires of the early eighteenth-century world, they have most often been seen as either allegories of, or allusions to, the English court under Queen Anne. Flimnap, the Lilliputian courtier, for example, has been read both specifically, as Walpole, and more generally, as a portrait of a "typical court favorite" of the period.[16] Alongside this critique of the values of a specific culture, however, the first two voyages also investigate the way value is assigned as people and things move between cultures. Like Robinson Crusoe, Gulliver arrives on his first island burdened with a plethora of European manufactures. Indeed, J. Paul Hunter has suggested that Gulliver's collection of objects—including a snuff box and a pair of pistols—constitutes part of the text's satire of the conventions of the early novel in general, and of *Robinson Crusoe* in particular.[17] It may be part of this parodic intertextuality that Gulliver, unlike Crusoe, almost immediately is made to give up his objects to the indigenous inhabitants of the island.

In a classic example of the satiric technique of making the familiar strange, Gulliver records his hosts' descriptions of these items. On the one hand, the satire here refers back to British culture: the Lilliputians' response functions as Swift's critique of technological dependence, as they deduce, for example, that Gulliver's watch is "some unknown animal or the god he worships" (28). Yet, on the other hand, the episode has more international implications; it works as a satire of the propensity of objects to fluctuate in meaning as they move from one culture into another. These objects then undergo what the anthropologist Nicholas Thomas describes as "a movement and displacement of competing conceptions of things, a jostle of transaction forms. . . . [They] change in defiance of their material stability."[18] The philosophy of the professors of Lagado, who are sure that objects will "serve as a universal language to be understood in all civilized nations, whose goods and utensils are generally of the same kind, or nearly resembling, so that their uses might easily be comprehended" (151), is here proleptically refuted. Instead, the Lilliputians give the watch not a "universal" meaning, but a radically contingent and historical one, as they conclude that the watch may be Gulliver's personal god. In other words, they are tempted to view the watch as a kind of fetish, a mode of understanding objects that the anthropologist William Pietz argues only appeared during the seventeenth century. It arose, he claims, with "the formation of inhabited intercultural spaces along the West African coast" where trade with Europe was conducted, "created by ongoing trade relations between cultures so radically different as to be mutually incomprehensible."[19] Like European traders in Africa, the Lilliputians conclude that the watch must have a purely personal value, as a pet, or as a deity, since they can find no use value or exchange value that accounts for its importance.

Just as the Lilliputian response indicates that European objects are not inherently valuable by virtue of being European, Gulliver's transportation of a number of farm animals out of Lilliput indicates that the value of indigenous items also mutates when they are brought onto European markets. Gulliver first presents these "rarities" both to convince the captain of the vessel that rescues him of his "veracity" and to procure his voyage home (63). Thereafter, these indigenous objects gradually move toward the status of commodities. Gulliver notes that:

> the short time I continued in England, I made a considerable profit by showing my cattle to many persons of quality, and others: and before I began my second voyage, I sold them for six hundred pounds. Since my last return, I find the breed is considerably increased, especially the sheep; which I hope will prove much to the advantage of the woolen manufacture, by the finess of the fleece. (64)

The Lilliputian animals at first become a commodified spectacle, shown to make a profit. As either rarity or spectacle, of course, the animals accrue value through their strangeness, rather than through their usefulness in English terms. But, finally, the animals enter into the ordinary market for wool. After Gulliver sells them, the sheep take their place in the most advanced English system of production in the late seventeenth and early eighteenth centuries—the woolen manufacture. One might read the sheep's oscillation between curiosities and commodities in this description as part of a satire of Gulliver's pretensions to success as a projector—he foolishly hopes that the tiny amount of fine wool gained from these animals will provide a new opportunity for profit. Yet, the sheep's trajectory through the English economic system also seems to intimate the way many curiosities and luxuries—such as sugar, tobacco, or silk—became necessary products tightly enmeshed in British economy during the early modern period. Indeed, raw wool was one of the significant colonial imports of the day, at least from the Celtic fringe, as Ireland, Scotland, and Wales all converted large tracts of land to pasturage in the face of English mercantile embargoes on other products.[20]

Gulliver's success with these animals might be said to indicate the profitability of exploration, even when unaccompanied by the violent appropriation of indigenous land, goods, or people. Yet, his control over the curious and rare items of other cultures and his success as a conveyer of these goods to English markets are both undermined by the events of his second voyage. If Gulliver's journey to Lilliput and back illustrates the text's interest in the mutability of culturally defined objects, his voyage to Brobdingnag reveals the narrative's concern with the way that bodies too are culturally defined, and may alter their use and value in cultural exchange. Gulliver finds that his status as an Englishman of the middling classes evaporates when he reaches Brobdingnag; almost immediately, he is put into the position of his Lilliputian sheep. The Brobdingnagian farmer who discovers him, "finding how profitable [he] was like to be, resolve[s] to carry [Gulliver] to the most considerable cities of the kingdom" (80). Gulliver moves from being the one displaying rarities to being himself the rarity displayed.

Dennis Todd has argued that this episode, along with Gulliver's display of the Lilliputian animals, and numerous other references to voyeurism in the narrative, stems from eighteenth-century England's fascination with fairs and other popular forms of entertainment. He notes that almost everything Gulliver sees on his voyages "could have been seen or experienced in a few days by anyone at the tourist sights, public entertainments, shows, spectacles and exhibitions in the streets and at the fairs of London."[21] While Todd's argument is thorough and convincing, he does not relate this peculiar commodification of leisure to imperialist expansion, preferring to see such fascination as part of a somewhat ahistorical critique of coherent identity. Clement Hawes, in contrast, reads the allusions in *Gulliver's Travels* to eighteenth-century displays of Africans and Native Americans as part of its critique of a colonialist ideology that objectifies cultural others. Yet, Hawes does not connect the psychological sources of racially inflected voyeurism to the economic underpinnings of British mercantile and colonial expansion.[22]

In the narrative itself, however, discussions of such spectacles are often, as with the account of Gulliver's Lilliputian sheep, followed by analyses of the shifting sources of value in an international economy, often focusing on the physical cost of the commodification of bodies. Gulliver, unlike the miniature farm animals, cannot adjust to his status as curiosity. "The frequent labours I underwent every day made in a few weeks a very considerable change in my health: the more my master got by me, the more insatiable he grew. I had quite lost my stomach, and was almost reduced to a skeleton. The farmer observed it, and concluding I soon must die, resolved to make as good a hand of me as he could" (81).

From Gulliver's point of view, being a spectacle is a kind of labor that consumes him; the farmer's extraction of profit from his activities literally melts the flesh off his bones. On one level, this reversal, in which Gulliver becomes the kind of spectacle he formerly controlled, is a critique of the objectification of difference that enables the observers' enjoyment of spectacle, a dynamic both Todd and Hawes describe. On another level, however, Gulliver's position here serves to highlight the potential commodification of human bodies as they move from one culture into another.

When the Brobdingnagian Queen liberates Gulliver from his position as spectacle by purchasing him, the transaction provokes Gulliver to speculate on the impact of such commodification on the relation between different national markets.

> [The Queen] asked my master whether he were willing to sell me at a good price. He, who apprehended I could not live a month, was ready enough to part with me, and demanded a thousand pieces of gold, which were ordered him on the spot, each piece being about the bigness of eight moidores; but, allowing for the proportion of all things between that country and Europe, and the high cost of gold among them, was hardly so great a sum as a thousand guineas would be in England. (82)

Gulliver's words both deny the possibility of an international trade governed by money, and hint at the possibility of such a system of exchange. On the one hand, the Brobdingnagians appear to have a market economy, in which objects, such as Gulliver, can be exchanged according to monetary values. Such an economic structure, especially one based on the familiar substance of gold, seems to suggest the potential for future economic contact between Britain and Brobdingnag. On the other hand, Gulliver also implies that their economy is incompatible with British conceptions of value. The bigness of their gold pieces, a result of the "proportion of all things between this country and Europe," signifies neither excessive wealth, nor their inaccurate valuation of Gulliver, but only extreme physical difference. Gold itself cannot provide a mutual system of value.

Gulliver says in Brobdingnag that "nothing is great or little otherwise than by comparison," but, in general, the disproportionate physical scales of the countries he visits work against the idea of intercultural contact (70). In this aspect of the narrative, at least, *Gulliver's Travels* makes it possible for the reader to compare British culture with these imaginary cultures, by reading them allegorically as versions of Britain. This makes it difficult to imagine a regular interaction between such seemingly contemporaneous societies, and thus short-circuits any explicit critique of mercantile or imperial expansion. The difficulty is produced mainly by physical disproportion, as Gulliver suggests when he dismisses the potential for colonial expansion into Lilliput or Brobdingnag: "The Lilliputians, I think, are hardly worth the charge of a fleet and army to reduce them, and I question whether it would be prudent or safe to attempt the Brobdingnagians" (236). The extent to which the narrative elaborates on these proportional relationships can thus be read as a narrative strategy for denying the potential value of Gulliver's activities for British imperialism. Gulliver's speculations about his own relative worth, however, mark a rare occasion in the text when the possibility of international trading networks is adumbrated; he cannot discuss the buying and selling of his own person without reference to an exchange rate between English and Brobdingnagian coin. Indeed, the ease with which Gulliver discusses the relative value of his own body here seems to indicate his complicity with a discourse of exchange that enables the commodification of human bodies in an international arena; he is, after all, prepared to take Blefuscans back to England along with their animals as a "sample" of their existence, and is only prevented from doing so by their king (62).

It is in this context that we must see the rarities that Gulliver brings out of Brobdingnag. Unlike the Lilliputian farm animals, these objects are all inanimate; nonetheless, they raise difficult questions about the relationship between the international trade in curiosities and the commodification of human bodies. As in the First Voyage, Gulliver produces these items to prove his "candor and veracity" (118) to the captain of the ship that rescues him:

> [I] showed [the Captain] the small collection of rarities I made in the country from when I had been so strangely delivered. There was the comb I had contrived out of the stumps of the King's beard, and another of the same material, but fixed into a paring of her Majesty's thumb nail, which served for the back. . . . I showed him a corn that I had cut off with my own hand from a maid of honour's toe; it was about the bigness of a Kentish pippin, and grown so hard, than when I returned to England, I got it hollowed into a cup and set in silver. . . .
>
> I could force on him nothing but a footman's tooth, which I observed him to examine with great curiosity, and found he had a fancy for it. (118–19)

Gulliver does not record the final fate of these "rarities," although he does display some giant wasp stings for profit, and eventually donates them to a university (89). Yet, the stings, unlike most of the rest of this collection, are not derived from human beings (insofar as the Brobdingnagians are human beings), and it is hard to account for Gulliver's interest in accumulating parings, droppings, and other castoffs from Brobdingnagian bodies. On one level, the passage may be satirizing the inability of European travelers to distinguish between valuable and inconsequential foreign objects; that is, it may be read as a parody of such scenes as Captain Cook describes from his voyages: "it was astonishing to see with what eagerness [the sailors] catched at everything they saw, it even went so far as to become the ridicule of the Natives, by offering pieces of sticks, stones, and what not to exchange, one waggish Boy took a piece of human excrement on a stick and held it out to every one of our people he met with."[23] Gulliver's desire to transform the maid of honour's corn into a beautiful and useful

European object might be seen as a similarly ridiculous perception of other cultures.

Yet, the status of these objects is ambiguous, to readers as well as to Gulliver: are they items of scientific interest, potential aesthetic objects, or of as little value as excrement? We might see that ambiguity, however, in the context of Nicholas Thomas's discussion of the place of the "curiosity" in early colonial discourse. While noting that such objects provoked "an infantile attitude which was excited and aroused by things, but which has no assertive intellectual framework within which the objects could be classified or hierarchized," Thomas points out that "there was a tension between an unstructured apprehension of diverse things and a scientific and imperialist project which affirmed certain relationships between European and indigenous people and made it possible to classify and differentiate those who might become the objects of colonialization."[24]

An "unstructured" or "infantile" attitude certainly colors the captain's fancy for the footman's tooth; presumably, he wants this object neither for profit, nor for scientific research, but simply because he finds it pleasing and curious. Yet, it is also possible to see how these objects might refer to an imperialist project of colonization. The hairs, nails, corns, and teeth Gulliver collects are not the most valuable parts of the Brobdingnagian body, but they nevertheless stand as the metonymic evidence for the existence of such a people. In displaying these objects, Gulliver hints at the possibility of showing those bodies. Since Gulliver's own experiences in Brobdingnag have established such spectacles both as a kind of debilitating labor, and as a way in which bodies are commodified, we can read this collection as a metonymy itself, hinting at the potential violence of transporting non-European bodies into international markets. Unclassifiable as they are, these bits of bodies signal the potential for Brobdingnagians to be taken apart, and put together again as objects of European manufacture — like the chair backs Gulliver makes out of the Queen's hair (101).

Gulliver's dealings with the Brobdingnagian women further illuminate the transformation of human relations into object relations in the Second Voyage. Gulliver's first encounter with the living bodies of these women produces no "other emotions than those of horror and disgust": "their skins appeared so coarse and uneven, so variously coloured, when I saw them near, with a mole here and there as broad as a trencher, and hairs hanging from it thicker than packthread" (95). As critics have noted, this disgust merely reverses Gulliver's identification with these repulsive bodies; despite the negative affect attached to his itemizing of the female body here, this episode also prompts a moment when Gulliver imagines himself in the feminized position of disgusting object.[25] After he faints at the smell of perfumed Brobdingnagian bodies, he remembers the sensitivity of a Lilliputian friend, and "suppose[s] that his faculty of smelling was as nice with regard to me, as mine was to that of this people" (95). By the time Gulliver returns to a European context, however, both his disgust at and his identification with the bodies of Brobdingnagian women have disappeared from his reaction to the maid of honor's corn. Harvested by his own hand, this body part is only an object for Gulliver, and an aesthetic object at that. The corn-goblet resembles the cups made out of exotica, such as ostrich eggs, coconut shells, and rhinoceros horns found in the collections of the Renaissance.[26] This association, however, tends to equate the Brobdingagian woman with the animals and plants of the colonial world; the shape and use of the cup mirror the shape and use of the Brobdingnagian breasts with which Gulliver is fascinated, but in an objectified and controllable form.[27] Here, the bigness of the Brobdingnagians is reduced to an oddly valuable smallness.

Of course, the ambiguous status of curiosities in early modern colonial discourse mediates any relationship between the Brobdingnagian body parts and an imperialism dependent on the commodification of non-European bodies. Yet, even while Swift's text disavows any explicit connection between Gulliver's travels and the exercise of British mercantile power, it also makes visible the workings of a discourse of exchange that might enable such a project. This imbrication of imperialism and the commodification of human bodies is perhaps most explicit in Gulliver's experiences among the Houyhnhnms. Houyhnhnmland has been read as both a utopia and a dystopia, which either forces Gulliver into a painfully clarified vision of mankind or pushes him over the edge into psychosis through its radical difference from his own culture.[28] Yet, despite its fantastic reversal of interspecies relations, in some ways Houyhnhnmland has a greater potential for contact with our own world than any of the other lands Gulliver visits.

Houyhnhnmland is the only country Gulliver explores that is not protected from English aggression by its physical and geographical difference from Europe. In explaining his reasons for withholding its location from the British government, Gulliver alludes to the consequences of such an encounter, rather than to its implausibility: "Their prudence, unanimity, unaquaintedness with fear, and their love for their country would amply supply all defects in the military art. Imagine twenty thousand of them breaking into the midst of an European army, confounding the ranks, overturning the carriages, battering the warrior's faces into mummy, by terrible yerks from their hinder hoofs" (236).

Gulliver's capacity to imagine such an encounter suggests that the possibility of interaction, even of commerce, exists between the two peoples—Gulliver even speculates that such contact may have taken place before his own adventures (238). This suggestion is supported by the circumstances of his arrival on the island; in contrast to his initial contact with the Lilliputians or the Brobdingnagians, Gulliver arrives in Houyhmhnmland ready to set up an inequitable, yet familiar, relationship of exchange between himself and the natives. His first action is to go "up into the country, resolving to deliver myself to the first savages I should meet, and purchase my life from them by some bracelets, glass rings and other toys, which sailors usually provided themselves with in those voyages, and whereof I had some about me" (180).[29] Gulliver seems to have already assumed that he will meet "savages," and that they will be so far outside his system of value as to take these "toys" as "payment" for his life.

Gulliver's expectations that he will meet a familiar form of indigenous culture go on for some time; even after he encounters a group of yahoos, he "pursue[s] the beaten road, hoping it might direct [him] to the cabin of some Indian" (181). Upon reaching a Houyhnhnm dwelling, he produces "some toys, which travellers usually carry for presents to the savage Indians of America and other parts, in hopes that the people of the house would thereby be encouraged to receive me kindly" (184). These initial responses seem to hint that Houyhnhnmland will be inside an imperialist geography in a way that the other cultures Gulliver visits are not. Paradoxically, the Houyhnhnms' innocence of European cultural forms also signals their cultural location;

they do not have a money economy, and Gulliver finds himself forced to explain the process of mercantile expansion to them (203). This economic difference, which the narrative presents as nobility and virtue, brings Houyhnhnmland closer to eighteenth-century stereotypes of native societies than are any of the other cultures Gulliver observes. Gulliver's expectation that the culture he encounters will be organized around a hierarchy of "savagery" and civilization is satisfied; the inferiority of the yahoos to the Houyhnhnms is clear to both Gulliver and his hosts. Thus, precisely because Houyhmhmnland differs from Brobdingnag, Lilliput, and Laputa in its economic organization, it seems more assimilable socially to a colonialist discourse dependent on the category of savagery to justify imperialist violence.

It is also in Houyhnhnmland that the psychic gap I have been discussing, between Gulliver's reactions to people and his reactions to things, most explicitly works to enable the commodification and brutalization of human bodies. Gulliver does not bring any rarities back with him to England when he leaves Houyhmhnmland; in this case, his reduction of bodies into useful objects is much more violent. In order to escape from the island, he builds a boat:

> I finished a sort of Indian canoe, but much larger, covering it with the skins of Yahoos well stitched together, with hempen threads of my own making. My sail was likewise composed of the skins of the same animal; but I made use of the youngest I could get, the older being too tough and thick.
>
> I tried my canoe in a large pond near my master's house, and then corrected in it what was amiss; stopping all the chinks with Yahoo's tallow. (227)

The way that Gulliver uses the yahoo skins here to make a vessel to take him back to England is, in a sense, the next stage in his strategy of using the hair, nails, and teeth of the Brobdingnagians to procure safe passage home on a European ship. No longer content to accumulate and display the human resources of other cultures, he begins to treat those bodies as raw materials to be transformed: first into a decorative object—the cup—then into an object that enables further exploration—a ship. While the Brobdingnagian body parts can be exchanged for safe passage, the yahoo body parts are *themselves* the safe passage.

Furthermore, the context of imperialism that the opening of the Fourth Voyage evokes puts the bodies of the yahoos in relation to the bodies that Europe most violently commodified in its pursuit of colonial power—those of African slaves. Recently, Laura Brown has delineated the extent to which Gulliver's descriptions of the yahoo body, most notably as "a perfect human figure; the face of it . . . flat and broad, the nose depressed, the lips large, the mouth wide" (186), are informed by contemporaneous European representations of Africans. This section of *Gulliver's Travels*, she argues, "is pervasively connected with—indeed essentially compiled from—contemporary evidence of racial difference derived from accounts of the race that was in this period most immediately and visibly the object and human implement of mercantile capitalist expansion."[30] This set of allusions reinforces the idea that the boat made of yahoo skins and yahoo bodies boiled down to tallow might stand in a metonymical relation to something outside the scope of Swift's narrative—the way non-English bodies provided the raw material for the items that guaranteed British imperial power and mercantile wealth. In this case, significantly, the object is a ship.

As he does in Brobdingnag, Gulliver experiences a moment of identification with the object of his own disgust in Houyhnhnmland; a female yahoo's lust forces him to "no longer deny that I was a real yahoo in every limb and feature" (215). The affect produced by this occasion—Gulliver claims that he was "never in [his] life so terribly frighted"—stands in contrast to his complete lack of feeling about those same bodies when they are transformed into shipbuilding materials. Gulliver's capacity both to identify with the yahoos and to use their skins as sails can be read as an early vision of the use of native bodies as the literal raw material of English expansion. Of course, Gulliver's ability to see yahoos as merely useful stuff is never fully stabilized in the narrative, and he reverts to his intensely felt "hatred, disgust and contempt" for (female) yahoos when he reencounters Mrs. Gulliver (233). Yet, his oscillation between these two poles of feeling—excessive negative affect and pragmatic objectification—may be interpreted as marking out the text's dual responses to cultural, and possibly sexual, difference. At its most extreme, such objectification is shown to lead to the possibility of valuing the bodies of cultural others simply as the raw material for interesting objects, like cups, or useful objects, like boats. While this dynamic may be seen as a general attribute of a mercantile, consumerist culture, in *Gulliver's Travels* it is exposed as also enabling British colonial expansion.

### "IT IS BUT SAYING NO AND YOU ARE SAFE"

If *Gulliver's Travels* examines the question of value in transnational settings in the imaginary arenas of fantastical countries, the pamphlets Swift wrote in the persona of M. B. Drapier take on that issue with great specificity and venom.[31] Ireland, he argues, has been reduced to the status of a colony by English economic policy, and that policy is slowly draining the country of its wealth. From the first letter, he contends that "the current Money of this Kingdom is not reckoned to be above Four Hundred Thousand Pounds in all; and while there is a Silver sixpence left, these Blood-suckers will never be quiet."[32] For Swift, Ireland's role as a source of English enrichment signified its colonial status. Of course, Ireland was already in effect a colony of England, but English mercantile policy increasingly restricted Irish trade and industry during the late seventeenth and early eighteenth centuries.[33] The Cattle Act and Navigation Acts of 1663 restricted the export of cattle to England and prohibited direct Irish trade with British colonies, forcing the Irish to buy colonial goods reexported from England. In 1667, cattle exports to England were completely prohibited, depressing the major industry of the day; Gulliver's plans for his Lilliputian cattle and sheep would have been illegal if he had obtained the animals in Ireland. In 1699, the English and Irish parliaments, now under William of Orange, passed a series of acts restricting the importation of raw Irish wool into England—the export of woolen manufacture was already prohibited.[34] These acts may have had little effect on the Irish economy, but they had great symbolic resonance, especially for members of the Anglo-Irish Ascendancy, such as Swift, who had no desire to give up their status as English subjects.[35] The acts seemed to make visible Ireland's dependence on a sovereign government with the power, like that held by the floating island of Laputa, to make their country an unproductive wasteland, depriving them even of sunlight.[36]

In this context, the grant of a patent to the Englishman William

Wood in 1722 to coin copper farthings and halfpence for use in Ireland caused enormous controversy. No one questioned the King's prerogative to grant the patent, nor did anyone dispute the fact that Ireland needed more small coins. The country's gold and silver supplies were rapidly diminishing, as the East India Company bought up Irish coin after the exportation of English money was prohibited. Furthermore, as in Brobdingnag, gold itself provided no universal standard of value; the exchange rate in gold differed between England and Ireland, and Irish merchants turned a profit by paying their English debts in silver, depleting the Irish supply.[37] Yet, the threatened introduction of the halfpence offended the Irish in two ways. In the wake of the Declaratory act of 1720 (which defined England's right to legislate for Ireland), the granting of a patent to an Englishman without consulting a single Irish governing body seemed to contradict any lingering Irish claim to being a kingdom, rather than a colony. The Drapier articulates his outrage at this misperception of Ireland's status in his third letter, "To the Nobility and Gentry of the Kingdom of Ireland":[38]

> Were not the people of *Ireland* born as *free* as those of *England*? How have they forfeited their freedom? Is not their *Parliament* as fair a Representative of the People, as that of *England*? And Hath not their Privy Council as great, or a greater share in the Administration of publick Affairs? Are they not Subjects of the same King? Does not the same Sun shine over them? And have they not the same God for their protector? Am I a Free-man in England, and do I become a Slave in six hours, by crossing the Channel?[39]

If Wood's coinage were introduced, the answer to the Drapier's last rhetorical question would become a resounding "yes." The second aspect of the Drapier's anger has to do with Ireland's impotence to challenge the monetary value assigned to the coins by Wood, and upheld by the corrupt institutions of England.[40] As Wood would surely introduce coins of debased value given the opportunity to do so, the wealth of Ireland would be depleted even further as people exchanged good coins for bad. The Drapier hyperbolically represents the disastrous effects of the resulting inflation by imagining a country squire and his wife arriving in town to shop, followed by five or six horses loaded with the necessary coin for the purchase.[41]

The Irish can resist this ruinous imposition, the Drapier argues, by exercising their underappreciated rights and powers as consumers; he tries to "show the Irish that they [have] within their power a weapon of economic retaliation against the legislative tyranny that had reached its climax with the Declaratory Act."[42] Swift did not invent this strategy; the Irish parliament had passed resolutions refusing English manufacture in 1703, 1705, and 1707, and local newspapers had promulgated the idea, although to little real effect.[43] In 1722, William King articulated the utility of refusing the coin, concentrating on the moral power of landlords: "We have only one remedy, and that is not to receive these [coins] in payments; the Patent obliges none but such as are willing of themselves, if therefore landlords . . . refuse to take their rents in brass . . . it will break the neck of the Project."[44] Swift's own agitation for home consumption of Irish products began in 1720, with the publication of his "Proposal for the Universal Use of Irish Manufacture." In 1724–25, he added Wood's halfpence to the list of English products that depleted Irish wealth. In "A Humble Address to Parliament," the Drapier objects to the purchase of "Indian Stuffs and Calicoes, or Woolen Manufactures imported from Abroad" as "there is no law of the Land obliging us either to receive such Coin, or wear such foreign manufacture."[45] The consumption of all these goods signifies Ireland's capitulation to colonial status.

The Drapier extends the agency of consumer choice from landlords to "Shopkeepers, Tradesmen, Farmers, and Common-People," and eventually to "The Whole People of Ireland." Differentiating between economic sanctions and physical violence, he urges them to use their untapped resources of refusal: "If a Highwayman meets you on the Road, you give him your Money to save your Life; but, God be thanked, Mr *Wood* cannot touch a Hair of your Heads. You have all the Laws of God and Man on your Side. When he, or his Accomplices, offer you his Dross, it is but saying No, and you are safe."[46]

The Drapier emphasizes the economic rather than the military context of anti-colonial resistance here. The fight against Wood's halfpence will be not a violent contest but a peaceful protest for the rights of royal subjects. The Drapier argues that the individual agency of choice can be mobilized against this imposition: "[the] patent . . . did not oblige anyone here to take [the coin], unless they pleased"—the coin can be rejected by "voluntary choice."[47] In light of the eminent legality and civility of this strategy, the Drapier calls upon his readers to "stand to it One and All: refuse this *Filthy Trash*. It is no Treason to rebel against Mr. *Wood*. His *Majesty* in his Patent obliges nobody to take these *Half-Pence*."[48] A consumer boycott of the coin suits the Drapier perfectly, as it targets the commodity without challenging Ireland's allegiance to the British king.

The Drapier thus reverses Gulliver's perspective on foreign objects. If *Gulliver's Travels* explores the way curiosities are valued as they enter Britain from the periphery of exploration, the *Letters* examine what happens when objects whose value is assigned by a colonial power are introduced into a subjugated country. As if they were imbued with the imperialist drive of their makers, the coins sometimes appear as alive as the human artifacts of *Gulliver's Travels* are dead. They lay claim to the peculiar agency of a virus, mindlessly penetrating the boundaries of the body; they "will run about like the Plague and destroy everyone who lays his Hands upon them"; "once [the halfpence] enters, it can no more be confined to a single or moderate Quantity, than the *Plague* can be confined to a few families."[49] Like the adventurers Gulliver describes, the coins will invade with the single instinct of destruction. But instead of that overt violence, the Drapier here suggests that colonial oppression will take a kind of bio-economic form, seeking to destroy the colonized body imagined organically. He has faith, however, in the consumer's immunity to such "pestilent" foreign objects; in the letter addressed "To the Whole People of Ireland" he acknowledges the rumor that Walpole plans to "ram [the halfpence] down our Throats," yet doubts that the coin "would stick in our stomachs."[50]

The Drapier balances this emphasis on individual immunity, agency, and choice against a vision of cohesive, resistant community. This community is, at least rhetorically, organized around the ritual practices of a tribe. He compares the halfpence to "the accursed Thing, which, as the Scripture tells us, the Children of Israel were forbidden to touch."[51] Sociopolitical coherence here becomes the shared recognition of a taboo about foreign substances. Breaking these taboos around consumption can only be accomplished by coercive violence, also represented at the scene of a shared meal. The exaggerated rhetoric of the English press, which claims that the Irish "must *either take these Half-pence or eat* [their] *Brogues,*"

> brings to [the Drapier's] Mind the known story of a *Scotch* Man, who receiving Sentence of Death, with all the Circumstances of *Hanging, Beheading, Quartering, Embowelling,* and the like; cried out, *What need all the* COOKERY? And I think we have Reason to ask the same Question: For if we believe *Wood,* here is a *Dinner* getting ready for us, and you see the *Bill of Fare*; and I am sorry the *Drink* was forgot, which might easily be supplied with *Melted Lead* and *Flaming Pitch.*[52]

The Scotch man ironically accuses his executioners of wanting to eat him, since they have gone to the trouble of cutting him to pieces. The threat of cannibalism hangs over the execution; the Drapier reverses the positions, imagining the Irish sitting down to a nightmare supper of money in which the food does not nourish, but kills. This literalization of the metaphors of enforced consumption continues, as the Drapier elaborately imagines the literal enactment of the English press's threat to make the Irish swallow the halfpence in fireballs. Such a threat is only infeasible because "the trouble and Charge of such an Experiment would exceed the profit," the Drapier concludes.[53] The community the Drapier imagines, then, coheres around the most physicalized aspects of consumption. He envisions an "inside" to the Irish community, which must be kept safe from the violent forced feedings of English mercantilism. The voluntary choice of refusal becomes corporeal self-defense.

In a letter addressed "To Lord Chancellor Middleton," the Drapier delivers a powerful manifesto for the rights of the middle-class consumer. He declares: "For my own Part, who am but one Man, of obscure Education, I do solemnly declare, in the Presence of Almighty GOD, that I will suffer the most ignominious and torturing Death, rather than submit to receive this accursed Coin, or any other that shall be liable to the same Objections, until they shall be forced upon me by a law of my own Country."[54] Here, the Drapier emphasizes his individual agency in resistance, the religious morality of his economic choices, and his alliance with those of "obscure education." He even intimates a kind of anti-colonial nationalism, distinguishing the laws of his own country from those imposed from outside.[55] The Drapier's allegiance to emergent capitalist modes of behavior is emphasized as well by his happy amazement that in the resistance to Wood's halfpence, "*Money*, the great *Divider* of the World, hath by a strange Revolution, been the great *Uniter* of a most *divided People*."[56] Thus, the Drapier articulates a powerful optimism about consumerist strategies of anti-colonial resistance. Subsequently, his beliefs were borne out by the repeal of Wood's patent; the repeal came about in large part as a result of the agitation of Swift's writings.

Swift's identification with the emergent bourgeoisie had its limits, however. His personal faith in a consumerist solution to Ireland's colonial status never quite matched the capitalist optimism of the Drapier, and the voice of the conservative Dean behind that of a progressive merchant occasionally shows through.[57] According to Michael McKeon, *The Drapier's Letters* can be read as an attack on "all the most hated features of the progressive phenomenon . . . [including] the alliance of governmental and monied corruption in the exercise of absolute colonialist power."[58] F. P. Lock, similarly, argues that the real nightmare of Wood's halfpence for Swift is that it signals the conversion of a land-based economy to one entirely based on money.[59] Such concern is evident in the second letter, as the Drapier claims that a "Landlord's Hand and Seal" is better security than any amount of Wood's brass halfpence.[60] Honest landlords, the Drapier hopes, will head up any boycott by urging their tenants to refuse the coin.[61] Thus, even at his most progressive, the Drapier does not imagine the individual consumer as fully autonomous, governed only by his or her own values and pleasures, as later writers were to do. Not only can the consumer be guided by the traditional power of the landlord, but he or she also can be governed by the wishes of the king. Although "compelling the Subject to take any Coin, which is not Sterling, is no Part of the King's *Prerogative*," the Drapier is "very confident, if it were so, we should be the last of his People to dispute it . . . from that inviolable Loyalty we have always paid his majesty[.]" The Drapier thus claims that there are still some stays upon the individual's status as absolute arbiter of his or her market decisions.[62]

### "THE MUSE OF POLITICAL ARITHMETIC"

*The Drapier's Letters*, then, are anti-colonial tracts in the sense that they argue for Ireland's constitutional equality with England as a subject nation of a British king. They do not advocate Irish independence, however, or argue for a unique and homogeneous Irish identity. On the contrary, the letters differentiate strenuously between Irish settlers of English descent and the native, wild, or savage Irish. In the letter addressed "To the Whole People of Ireland," for example, the Drapier bemoans the fate of English settlers in Ireland:

> One great Merit I am sure we have, which those of *English* birth have no pretence to; that our Ancestors reduced the Kingdom to the Obedience of ENGLAND; for which we have been rewarded with a worse Climate, the Privilege of being governed by Laws to which we did not consent; a Ruined Trade, a House of *Peers* without *Jurisdiction*; almost an Incapacity for all Employments, and the Dread of *Wood's* Half-pence.[63]

Indeed, one of the Anglo-Irish's greatest fears was the dissolution of distinctions between the two groups. The Drapier admits that the English already "look upon us as a Sort of *Savage Irish*, whom our Ancestors conquered several Hundred Years ago."[64] It follows, then, that the strategies the Drapier recommends, refusing English goods and substituting home manufacture, are designed to ameliorate the condition of the Anglo-Irish bourgeoisie and Protestant landowners, not the rural, Catholic majority of Ireland's inhabitants.

When the native Irish do appear in Swift's writings of the later 1720s, they bear a noticeable resemblance to the yahoos of *Gulliver's Travels*.[65] Like the yahoos, the Irish were seen by many to be a degraded, racially inferior, pastoral people, only marginally removed from the animals they tended.[66] Yet, Swift's discussion of the dehumanization of the native Irish is more complex than simple prejudice or contempt. He suggests, instead, that since they are forced to struggle with livestock for space and sustenance, they can hardly avoid becoming animalistic themselves. Swift was outraged by the fact that despite the economic restrictions imposed on Ireland during the early eighteenth century, landowners preferred to keep their lands as pasture rather than using them as tillage. With regard to sheep-raising, he contends that

> [t]here is something so monstrous to deal in a Commodity (further than for our own Use) which we are not allowed to export manufactured, or even unmanufactured, but to one certain Country, and only to some few

Ports in that Country; there is, I say, something so sottish, that it wants a Name, in our Language to express it by: and the Good of it is, that the more Sheep we have, the fewer human Creatures are left to wear the Wool or eat the Flesh. Ajax was mad when he mistook a flock of Sheep for his Enemies: But we shall never be sober, until we have the same way of thinking.[67]

In this economic travesty, sheep invade human territory, displacing and destroying the original inhabitants. This reversal mocks Swift's ideal of a self-sufficient island economy by creating more commodities than consumers. Swift critiques the paradoxes of colonial production under mercantilism here, but he also implicitly comments on the way these conditions effect perceptions of the colonized subject. As livestock become people, people become livestock. Placed in competition with sheep, the native Irish are rendered almost indistinguishable from them. In the "Answer to the Craftsman," for example, Swift suggests that when the Irish "changed the Blood of Horses for that of their black Cattle" in their diet, they "by Consequence, became less warlike than their Ancestors": thus, the Irish take on the qualities of the animals they eat.[68] As Irvin Ehrenpreis notes with regard to "A Modest Proposal": "treated as cattle, and as passive as cattle, the Irish are figuratively reduced to pieces of beef."[69] It is in this context that we can read the moment in "A Letter to the Archbishop of Dublin, Concerning the Weavers" when Swift admits that he must often examine "whether those animals which come in [his] way with two legs and human faces, clad and erect, be of the same species with what I have seen very like them in England, as to the outward Shape, but differing in their notions, natures and intellectualls more than any two Brutes in a forest."[70] Swift probably never fully identified himself with or even sympathized with the native Irish, but like the yahoos, his images of them can be read as depicting degradation rather than a natural condition.[71]

In a colonial economy under mercantilism, the absurd reversals continue. Sheep and cattle occupy land that should belong to people and their crops, and, since such livestock cannot be exported, people themselves take on the qualities of portable goods. In other words, the Irish themselves become the most valuable raw material on offer, exportable for profit. For example, in the *Intelligencer* No. 19 (December 1728),

Swift has "a country gentleman" from the North of Ireland explain the value of Irish immigration to America in these terms:

> The truth of the Fact is this: The *English* established in those colonies, are in great Want of Men to inhabit that Tract of Ground, which lies between them and the *wild Indians*, who are not reduced under their Dominion. We read of some barbarous people, whom the Romans placed in their Armies, for no other Service than to blunt their enemies' Swords, and afterwards to fill up Trenches with their dead Bodies. And thus our People, who transport themselves, are settled in those interjacent Tracts, as a Screen against the Assaults of the *Savages*.[72]

While the Irish, in this instance primarily Presbyterians from the North, go to America of their own free will, their value there is determined in the most materialist terms: the mass of their bodies will blunt swords and later function as landfill. Like animals, they are valued not for their initiative, or even for their labor power, but simply as space-filling raw material.

In a pamphlet written the same year, "Maxims controlled for Ireland" (1728), Swift meditates on how Ireland might profit by this export of raw materials. He ironically proposes that the country sell off its inhabitants as slaves:

> It is an undisputed Maxim in government, that people are the riches of a nation, which is so universally granted, that it will hardly be pardonable to bring it in doubt. And I will grant it to be so far true, even in this island, that, if we had the African custom or privilege, of selling our useless bodies for slaves to foreigners, it would be the most useful branch of our trade, by ridding us of a most unsupportable burthen, and bringing us money in the stead.[73]

In exploring the possibility that human beings might become export goods, Swift is playing on an ideal of mercantile policy. According to both Louis Landa and George Wittkowsky, Swift had a longstanding interest in the principle that "people are the riches of a nation"—the idea prevalent in late seventeenth- and early eighteenth-century mercantilist thought, according to which national wealth should be reckoned by assigning a value to individual bodies.[74]

In the Irish context, this principle has often been associated with the work of William Petty, the originator of the science of "political arithmetic." In his work on the Down Survey for Cromwell (so-called because it was written down), Petty sought to quantify the land of Ireland, and the people who lived on it, so as to enable the payment of English investors and soldiers. As Wittkowsky notes, "one effect of the rise of political arithmetic was the intensifying of the tendency to regard human beings as commodities."[75] And, for Petty, not all human beings had the same value. Considering the losses of the "late rebellion," he calculates:

> The value of people, Men, Women and Children in *England*, some have computed to be 70 l. *per* Head, one with another. But if you value the people who have been destroyed in *Ireland*, as Slaves and Negroes are usually rated, *viz.* at about 15 l. one with another; Men being sold for 25 l. and Children 5 l. each; the value of the people lost will be about 10,355,000 l.[76]

Thus, Swift's suggestion that the native Irish might be valued in the same way as African slaves has some historical precedent.[77] In the "Answer to the Craftsman" (written in 1730, but published posthumously), we can see his satirical engagement with the elaborate statistics of political arithmetic. Here, Swift ironically calculates how much money Ireland will save by allowing the kings of France and Spain "leave to carry off Six thousand Men between them" as mercenary soldiers: "By computing the Maintenance of a tall, hungry *Irish* Man, in food and cloaths to be only at Five Pounds a Head, here will be Thirty Thousand Pounds *per Annum* saved clear to the Nation, for they can find no other Employment at Home beside begging, robbing, or stealing."[78] Wittkowsky remarks that Swift wrote "A Modest Proposal" with the aid of the "muse of political arithmetic," but we might extend that inspiration to other of his Irish Tracts, with their interest in the dehumanization and exportation of the native Irish.[79]

What is particularly interesting about these tracts is their recognition of the global context in which these commodified bodies circulate. Scotch-Irish Presbyterians leave Ireland to fill a need in North America; Irish soldiers are profitably employed in the armies of mainland Europe. Only from an international perspective could a comparison between Irish and African bodies make any sense. In these texts,

Swift suggests that one implication of Britain's mercantile policies is that some places will be depopulated, in order that the bodies can be shipped around the world, wherever the empire's need is greatest.[80] These bodies might be required as workers, or as soldiers, or they might simply be used as raw materials, to fill a trench or stop a gap. A harsh satire of the principles of political arithmetic merges with Swift's criticism of England's mercantile policies in these passages, as he imagines the bodies of the native Irish dehumanized, commodified, and exported. He may have felt a certain amount of contempt for the rural Catholic Irish, but it does not prevent him here from criticizing the system that transformed them from productive laborers to dehumanized bodies.[81] In this context, the density of cultural signifiers attached to the yahoos in *Gulliver's Travels*, which have led critics to read them as versions of Africans, the native Irish, generalized human savagery, or some overdetermined combination of the three, makes sense. All these beings were contemporaneously victims of the dehumanization that turned them into the raw material, the fuel, of a more "civilized" society. One might even say that Swift's Irish writings of 1728 to 1730 take up the questions of *Gulliver's Travels* in a much more specific setting. These texts, too, tell the story of the circulation of colonial objects, and the pernicious systems used to assign value to them. In the tracts, however, those objects are the recognizable bodies of the Irish, and their commodification is the oppressive consequence of England's economic violence toward Ireland.

Written during the same period, "A Modest Proposal" (1729) begins by presenting itself as a solution to just this problem: the export for profit of excess Irish bodies. The Proposer addresses the fate of "*helpless infants* . . . who, as they grow up, either turn *Thieves* for want of Work; or leave their dear *Native Country, to fight for the Pretender in* Spain, or sell themselves to the *Barbadoes.*"[82] He further connects the situation of the poor in Ireland to the conditions of other British colonies, by claiming that much of his information about eating children comes from "a very knowing *American.*"[83] The "Proposal," however, works precisely to prevent the potential migration of these bodies to other colonial scenes; as consumable goods, they will be most profitable in their home markets. Thus, "A Modest Proposal" applies the Drapier's consumerist solutions for mercantile oppression to the dehumanization and commodification of colonized bodies revealed in other of Swift's Irish tracts—with horrifying results.[84]

What makes "A Modest Proposal" such a compelling and unanswerable vision of the colonial condition is that it both admits the allure of consumerist strategies of colonial resistance and shows the terrifying limits of those methods. Unlike later writers, who had unbridled optimism about the power of ordinary consumers, the conservative Swift eventually saw them as potential monsters, carrying the reification of human relationships to a logical extreme. The sustained darkness of the pamphlet's satire has been read as part of Swift's increasing hopelessness about the efficacy of popular resistance to government policies. The widespread protest against Wood's halfpence, instigated in part by Swift himself, had successfully voided Wood's patent. Yet, Ireland's political and economic conditions did not change for the better in the following five years.[85]

The consumerist optimism of *The Drapier's Letters* visibly dissipates, for example, in the pamphlet's revision of the Drapier's idealized community, sustained by ritualized consumption practices. In the *Letters*, that scene is one of "tribal" resistance, as the Irish are urged to regard the halfpence as taboo. For the Drapier, such a commitment can only be broken by coercive violence inflicted from outside, as when the Irish are threatened with a forced feeding of coin equivalent to fireballs or molten lead. In "A Modest Proposal," however, one class of Irishmen is imagined as feeding off another in a scene of mutual destruction, as "social unanimity is broken down by mastication and digestion."[86] The Drapier, furthermore, imagines both the native Irish and the Anglo-Irish as curiosities in the eyes of English subjects; "upon the arrival of an Irish man to a Country Town," he says, "I have known Crouds coming about him, and wondering to see him look so much better than themselves."[87] The Proposer, in contrast, unrelentingly represents the native Irish as the raw material for commodities, the Anglo-Irish as cannibalistic consumers. Like the yahoos at the end of Gulliver's fourth voyage, the native Irish have reached the point where they are more valuable as things than as laborers who produce things.

A number of critics have argued that this shift, from colonial oppression to self-destruction, represents Swift's growing tendency to blame the Irish for their own misery.[88] This may be true, but his contempt for the Irish here is certainly combined with a pointed satire of the consumerist strategies of the Proposer—a critique of the progressive bourgeoisie much stronger than that glimpsed in *The Drapier's Letters*. Although Swift continued to promulgate home consumption in later tracts, "A Modest Proposal" seems to reveal a certain loss of faith in consumerist solutions to the inequities of colonial production. The unjust conditions of English colonial rule and mercantile policy have transformed the native Irish into dehumanized and exportable commodities, and changing consumer practices to keep those bodies and the profits they produce at home will not reverse that process. Irish ladies might be convinced to buy gloves made of Irish skin instead of French silk through a sense that they are ameliorating the conditions of the poor. But this ethical, nationalistic practice merely implicates the colonial consumer in the oppressive economic policies of England.[89]

Indeed, in convincing consumers to turn cannibal, the Proposer can be seen not as advocating progress, but rather as returning the Irish to the worst moments of their past. Swift was familiar with the long association between the Irish and cannibalism from Thomas Sheridan's exploration of it in the *Intelligencer* (no. 18, November 1728), if not from other sources, and drew on those accounts when he wrote "A Modest Proposal."[90] Depictions of the Irish as cannibals possibly originate in Giraldus Cambrensis's *Topography of Ireland*, written in the late twelfth century, and continue in Edmund Spenser's late sixteenth-century images of the survivors of the Munster wars: "[they] did eat of the dead carrions . . . yea and one another soon after in so much as the very carcasses they spared not to scrape out of their graves."[91] They appear in similar terms in Fynes Morrison's account of the aftermath of Tyrone's Rebellion in his *Itinerary* (1617). Sheridan, summarizing the worst of Morrison's stories in the *Intelligencer*, focuses on the way cannibalism perverts the conventionally nurturing relationships between women and children.

> [A] poor widow of *Newry*, having six small children, and no food to support them, shut up her Doors, Died through despair, and in about three or four Days after, her children were found Eating her Flesh. . . . at the same time, a discovery being made of Twelve Women, who made a practice of stealing Children, to Eat them, they were all burned, by order of Sir *Arthur Chichester*, then Governour of the *North* of *Ireland*.[92]

Children eat mothers, and mothers eat other peoples' children; the economic ruin that follows in the wake of colonial conquest thus destroys the most minimal bonds of community. In "A Modest Proposal," the Proposer envisages "modernizing" a similar recourse to cannibalism through the rational dynamics of the market.

Carole Fabricant claims that Swift recognized "close ties between Ireland's self-destructive tendencies and England's brutal oppressions," while Claude Rawson attributes Swift's "cannibal slur" to the belief that "this is what the savages do anyway, or (equally pertinent) that the whole Irish nation is driving its poor to such things."[93] Yet, whether Swift blames the English or the Irish for their susceptibility to cannibal solutions, he does seem to deflate any claim for Irish progress or modernity here. Significantly, the best-known accounts of cannibalism derive from the Elizabethan conquest of Ireland, which followed a "scorched earth" policy of devastation in order to "deprive the Irish of food, succour and recruits," and aimed to "make Ireland 'a razed table' upon which the Elizabethan state could transcribe a neat pattern"[94] — the era, in other words, that brought Ireland into the age of imperialism. Irish cannibalism, then, can be read as evidence of the continuing process of brutal colonization. Invoking the practice in "A Modest Proposal," Swift collapses the temporal distance between the "savage" world England labored to subdue in the sixteenth century and the "civilized" world of Ascendency culture.

Toward the end of "A Modest Proposal," the Proposer compares Ireland unfavorably to several other societies thought to be cannibalistic. The Irish, he contends, have failed in "learning to love [their] Country, wherein [they] differ even from LAPLANDERS, and the Inhabitants of TOPINAMBOO." This comparison reiterates the Proposer's claim that the misery of his country is unique, and the extremity of his scheme suits "this one individual Kingdom of IRELAND, and . . . no other that ever was, is, or I think ever can be upon Earth."[95] Yet, even as this formulation insists on Irish exceptionalism, it simultaneously makes available the connections between Ireland and other "savage" landscapes. This rhetorical construction occurs with some frequency in Swift's writings about Ireland. We have seen it already in the idea that Africa manages its excess population better than Ireland does, by feeding slaves to the empire. And in the *Intelligencer*, the northern landowner admits, "I see nothing left to us but to truck and barter our Goods, like the wild Indians, with each other; or with our too powerful Neighbors; only with this Disadvantage on our side, that the Indians enjoy the product of their own Land whereas the better half of ours is sent away, without so much as a Recompence in Bugles or Glass in Return."[96] Here, Ireland's economic relation to England is revealed to be worse than the conventional imperialist exchange of valuable raw materials for trinkets. Swift's objective is clear; he argues that Ireland should be rescued from such comparisons, restored to a condition of equality with England. Yet, the comparisons collapse spatial distance in much the same way that the treatment of cannibalism in "A Modest Proposal" collapses temporal distance, creating suggestive links between Ireland and the colonial periphery.

The rhetoric of these passages emphasizes the paradoxes of Swift's status as an anti-colonial writer. On the one hand, he continually points out that Ireland's condition, and its misery, are unique, not least because the country deserves to be treated as an equal partner by England. He tries to write himself and the Anglo-Irish out of their colonial status. On the other hand, he cannot illustrate this point except by comparing Ireland to the other savage wastelands of the world, many of them the scenes of imperial conquest. Even the Drapier admits that "As to Ireland, [the English] know little more than they do of Mexico; further than it is a Country subject to the king of England, full of Boggs, inhabited by wild Irish Papists; who are kept in Awe by mercenary Troops sent from thence."[97] He recognizes that the English see Ireland as a colony like Mexico, full of rebellious subjects who need to be kept in check by imperial troops. In the English imagination, the place of the Anglo-Irish, loyal and deserving subjects of the king, the position from which Swift hopes to speak, disappears into the dichotomy of colonizer and colonized; as an Anglo-Irish writer, Swift speaks from a position he knows to be invisible. Paradoxically, what emerges instead from Swift's attempts to differentiate between the Irish and the rest of the world is an implicit continuum between conditions in Ireland and the more far-flung enterprises of English empire-building. One could even say that Swift's writings of the 1720s, from *Gulliver's Travels* to "A Modest Proposal," register the impact of the Treaty of Utrecht, signed in 1713, which granted England a monopoly on the American slave trade; they make visible a synchronic connection between Africans, Irish, and yet-to-be-discovered types of yahoos, based on England's imperial need to commodify and transport the valuable raw material of colonized bodies. By the end of the decade, the conservative Swift, unlike later writers, came to believe that no amount of organized consumer practices could halt this lamentable process.

Chapter 3

# Foreign Objects, Domestic Spaces

*Transculturation in* Humphry Clinker

England's colonial possessions seem very far away in Smollett's
*Humphry Clinker.* On the contrary, the novel has been called both a
"comic Pastoral poem in prose" and a "picaresque ramble," because it
concerns a domestic journey. Not only does it primarily move across
the domesticated spaces of England and Scotland, but it also focuses
on a domestic group—a household organized around familial relations.[1] This conventional social organization finds a mirror in the text's
formal structure; just as the Bramble party's road trip casts a fresh perspective on traditional relationships, so does the narrative put a new
twist on the epistolary novel. Yet, the novel's recourse to such generic
ideals has been read on occasion as a defensive bulwark against the
social ills of late eighteenth-century England, a litany of exhaustively
cataloged conflicts that continually threaten to interrupt the Bramble
party's journey.[2]

Indeed, the encyclopedic nature of the novel seems linked to its particular brand of epistolarity. Its letters provide a multiplicity of perspectives, what Eric Rothstein calls a "compound eye, in whose multiple
vision the authority of the novel consists."[3] Hazlitt labeled the effect of
this structure "gossiping," a term that "highlights one of the novel's
most conspicuous features: the wealth of historical, biographical, autobiographical, economic, political, social, geographical, and topographi-
cal data that the characters see, use, hear about, discuss, and report
back to their internal readers."[4] Recent readings of *Humphry Clinker*
have given pride of place to this gold mine of cultural information;
scholars have looked to the novel to elucidate such issues as changing
conceptions of the poor, the debate over agricultural reform, the sexual
anxiety provoked by popular castrato singers, and attitudes toward the

growing fashion market, among others.[5] In addition, critics have demonstrated the importance of Smollett's own origins to the novel's concern with the construction of a British identity that could incorporate Scotland as well as England.[6]

This chapter aims to demonstrate that the novel's concerns extend even further afield — into the colonial arena of the Americas.[7] Furthermore, it argues that even within domestic spaces, the problems posed by colonial expansion can be perceived, and that it is precisely those problems that provoke the anxiety over the dissolution of English domestic self-sufficiency that is one of *Humphry Clinker*'s most persistent concerns. The primacy of this concern may not be immediately apparent, embedded as it is in a more legible anxiety over England's changing class structure. But, by concentrating on the novel's representation of colonial relations, I not only want to make visible the growing connectedness of English and colonial society in the period, but also to reveal the work the novel performs to neutralize any textual evidence of this increasing interdependence, and to erect instead a compensatory fantasy of English self-sufficiency. This fantasy of self-sufficiency, of an impenetrable national identity, seems to me to be one of the most durable legacies of the eighteenth century, and to hold a central place in the organization of Smollett's novel.

*Humphry Clinker*'s depiction of the effects of England's colonial relations on domestic life in some ways replicates the representational strategies used by Swift. Smollett, like Swift, uses foreign objects both to objectify the military and economic structures of international relations, and to render those relationships repellent by investing them with excessive negative affect. The novel mobilizes a kind of Swiftian disgust around suspicious items, especially foodstuffs, in an attempt to render social and cultural mixing reprehensible. Unlike Swift, however, Smollett investigates the entrance of those items into England's domestic spaces. Furthermore, his novel registers a later moment in the development of colonial ideology in eighteenth-century England, investigating the country's growing reliance on the products of the colonial periphery. *Humphry Clinker* describes the dynamics of a culture irrevocably enmeshed in an international economy.

I want to begin with the story of a journey that reverses the usual trajectory of colonial expansion: Captain Lismahago's voyage back from the Native American tribe that adopts him to the heart of English domestic space as Tabitha Bramble's husband. Captain Lismahago's return is only the novel's most graphic example of the intrusion of the colonial world into English domestic life. Like Lismahago, numerous new commodities made their way back from the New World during the first half of the eighteenth century. To cite one of Smollett's own lists, "sugar, rum, tea, chocolate, and coffee"[8] all became part of everyday English life during that first phase of imperial expansion. As James Bunn notes, "tea and porcelain now seem so iconistically English that one must recall . . . [that] what seems to be the very soul of Englishness might recently have been imported and assimilated by a syncretic culture."[9] The influx of these substances, then, was one of many material tokens intimating that England's colonial expansion had not only created syncretic cultures in the colonial arena but might also challenge the country's idea of itself as a coherent, homogeneous society.[10]

This increase in the consumption of colonial foodstuffs triggered a concern for the national integrity of England itself. We have already noted the presence of nationalist rhetoric in attacks on consumerism like Hanway's "Essay on Tea." Hanway, in a sense, calls for the English to stop emulating the Chinese in consuming Chinese products. In doing so, he draws on a critique of consumerist mimicry established earlier in the eighteenth century by such writers as Lady Mary Wortley Montagu. For example, in the first issue of her anonymous periodical, *The Nonsense of Commonsense*, Montagu argues that the poor have been "reduced now to a very low ebb by the Luxury and ill taste of the Rich, and the fantastic mimicry of our Ladys, who are so accustomed to shiver in silks, that they exclaim at the Hardships of Warmth and Decency." She recommends that such ladies forsake French silk for English wool and "appear in a Habit that does Honnour to their own country and would be a universal benefit to the Nation."[11] Criticism of English imitation of French habits continued into the middle of the century, in the writings of Samuel Johnson, among others, who writes in *London*: "Behold the warrior dwindled to a beau; / Sense, freedom, piety refin'd away, / Of France the mimic, and of Spain the prey." Smollett, particularly in the character of Mrs. Baynard, reiterates such contempt for English mimicry of the French. Yet, he also broadens this rhetoric to include the way English consumers are distorted by their consumption of the new products of international and imperial trade.

In Smollett's *Humphry Clinker*, published in 1771, one can judge the gravity of such a challenge through the narrative's vision of the dangerous consequences of intercultural contact. The novel's anxiety about the economic changes wrought by merchant capitalism centers on the transculturation of England threatened by the foreign luxury goods that mercantile trade brought back into the country. For the text, these luxury goods are most exemplarily foodstuffs, whose penetration of individual digestive tracts replicates the penetration of English culture by its supposedly subjugated colonies. Indeed, "by far the largest group [in percentages of total imports during the period] is that which the officials describe as 'grocery' and which consisted of tea, coffee, sugar, rice, pepper and a variety of other tropical, semi-tropical or oriental produce."[12] The growing necessity for such imports undermined England's claim to national self-sufficiency, especially during the period in which *Humphry Clinker* was written: "between 1765 and 1774 . . . homegrown supplies [of food] were insufficient to meet the needs of a growing population."[13] Smollett's novel views these economic developments as threatening—it figures the process of intercultural exchange as a kind of poisoning, newly possible at the domestic table.

Alongside this fantasy of incorporation, in which cultural difference is fantasmatically transformed into a foreign object looking to take up a destructive residence inside English bodies, we can read a compensatory defense of national identity. The problem of how to assimilate, or acculturate, other cultures, economically or socially, is redacted into a problem of oral consumption: to avoid becoming the other, one must simply avoid eating the other. *Humphry Clinker* represents the economic and military relations between the metropolis and the periphery as object relations, and in this way attempts to neutralize the cultural anxiety surrounding transculturation. In other words, this strategy of literalization can be interpreted as a textual response to the importance of commodification in structuring colonial ideology during this period. Out of the novel's insistently corporeal and oral figurations of changing patterns of economic consumption, a nascent fantasy of disconnection emerges, expressing a desire for England to disentangle itself from the cross-cultural connections of mercantilism. Such a fantasy, of course, could only be motivated by a clear vision of the collapsing distinctions between foreign sites of capital accumulation and domestic spaces of consumption.

### LISMAHAGO'S TRANSCULTURATION

During the second half of the eighteenth century, England's closest commercial ties were with her American colonies, a historical dynamic that is well illustrated by *Humphry Clinker*. Like almost all eighteenth-century English novels, it refers to the colonies frequently, as a convenient offstage site for capital accumulation, or as a respectable outlet for entrepreneurial energy.[14] The novel contains only one extended anecdote about colonial life, however: Captain Lismahago's account of his captivity among the Miamis in North America. Critics have often pointed to the topicality of this story, and have used it as evidence of Smollett's extensive knowledge of historical sources. Louis Martz, for instance, claims that Lismahago's adventures are based on episodes from the "History of Canada," which appeared in the *British Magazine* from 1760 to 1763, while T. R. Preston argues for the equal importance of Cadwallader Colden's *History of the Five Nations* (1727) in the formulation of these events.[15] One could undoubtedly find many more relevant historical accounts, given the British preoccupation with the conquest of North America during the 1760s. Yet, the multiplicity of possible sources for Lismahago's adventures points as much to the repetition of certain images in eighteenth-century accounts of Native Americans as it does to Smollett's own extensive historical knowledge. I would claim, as well, that these images enact different versions of a problematic scenario for the English during this period: the meeting of two distinctly different cultures in an imperialist setting.

The term "transculturation" seems particularly appropriate for the British experience in North America; the possibility of the "creation of new cultural phenomena" was always present in North America, not least because the indigenous residents of that area were not immediately eradicated, as were those of the Caribbean islands.[16] Instead, although the native tribes were numerically small, James Axtell, for one, has claimed that the battle for hegemony south of the Canadian Shield was primarily waged in terms of cultural conversion: he argues that "the contest for North America was fought largely in times of declared peace, with weapons other than flintlocks and tomahawks."[17] To their advantage in this struggle, the Northeastern tribes were disconcertingly capable of absorbing Europeans into their communities.[18] The colonial encounter in the North American woods was more complicated than simple imperial aggression—as can be seen from Lismahago's adventures.

Indeed, Smollett's rendering of his story takes the form of a parody of the narrative convention that encompassed these complicated relations, the captivity narrative. Captivity narratives, accounts of Europeans forcibly exposed to Native American cultures, themselves encapsulate the ambiguities of transculturation by pointing out a secondary meaning in the word itself: the ability of individuals to move across, or through, cultures. Although the burden of these early American documents is usually to illustrate the protagonist's suffering in a supposedly savage society, such narratives must somehow accommodate the fact that he or she has survived these hardships, having adapted sufficiently to Native American customs to return alive. The tension in these narratives between the fact of survival and the cultural imperative to establish the savagery of Native American tribes becomes apparent when Rachel Plummer, abducted by the Comanche in 1836, writes "I have withheld stating many things that are facts, because I well know that you will doubt whether any person could survive what I have undergone."[19] Because the reader must continue to doubt that "life" as Europeans construe it is possible inside a Native American tribe, Plummer elides material descriptions of the "facts" of her captivity. The coding of cultural adaptation as inhuman suffering is incompatible with the "fact" of her survival; the narrative ellipsis can be read as an ideological aporia.

Lismahago's narrative rehearses this central ambivalence in English representations of Native American captivities—the contradiction between documenting the adaptability of cultural identities and reasserting the superiority of European social values. Two moments central to many accounts of the tribes of Northeastern America reappear in Lismahago's story: the Algonquin torture ritual of making prisoners "run the gauntlet" (also called bastinado) and their subsequent practice of either adopting such prisoners into the tribe or cannibalizing them. These rituals, although violent, were seen by eighteenth-century observers as the means by which Native American tribes appropriated and transformed foreign cultures. Europeans saw these rituals as evidence of a tribe's ability to retain its social coherence in the face of a colonizing invasion—a quality they found admirable as well as threatening.

The resonance of the scene of cross-cultural adoption for a culture, which, like eighteenth-century England, was concerned with colonial acquisition, becomes apparent in Cadwallader Colden's analysis of the phenomenon. Colden, one-time governor of New York and a historian of eighteenth-century colonial relations, links the practice of adopting prisoners of war with imperial expansion. In his *History of the Five Nations*, published in 1727, he remarks:

> They strictly follow one Maxim, formerly used by the *Romans* to increase their Strength, that is, they encourage the People of other Nations to incorporate with them; and when they have subdued any People, after they have satiated their Revenge by such cruel Examples, they adopt the rest of their Captives; who, if they behave well, become equally esteemed with their own people; so that some of their Captives have afterwards become their greatest *Sachems* and *Captains*.[20]

The ability of the Northeastern tribes to "incorporate" and "adopt" foreigners into their own society without diminishing their own cultural integrity fascinated European observers. This principle of absorption, especially when linked to ideas of "Roman strength," seems to provide a model for a successful, expansionary encounter with another culture. Such native tribes manage to bring foreigners into their culture without challenging their dominant social system, and while continuing to patrol rigorously the borders of that society. Thus, Smollett's Miamis are able to do what the English cannot: in Lismahago's words,

> The Indians were too tenacious of their own customs to adopt the modes of any nation whatsoever. . . . [N]either the simplicity of their manners, nor the commerce of their country, would admit of those articles of luxury which are deemed magnificence in Europe; and that they are too virtuous and sensible to encourage the introduction of any fashion which might help to render them corrupt and effeminate. (189)

If colonial expansion has occasioned the luxury that corrupted English society, then, in Lismahago's view, the Miamis' tenacious belief in their own culture has enabled them to maintain their virtue: in this case, the colonial encounter violates Europe, rather than the New World.

Eighteenth-century commentators' admiration for the strength and durability of native cultures has its double in a contrasting vision of this encounter. In this nightmarish version of social absorption, the captives are eaten; cannibalism too somehow allegorizes the meeting of two cultures. These two possibilities—cannibalism or adoption—seem to function as positive and negative versions of the same event in the eyes of their European victims. Both options focus on Native American social "tenacity"; both adoption and cannibalism ultimately work to maintain social coherence. The eighteenth-century equation of cultural and gastrointestinal absorption implies a certain vision of how intercultural confrontations might be negotiated. On one hand, such images of Native Americans glorify an image of Roman, imperial virtue as the model of cultural expansion, while, on the other hand, they outline the threat of the literal disappearance of European culture into the belly of America. But, in both cases, texts like Colden's imply that when two cultures meet, one must be incorporated, whole, inside the other.

Lismahago's experience, however, represents a third option; his story has more to do with cultural syncretism than with either destruction or absorption. Jery Melford's transcription of Lismahago's version of these events reads like this:

> [Lismahago and Murphy] fell in with a party of Miamis, who carried them away in captivity. The intention of these Indians was to give one of them as an adopted son to a venerable sachem, who had lost his own in the course of the war, and to sacrifice the other to the custom of the country. Murphy, as being the younger and handsomer of the two, was designed to fill the place of the deceased, not only as the son of the sachem, but as the spouse of a beautiful squaw, to whom his predecessor had been betrothed; but in passing through the different whigwhams [sic] or villages of the Miamis, poor Murphy was so mangled by the women and children, who have the privilege of torturing all prisoners in their passage, that, by the time they arrived at the place of the sachem's residence,

he was rendered unfit for the purposes of marriage: it was determined, therefore, in the assembly of the warriors, that ensign Murphy should be brought to the stake and that the lady should be given to Lieutenant Lismahago, who had likewise received his share of torments, though they had not produced emasculation.—A joint of one finger had been cut, or rather sawed off with a rusty knife; one of his great toes was crushed into a mash betwixt two stones; some of his teeth were drawn, or dug out with a crooked nail; splintered reeds had been thrust up his nostrils and other tender parts; and the calves of his legs had been blown up with mines of gunpowder dug into the flesh with the sharp point of the tomahawk. (188)[21]

The Miamis then make "a hearty meal upon the muscular flesh which they pared from the victim" and marry Lismahago to the sachem's daughter Squinkinacoosta (188). Although the passage outlines the usual options of incorporation—Murphy is eaten while Lismahago is adopted—its descriptive focus is on the violence of running the gauntlet. The injuries Lismahago sustains to his extremities form the basis of the text's vision of his transculturation—his movement from one culture into another.

The significance of this particular form of violence underlines the fact that these descriptions are the aspect of his historical sources that Smollett most painstakingly replicates in *Humphry Clinker*.[22] Smollett's description of the structure of the gauntlet is so similar to Cadwallader Colden's as to seem a simple repetition.[23] The more brutal instances of dismemberment may well have come from Smollett's own *British Magazine*, which began to publish the "History of Canada" in 1760.[24] This serial abounds in the same descriptions of the ripping and tearing of bodies as does *Humphry Clinker*. To cite just one example: "[one prisoner] had been tortured according to custom. One hand had been crushed between two stones, and one finger torn off: they had likewise chopped off two fingers of the other hand; the joints of his arms were burnt to the bone, and in one of them was a dreadful gash or incision."[25] The central role these details play in Lismahago's story suggests that the gestures of paring and grinding down of European bodies provide Smollett's novel with appropriately corporeal images for the experience of transculturation on the North American frontier. Lismahago's captivity narrative represents the dispersal of the Euro-

pean body in pieces; teeth, fingers, and other body parts disappear into
the Native community. In this way, the diffuse operations of cultural
change are reduced to discrete, physical losses.

Lismahago's account, however, wrestles with the central ambiguity
of captivity narratives. His absorption into the Miamis, despite the
physical suffering it occasions, illustrates a historically new transience
in cultural identifications. Running the gauntlet of the Miamis rather
brutally reshapes him, true—leaving him missing a few teeth and fingers; but it does not disempower him, or, the text stresses, emasculate
him. In fact, he is "elected sachem, acknowledged first warrior of the
Badger tribe, and dignified with the epithet of Occacanastaogarora,
which signifies *nimble as a weasel*" (189). He enters into a miscegenous
union with Squinkinacoosta, and produces a son among the Miamis.
Yet, significantly, Lismahago begins his journey back to England when
he is "exchanged for an orator of the community, who had been taken
prisoner by the Indians that were in alliance with the English" (189).
The principle of adoptability thus renders individuals both replaceable
and portable—Lismahago moves as easily between cultures as one of
his own furs. In this case, cultural exchange is literalized by the mobility of bodies through the communities that are no longer able to
anchor them.

In addition, we should remember that, as a Scottish soldier, Lismahago is in some ways already the human equivalent of the commodities mentioned at the beginning of this chapter. While perhaps
not as drastically dehumanized as the native Irish who preoccupied
Swift, a remarkable number of Scots entered the circuits of empire in
the eighteenth century, particularly after the failed rebellion of 1745.
Indeed, a late eighteenth-century mode of thinking about the Scottish
was as a pool of surplus population, destined, like the Irish, to fill the
empire's various and sundry needs; one reformer believed that the
country might become "*a People-Warren* for supplying [the] King with
brave soldiers and sailors and the more fertile parts of the kingdom with
faithful servants of every description."[26] Matthew Bramble seems to par-
take of this view when he suggests that the Highland Scots might do
more good for Britain outside their own territory than within it. Their
traditional mode of husbandry, he argues, leads them into "that idle-
ness and want of industry, which distinguishes these mountaineers in

their own country"; but "when they come out into the world, they become as diligent and alert as any people upon the earth" (245). He notes that "these Scots make their way in every corner of the globe" (209). Lismahago, then, can be read on one level as representative of the many Scots who moved between the heterogeneous cultures of Britain during the period, including Smollett himself.

Indeed, as Robert Crawford reminds us, Lismahago tells his story just as the Bramble party is preparing to cross the border from England into Scotland. Both Crawford and Katie Trumpener propose that this placement triangulates England, Scotland, and the American colonies, in order to place Scotland on the side of domestic "civilization"; "the Scotland to be presented to these Welsh visitors appears all the more refined by contrast with the account of the Amerindian" barbarity in Lismahago's tale.[27] Trumpener argues that this contrast functions to prevent Scotland from being perceived as an English colony; the novel works against the danger "that an imperial view of subject cultures will inform English views of Scotland. Recounted to Anglo-Welsh travelers on the eve of their arrival in a Scotland they expect to be backward and savage, Captain Lismahago's tale is cautionary, warning them not to recast the Scots in the role of militant primitives."[28] These points are plausible, but even as Lismahago stabilizes the relationships between the heterogenous territories he traverses, he also brings a certain instability in cultural identifications into the heart of the Bramble family circle.

His first encounter with the Bramble party reveals his physical difference: "his hat and periwig falling off, displayed a head-piece of various colours, patched and plaistered in a woeful condition" (182). He has, he explains, been scalped. Rendered alien in this way, he gains Othello's skills as a lover: Tabitha *did seriously incline her ear—* indeed, she seemed to be taken with the same charms that Captivated the heart of Desdemona, who loved the Moor *for the dangers he had past*" (189). In what is, once again, a syncretic collapse of the many cultures inhabiting North America, Lismahago has the eloquence both of the African Othello and of the Native Americans among whom he has lived: he owes his presence in England to being exchanged with a tribal orator. Along with his external changes, Lismahago has acquired a style of speech associated with exoticism and seduction; he has assumed the Miamis' ability to take captives and so "captivates" Tabitha. If the novel uses these tropes to satirize the rather ungainly couple of Tabitha and Lismahago, it also, through these images, acknowledges the recognition triggered by such American concepts in late eighteenth-century England. Through this chain of associations, Lismahago's marriage to Tabitha becomes as much an interracial union as his marriage to Squinkinacoosta was—he represents the presence of creolized North America on English domestic soil.

Lismahago's wedding gift to Tabitha, a "fur cloak of American sables, valued at fourscore guineas" reinforces the aura of scandal surrounding their union (331). Not only does this costume complete the doubling of the two wives by dressing them alike, but it also figures Lismahago's position as a trader, and therefore points to his part in the machinery of colonial expansion. Owing to his transformative experiences, Lismahago is a foreigner both among the Miamis and among the English, but his position as a trader bridges the two worlds. Furthermore, his samples of colonial goods are not merely curiosities but are also tokens of transculturation, forming the links of a chain of commerce binding the sites of colonial production to the sites of domestic consumption.

*Humphry Clinker*'s description of Lismahago's sojourn among the Miamis contains three possible models of intercultural contact: an image of cultural expansion, centering on the Native American practice of adopting war captives; a vision of cultural obliteration focused on the threat of cannibalism; and, finally, a scenario of cultural syncretism, which finds its economic equivalent in trading, and its corporeal image in the dispersal of bodies along the gauntlet. The remainder of this chapter will examine how these possibilities, particularly the last, function in the greater part of *Humphry Clinker*, which takes place in domestic territory.

### DOMESTIC TIDES

If Lismahago's narrative illustrates the growing, inextricable net of connections linking England to her colonial possessions, then the novel's domestic scenes figure those connections in a particularly mediated way. Using the same strategy of corporealizing cultural change as the inserted captivity narrative, *Humphry Clinker* imagines English bodies to be under attack by the forces of mercantile accumulation. These forces are materialized in the catachrestic "tide of luxury." The instability of the world through which the Bramble party travels is consistently denoted by images of fluidity. Social disintegration is a "flood of luxury and extravagance," which can turn a city into a "mere sink of profligacy and extortion" (56); the "tide of luxury" (87) ends in "one vile ferment of stupidity and corruption" (87). These metaphors are a typical eighteenth-century method of describing an economy governed by mercantilism, and a society newly reshaped by trade: as Lismahago explains, trade "is a continual circulation, like that of the blood in the human body, and England is the heart to which all the streams which it distributes are refunded and returned" (268). In this characteristic trope, trade and the human body are brought into relation through images of fluidity—the individual body becomes a figure for the cultural body of England.

In Bath, these metaphors for social instability assume a different guise, one which proves perilous for individual bodies. Here, the ebb and flow of commerce is mirrored by the waters of the baths, which become a literal medium of corporeal contamination. But this metaphoric transference, from the economic to the corporeal, does more than simply mirror economic changes in literary terms. It works to neutralize the threat posed by shifting power relations between social classes in England by figuring them as a danger against which individual bodies can actually defend themselves. This representation erects the fantasy that if the baths can be purified, and if foreign substances can be expelled from the body, then the changes in English class structure wrought by cross-cultural economic connections can be reversed. At the same time, this literalization needs to be read as a version of the objectification inherent in a commodity culture. In other words, even as the narrative criticizes the influx of colonial luxury, and the resulting reorganization of class structures, it relies on the individual's power to refuse particular objects, a strategy of resistance only possible in a social world organized around the consumer's relation to a plethora of available commodities.

Smollett's Bath is most obviously scandalous because of the indiscriminate mixing of social classes that takes place there, yet the novel makes rhetorical links between this scandal and the process of imperial expansion. Such links can already be seen in Matthew Bramble's claim that:

> All these absurdities arise from the general tide of luxury, which hath overspread the nation, and swept away all, even the very dregs of the people. Every upstart of fortune, harnessed in the trappings of the mode, presents himself at Bath, as in the very focus of observation—Clerks and factors from the East Indies, loaded with the spoil of plundered provinces; planters, negro-drivers, and hucksters, from our American plantations, enriched they know not how; agents, commissaries and contractors, who have fattened, in two successive wars, on the blood of the nation; usurers, brokers, and jobbers of every kind; men of low birth, and no breeding, have found themselves suddenly translated into a state of affluence, unknown to former ages. (36)

All of these "upstarts of fortune," aside from the usurers, brokers, and jobbers, have been "translated" into affluence either in or through colonial and foreign ventures. Bramble's method of description itself underlines the disruption such an influx of mercantile wealth produces at Bath. He lists the types of people to be found in the city in no partic- ular order, as if they themselves were commodities adrift in the "tide of luxury." Laura Brown has identified the presence of such random lists in eighteenth-century texts like "The Rape of the Lock" as the "rhetoric of acquisition"; she claims that in such "catalogues the simple list of goods carries a raw and inherent fascination" for "mercantilist dis- course."[29] But in Smollett's list, this acquisition has taken on a threat- ening edge. The "blood of the nation" is set in a negative economy with the various oceans the traders and soldiers cross to make their profits: the former is depleted to swell the "tides of luxury." To account for such anxiety, James Bunn proposes that the danger surrounding random collections was in fact part of the threat mercantilism posed to English cultural identity: "So prodigious, yet so patternless seemed the import of luxuries from cultures distanced in space and time, that the effect seemed to have a life of its own, as if Pygmalion's beloved grew grotesque. According to that kind of metaphorical thinking, a growing mass of exotic imports overburdened the foundation of native English liberties and made them 'precarious.'"[30] The very patternlessness of the collection of riches at Bath, and the syntax of iteration this accumula- tion provokes, signal irreversible cultural changes. The source of such changes is located in wealth imported from abroad. In the half century between "The Rape of the Lock" and *Humphry Clinker*, the not-so-metaphorical oceans of trade ceased to swell the English spirit and began to dissolve its cultural borders.

The historical specificity of Smollett's anxiety over the influx of capital from colonial trade can be seen by comparing two satirical poems about Bath by Christopher Anstey. While the first of these poems, *The New Bath Guide*, published in 1766, may have influenced *Humphry Clinker* in other ways, it contains no references to colonial capital. The second, however, "An Election Ball," published in 1776, contains many such references, not only concrete instances ("Miss CURD [danced] with a partner as black as OMIAH") but also extended similes, such as:

> Alas! my dear wife, I can never describe
> Bath's beautiful Nymphs, that adorable Tribe,
> Who like Mexican Queens in the picture you may
> Have seen of the Court of the great Montezuma
> Set in solemn array, and diversify'd plume
> That shed o'er their charms its delectable gloom. (28)

One might speculate that the density of such references in both Smollett and Anstey springs from the end of the Seven Years' War and its related American conflicts in 1763.[31] Colonial trade expanded during the war, bringing the kind of new capital Smollett describes into metropolitan centers. At the same time, however, the war was so expensive that Britain was forced to levy new taxes on its colonial possessions to pay for the cost of fighting to protect them. Thus, paradoxically, the very wealth that streamed into British cities, like Bath, after the war became a sign of Britain's dependence on her colonial subjects.[32]

The corrosive effects of these tides of luxury are literalized in the contaminating waters of Bath. *Humphry Clinker's* extensive description of the baths transforms economic developments into waters that break through the physical defenses of the body just as mercantile accumulation has broken down the social barriers between landed gentry like the Brambles and the world of commercial enterprise. Matthew Bramble exclaims that "we know not what sores may be running into the water while we are bathing, and what sort of matter we may thus imbibe; the king's-evil, the scurvy, the cancer and the pox" (44).[33] Here, a particularly virulent form of social mixture becomes a problem of ingestion—the mouth can no longer control what it "imbibes." On an only slightly more hysterical note, Bramble declares:

> it is very far from being clear with me, that the patients in the Pump-room don't swallow the scourings of the bathers. I can't help suspecting, that there is, or may be, some regurgitation from the bath into the cistern of the pump. In that case, what a delicate beveridge is every day quaffed by the drinkers; medicated with the sweat, and dirt, and dandriff, and abominable discharges of various kinds, from twenty different diseased bodies, parboiling in the kettle below. (45)

While Bramble's exaggerated disgust might be itself the object of some satire here, I would argue that this description of uncontrollable oral intake, and of the promiscuity of contact within the baths, seems to pierce that narrative distance. "Twenty different diseased bodies," rather than simply one, combine in what "the patient" unwittingly drinks. Boiled together, these bodies form an indistinguishable mass; not only do individual bodies indiscriminately mix, without regard for social hierarchy, as in Bramble's description of the crowds at Bath, but bits of originally discrete bodies also combine in threatening ways. By swallowing this "beveridge," the patient incorporates the matter of social reorganization, which will begin to destroy him from within his own body.

Thus, the tides of luxury are conflated with the tides of bodily fluid that seek to breach corporeal barriers. At times, in *Humphry Clinker's* Bath, it is impossible to tell where bodily fluids end and the tide of luxury begins: "Imagine to yourself a high exalted essence of mingled odours, arising from putrid gums, imposthumated lungs, sour flatulencies, rank arm-pits, sweating feet, running sores and issues, plasters . . . assafoetida drops, musk, hartshorn, and sal volatile; besides a thousand frowzy steams, which I could not analyse" (63). Here, using the same rhetorical technique with which he listed the components of threatening crowds, and alluding to the same social disruption, Matthew Bramble describes the smell of a typical ball. The channels that normally contain such bodily fluids seem to have dissolved, leaving "running sores" to stream uncontrolled into a public space. No longer attached to a discrete body, such "issues" are indistinguishable from commercially available liquids. Once again, the incoherent mixture of smells, as much as their disgusting nature, heightens the disturbing quality of this description. This anxiety is syntactically marked; names for contaminating bodily fluids slide into names for medications, without even a semicolon to signal the transition.

This confusion over the limits of individualized bodies links social disruption inside England with the cultural confusion of the colonial arena. The dissection of bodies into their component parts at Bath narratively replicates the results of the gauntlet Lismahago runs in North America. In Bath, as in Miami territory, the decomposition of the English body becomes a sign for the dissolution of English social structure. The scrofulous flakes of skin Matthew Bramble fears simply represent an even more radical atomization of the human body; in fact, Bramble's opening sentences refer to his own battered state, he is "as much tortured in all [his] limbs as if [he] were broke upon the wheel" (7). Yet, in both situations, such fragmentation results from the promiscuous proximity of bodies. The threat posed by the crowds at Bath partly arises from the surprise of such undisciplined activity in a supposedly regulated space: the streets of an English town suddenly resemble uncharted colonial territory, spaces alternately deserted and strangely overpopulated.

The connection between such isolated crowds and colonial expansion is reinforced by Smollett's autobiographical account of the European experience in the Americas, as described in *Roderick Random*. Here, in a fictionalized description of Smollett's own stint as a naval doctor on the English expedition to Cartagena, English bodies are crowded into dissolution:

> The sick and wounded were squeezed into certain vessels, which thence obtained the name of hospital ships, though methinks they scarce deserved such a creditable title, seeing none of them could boast of either surgeon nurse or cook; and the space between decks so confined, that the miserable patients had not room to sit upright in their beds. Their wounds and stumps being neglected, contracted filth and putrefecation, and millions of maggots were hatched amid the corruption of their sores.[34]

Like Lismahago's fingers, these sailors' limbs have been amputated in their voyage to the New World, their bodies radically reshaped. In fact, ironically enough, their presence in the Caribbean is due to a war itself instigated by the crime of dismemberment—the War of Jenkins' Ear.[35] Obviously, the injuries sustained by these soldiers are much more severe than the damage done to bodies at Bath. Furthermore, the agents for their injuries are clear in the colonial arena—they are at war with the Spanish—while in England, bathing bodies seem to disintegrate of their own accord. Yet, the underlying similarity between these images of corporeal dissolution may allow us to posit that the bodies in Bath are also subject to the consequences of imperial expansion; they are as vulnerable as Lismahago to the loss of physical and cultural integrity seemingly attendant on intercultural contact. If the scenes in Bath represent such effects without a cause, it may be because they refer metonymically to colonial violence.

The similar tropes the novel employs in these geographically disparate scenes can be read as its strategy for representing the actual economic links between English cities such as Bath and British imperialism in the Americas. Robert Giddings points out that "colonial expansion by means of war, and the wealth from the West Indian slave trade—these are the major sources of the wealth and luxury so frequently noted by commentators of the time."[36] The connections formed by the Atlantic trade routes between Bath and the Americas introduce a third term to the text's representation of the forces changing English culture. Just as the tides of luxury have their internal equivalent in contaminated bodily fluids, they have an external equivalent in the ocean waters that facilitate trade. Thus, the anxiety surrounding liquid images in *Humphry Clinker* proves to be totalizing and insistent; any stream, either inside or outside the body, becomes a literalization of the problem of social fluidity.[37]

For this reason, when the Bramble party escapes from a watery grave, the event carries far more ideological weight than a simple accident. Jery Melford explains that:

> in crossing the country to get into the post road, it was necessary to ford a river, and we that were a-horseback passed without any danger or difficulty; but a great deal of rain having fallen last night and this morning, there was such an accumulation of water, that a millhead gave way, just as the coach was passing under it, and the flood rushed down with such

impetuosity, as first floated, and then fairly overturned the carriage in the middle of the stream. (300)

This swollen stream seems another version of the putrid waters—internal and external—of Bath, which also constantly overflow their bounds, and thus another embodiment of the ravaging ebb and flow of trade. The Bramble party's submersion in the stream literalizes their experience of the disorganization of English culture.[38] But they are rescued from this particular mishap—Humphry "flew like lightning to the coach, that was by this time filled with water, and, diving into it, brought up the poor 'squire, to all appearances deprived of life" (301). Although the revelation of Humphry's paternity this incident precipitates seems largely irrelevant to the plot of the novel, the fact that Humphry is Matthew Bramble's illegitimate son does reassert the importance of familial connections in a world where all non-economic relationships seem to be disintegrating. Only the power of filial loyalty, and the stable social hierarchy it implies, can pump the river water out of Matthew Bramble's lungs, and stem the tide of luxury.

The references to liquid in *Humphry Clinker* may seem to work on many discursive levels, through metaphors, images, and descriptions of events. Yet, when this diffuse group of tropes is read through the organizing framework of a late eighteenth-century ideology of colonialism, it can be seen as figuring the causes of the cultural changes brought about by colonial expansion and the mercantile wealth such expansion produced. Both the new fluidity of cultural space and the new fluidity of social classes are rhetorically literalized in the fluids, bodily and otherwise, that seem to be carrying out a concerted attack against the Bramble party. Any moment in which one of the party can deny these fluids access into his or her own body, or can gain control over his or her own oral intake—for example, Humphry's rescue of Matthew Bramble, or Matthew's refusal to participate in Bath society—can be read as the text's imagined solution to the problem of class structures rendered unstable by mercantile accumulation and colonial capital. In this way, the novel's insistently corporeal representations of transculturation perform the textual work of neutralizing these socioeconomic disruptions, and its literalizing rhetoric promises that otherness will never be assimilated as long as it is denied access to the individual body.

Paradoxically, however, the novel's emphasis on the power of individual refusal to regulate the exchange of objects signifies its own involvement in the increasing commodification of social relations, a tendency it seemingly abhors. Furthermore, the fact that the novel imagines the need for the individual regulation of consumption can be seen as a reaction to the disappearance of any contained site of cultural exchange; the images of dismemberment we might associate only with Lismahago's narrative appear in descriptions of England as well as in descriptions of America. What might be called the material effects of transculturation are not localized, but occur across British culture — in the colonies and on domestic soil.

## CANNIBALISM AND HOME-GROWN FOOD

I have been arguing that *Humphry Clinker* transforms the social effects of economic consumption into a physiological problem of oral consumption, an objectification that signals its involvement in a commodity culture. This transposition allows the novel to imagine a solution to those problems — a fantasy of harmless ingestion. If it figures the transculturation of English culture as a kind of poisonous physical incorporation of cultural difference, then it describes, in compensation, an ideal of cultural self-sufficiency, centering on pure English food. While the narrative recounts with horror the uncontrollable intake of various fluids, not least the diseased bodily fluids ubiquitous at Bath, it also extends that horror to contaminated foods. Perhaps the most succinct example of the danger of eating occurs in Scotland, where the haggis puts Jery Melford "in mind of the history of the Congo, in which [he] had read of negro's heads sold publically in the markets" (214). As a number of critics have noted, Smollett's novel has pronounced "Scotophilic" tendencies; it attempts to integrate Scotland into a coherent British nation, while retaining a certain pride in its specific regional culture.[39] This rhetoric, as Trumpener suggests, militates against the possibility of Scotland's being seen as simply another colonized pool of commodified bodies for the empire. Yet, the narrative cannot eradicate this aspect of Scotland's status completely, as this brief moment of satiric excess reveals; the haggis, figured as an African head, suggests an analogy with the Scottish bodies and parts of bodies circulating through British colonial space. As Smollett wrote of Scottish soldiers after Culloden: "the survivors have since literally washed away their offenses with their blood; witness their bones now bleaching in almost every corner of the globe—at Cape Breton, Ticonderoga, Fort du Quesne, in Guadaloupe and Martinique, before the walls of Pondicherry."[40] The passage is reminiscent not only of Lismahago's colonial dismembering, but also of Swift's similarly half-satiric comparison of the Irish to African slaves, and even of the cannibalized bones Crusoe finds on his island's shore. The bodies of the Scottish, like those of the Africans and Irish, are potential raw material, to be taken apart and sold at the markets of empire.

Characteristically, these connections are mediated through the disgusting affect of foreign food; eating the haggis becomes cannibalism, literally taking the colonized other inside oneself. The destructive presence of that internalized other is signified as well by the suggestion that the British, through their economic practice of trading with supposedly inferior nations, have adopted the eating rituals of "savages." Throughout the novel, food, as a possible agent of the collapsing difference between England and the colonial arena, is suspect. This suspicion is not confined to food actually produced in the colonies, but rather extends to any food associated with the growing intercourse between different social classes occasioned by colonial capital. One can begin to see the formulation of this problem, and its corresponding solution, in Matthew Bramble's tirade on the corruption of London town life:

> If I would drink water, I must quaff the maukish contents of an open aqueduct, exposed to all manner of defilement; or swallow that which comes from the river Thames, impregnated with all the filth of London and Westminster. . . . The bread I eat in London, is a deleterious paste, mixed up with chalk, alum and bone ashes. . . . I shall conclude this catalogue of London dainties, with that table-beer, guiltless of hops and malt, vapid and nauseous; much fitter to facilitate the operation of a vomit, than to quench thirst and promote digestion. . . . [Londoners] may, for aught I care, wallow in the mire of their own pollution. (119–21)

Even these excerpts from what is a three-page rant demonstrate that the same tropes operate here as in Bramble's description of Bath.

Contaminated liquids not only create internal discomfort, but also coagulate into an external "mire." Furthermore, it is not clear whether the contents of that mire are simply contaminated foodstuffs, or also the "vomit" they provoke. There is no way of knowing, in London, whether the food one consumes is human waste or other organic matter. An anxiety about class mobility, expressed as a fear of the incorporation of poisonous objects, emerges in the novel whenever, as in London and Bath, the difference between human and nonhuman substances dissolves into a continuum of contaminated matter.

Matthew Bramble reveals that it is the foreign nature of such food, its importation, which is so destructive, when he contrasts London to his nutritional ideal. At Brambleton Hall, he claims:

> I drink the virgin lymph, pure and crystalline as it gushes from the rock, or the sparkling beveridge, home-brewed from malt of my own making . . . ; my bread is sweet and nourishing, made from my own wheat, ground in my own mill, and baked in my own oven; my table is, in a great measure, furnished from my own ground; my five-year old mutton, fed on the fragrant herbage of the mountains, that may vie with venison in juice and flavor; my delicious veal, fattened with nothing but the mother's milk, that fills the dish with gravy; my poultry from the barn-door, that never knew confinement, but when they were at roost; my rabbits panting from the warren; my game fresh from the moors; my trout and salmon struggling from the stream; oysters from their native banks; and herrings, with other sea-fish, I can eat in four hours after they are taken—My sallads [sic], roots and pot-herbs, my own garden yields in plenty and perfection; the produce of the natural soil prepared by moderate cultivation. The same soil affords all the different fruits which England may call her own, so that my desert [sic] is every day fresh-gathered from the tree; my dairy flows with nectarious tides of milk and cream, from whence we derive abundance of excellent butter, curds and cheese; and the refuse fattens my pigs, that are destined for hams and bacon. (118)

I quote this description at such length in order to demonstrate that Bramble's description of rural purity is at least as excessive as his description of metropolitan corruption. Here, however, colonial foodstuffs are replaced by the "fruits England may call her own" and the tides of luxury by the "nectarious tides of milk." Syntactically, Bramble's reiteration of possession—"my veal . . . my sallads . . . my desert [*sic*] . . . my pigs"—adds coherence to a list that in its iterative construction resembles his description of the confusion at Bath. Furthermore, his documentation of the original location of each item, and of its exact distance from his table, inscribes a precise loop of consumption—from orchard to refuse to bacon in a model of self-sufficiency. This contained domesticity seems a refuge from the contaminated and contaminating food of London and, metonymically, from the social changes that disrupt that urban space.

This description of Brambleton Hall has deep roots in classical and Augustan ideals, and has been taken as evidence of the novel's investment in a Horatian pastoral utopia.[41] Yet, it is exactly this self-contained nutritional system that is already, from the start of the novel, undermined at Bramble's home. The "nectarious tides of milk" do not always end up on the Brambles' table, because Matthew's sister Tabitha often sells them at the local market. Here, another step in the novel's systematic localization of the sources of social change becomes clear; since women have control of the family's food intake, the guilt of contamination falls on them. The depth of Tabitha's transgression is revealed; instead of a domestic manager, facilitating the passage from field to table, she is a "domestic daemon" (74), breaking down the barriers between Brambleton Hall and the world of commerce. Tabitha's unpaid and denigrated domestic labor, occasioned by her dependence on her brother, leads her to enter the contaminating world of trade. It is for this reason that she is an appropriate partner for Lismahago; she is a domestic entrepreneur, even as he is a colonial entrepreneur. Tabitha recognizes her exchange value on the marriage market, just as Lismahago acknowledges his own exchangeability in the colonial arena. This repeated moment of self-reification links Tabitha's transgression of her gender and class roles—her attempt to alter her dependent spinsterhood into independent wealth and marriage—with the cultural transgressions of colonial captivity. This set of correspondences between Tabitha's domestic labor and Lismahago's colonial adventures reveals that conditions at Brambleton Hall may not be as separate from the dynamics of empire as Matthew Bramble would like to believe.

Yet, even as Tabitha's actions double Lismahago's, her crime is also peculiarly female; the novel only levels the charge of mishandling food at women. For example, at the table of the exemplary bad woman of *Humphry Clinker*, Mrs. Baynard, Matthew Bramble finds that

> as to the repast, it was made up of a parcel of kickshaws, contrived by a French cook, without one substantial article adapted to the satisfaction of an English appetite. The pottage was little better than bread soaked in dishwashings, lukewarm. The ragouts looked as if they had been once eaten and half digested. . . . The desert [*sic*] consisted of faded fruit and iced froth, a good emblem of our landlady's character; the table beer was sour, the water foul, and the wine vapid. (283)

Mrs. Baynard's food shares many of the characteristics of London food; her beer is bad, her water contaminated. Like London food, as well, it is impossible to tell which stage of the digestive cycle it occupies; her guests might as well be eating "the mire of their own pollution" as the "half digested" ragouts. In this case, however, the corruption is not a generalized phenomenon, but firmly the responsibility of the hostess. She is identified by the food she serves, emblematized by her "faded fruit and iced froth." If the ingestion of contaminated food is a moment that the text invests with all its diffuse anxieties about the influx of colonial capital into England, then, in this scenario, a woman becomes the agent of the transmission of such food into the English body. In this misogynist dynamic, the text finds a scapegoat for the social changes it fears.

The central part played by women in the transfer of external corruption into internal physical systems is illustrated as well by the only distinct figure to emerge from Matthew Bramble's catalogue of London muck. Toward the conclusion of his rant, he notes that "It was but yesterday that I saw a dirty barrow-bunter in the street, cleaning her dusty fruit with her own spittle; and who knows but some fine lady of St. James parish might admit into her delicate mouth those very cherries, which had been rolled and moistened between the filthy, and, perhaps, ulcerated chops of a St. Giles huckster (120)." The fruit dangerously mediates social mixture—it carries the spittle of a poor woman into the mouth of a rich one. This oral transmission of bodily fluid by the agency of a cherry once again insists that the mouth is the primary orifice by which social corruption passes into the human body. Significantly, this exchange is a commodified one, and it occurs between women, who here occupy both ends of a distasteful trade. In this instance, as at Mrs. Baynard's table, and in the demonization of Tabitha, women are made responsible for both the contamination of food, and for the appearance of that contaminated food at the domestic meal. Tabitha, who herself both sells food at market and provides a market for luxurious colonial goods, marks the disappearance of distinctions between the roles of the fine lady and the St. Giles huckster.

The concomitant threat in Mrs. Baynard's food is the suggestion of a connection between contaminated foods, and a foreign, and often colonial, origin for their contamination. Her table has nothing "adapted to the satisfaction of an English appetite" because it has been prepared by a French cook. Furthermore, Matthew Bramble contemptuously denotes the "kickshaws" she serves by the same word that the Duke of Newcastle uses to identify one of the Five Iroquois Nations (109). The word "kickshaw" is itself a creolized nonsense word, meaning "fancy thing" and derived from the French "quelque chose"; this misnaming of both distasteful food and indigenous peoples rhetorically links the colonial sphere with Mrs. Baynard's table. The linguistic connection suggests a more metaphorical association; the dinner party replicates the destruction of Native American tribes by English colonial expansion, as well as indulging in American-style cannibalism, by eating the "kickshaw" that might also be the nauseating body of the colonized subject.

In this context, Matthew Bramble's earlier reference to the fate of men "who are ruined by extravagance [and] fall a sacrifice to the ridiculous pride and vanity of silly women, whose parts are held in contempt by the very men whom they pillage and enslave" makes sense; he links the disruption caused by female domestic mismanagement with the socially destructive ties between England and her colonies (283). Bramble figures men as the victims of this imperial aggression—financially raped by pillaging women. Among the Miami it is "the women and children, who have the privilege of torturing all the prisoners in their passage," because "the Women are much more cruel than the Men" (188). Women occupy both ends of the chain of imperial plunder, are both its object and its subject, even as they occupy both ends of the scandalously filthy exchange in the fruit market. The social transgression of that commercial exchange echoes the scandal of Tabitha's union with Lismahago, the miscegenous nature of which is also indicated by the transmission of a luxury good—a fur coat. Although Tabitha might claim that she is herself enslaved by the disempowered position of women within the domestic space, the novel in general works to establish the culpability of such women (43). The chain of associations between food produced or procured outside the home, sites of savage cannibalism, and the social disruption caused by colonial capital runs persistently through *Humphry Clinker*—linked metonymically by the figures of trading, pillaging, and socially transgressive women, like Tabitha, Squinkinacoosta, and Mrs. Baynard. The domestic space, although ideologically privileged, is never secured, never purified, never self-sufficient.

*Humphry Clinker* is organized around a distinction between a cultural inside and outside, made literal through reference to the inside and outside of actual English bodies. Paradoxically, the problem of how to refuse the assimilation of alien cultures is most pressing inside the heart of English domestic life—in the female province of the domestic meal. The novel's concern with consumption, most localized in these descriptions of the dangers of foreign or contaminated foods, stems from an anxiety over the transculturation of English society. It primarily imagines the process of transculturation as a threat against the English body, which is in constant danger of being absorbed by a cultural other, or of unwittingly incorporating that dangerous other inside itself. The remedy for this corporeal problem is physical as well; by purifying and regulating its oral consumption, the body will remain sealed to otherness. Thus, the novel works through problems of intercultural contact according to the logic of incorporation; it imagines that when two cultures meet, one must inevitably overwhelm, swallow, or otherwise incorporate the other. This process is dangerous for both the swallowed and the swallowing, as the former becomes a destructive object lodged within the latter. Yet, while the novel vilifies foreign objects, investing them with a supererogatory disgust, its solution itself rests on some of the assumptions of the commodity culture the narrative ostensibly critiques; the efficacy of nonconsumption relies on the power of an individual consumer to discriminate among available products.

## INTERNAL HETEROGENEITIES

As the eighteenth century entered its last quarter, the discourse of consumerist abstention Smollett inherited from earlier writers like Swift found a new political focus in the movement against slavery. The strategies *Humphry Clinker* imagines will keep England and English consumers safe were directed next against colonial injustice in the 1790s campaigns against slave-grown sugar. These campaigns, discussed in the following chapter, reveal that in its discomfort with the changes wrought by colonial and mercantile expansion, Smollett's novel proved prescient about England's changing attitudes toward its American possessions. In particular, the loss of the North American colonies in 1783, after a long war that aroused a great deal of ambivalence, made real some of the cultural anxieties about the security and stability of national identity adumbrated in *Humphry Clinker*. As Kathleen Wilson argues, "the American war brought into sharp relief the tension between empire and nation." The Revolution revealed that

> The various hierarchical visions of . . . domestic policy were recognizably, if irregularly, mapped onto the imperial one, and the incompatibility of the rights of English people and those of Britons laid bare—the first must always take priority over the second, and national belonging kept within strict territorial, cultural, and, increasingly, racial bounds.[42]

Thus, despite the utopian hope that the nation-state could be imagined as a homogeneous entity, the heterogeneous and conflicted nature of the empire demonstrated that not all Britons could be guaranteed the same liberties.

In the last decades of the eighteenth century, this heterogeneity, and internal difference—the kind of fragmented and transcultural identity inhabited by Lismahago—became more culturally visible—present, for example, in the collected letters of the former slave Ignatius Sancho, published in 1782. These letters register both a patriotic disgust with the current condition of England and a new flexibility in cultural identification. "Government is sunk in lethargic stupor—anarchy reigns," Sancho wrote in 1780 after the Gordon riots: "When I look back to the glorious time of a George II. and a Pitt's administration, my heart sinks at the bitter contrast—. We may now say of England, as was heretofore said of Great Babylon—'The beauty and the excellency of the Chaldees is no more.'" Sancho here sounds as identified with and nostalgic for a better England as Matthew Bramble, even employing the flexible, emotional style of the epistolary novel. Yet, he was equally capable of dissociating himself from his adopted nation's problems. The previous year he had noted that: "The present time is rather *comique*.—Ireland almost in as true a state of rebellion as America.—Admirals quarrelling in the West-Indies—and at home Admirals that do not choose to fight.—The British empire mouldering away in the West—annihilated in the North—Gibralter going—and England fast asleep—. . . . For my part, it's nothing to me—as I am only a lodger—and hardly that." Seemingly content to do business in England—he owned a tobacco shop—and raise his family there without worrying about imperial policy, Sancho declared to a correspondent, "what a plague is all this [political unrest] to you and me?"[43]

A few years later, however, another former slave, Olaudah Equiano (1789), gave a more political spin to the heterogeneity possible in British identity. In his autobiographical account, an early and widely read salvo in the war against slavery, Equiano wrote:

> I believe there are few events in my life which have not happened to many; it is true that the events of it are numerous; and, did I consider myself an European, I might say my sufferings were great; but, when I compare my lot with that of most of my countrymen, I regard myself as a *particular favourite of Heaven*, and acknowledge the mercies of Providence in every occurrence of my life.[44]

Equiano here strategically positions himself somewhere between Europeans and Africans—his own countrymen. He does not admit to considering himself European, but imagines what the consequences would be if he did; indeed, the arguments against slavery he provides hinge on the possibility of such transcultural identification. And yet, Equiano does not present himself as fully African either; his experiences, not to mention his literacy and command of Christian discourse, have made him exceptional among that group. The writings of former slaves like Sancho and Equiano were important to the abolitionist movement, and it is their authors' ability to move between worlds, to explain the horrors of the colonies to metropolitan audiences, that made them so powerful. The transculturation Smollett recognized, experienced, and deplored in 1771 reached its next crisis in the struggle over Caribbean slavery.

## Chapter 4

# Women and the Politics of Sugar, 1792

In the last decade of the eighteenth century, West Indian sugar became
an important symbol of the proliferating chains of interdependence
between England and her Caribbean colonies. Grown in the farthest
reaches of the British Empire, sugar was eaten in the intimacy of
British homes; it linked colonial sites of the production of raw materials with the domestic sites of their consumption. To analyze the discourse surrounding sugar consumption in the late eighteenth century
is thus to examine the intersection of colonial policy and domestic policy. Such an analysis also must interrogate the semantic slippage
between "the domestic," meaning British national territory, and "the
domestic," meaning the interior of the family. Defining these two
domestic sites in terms of one another helps to reveal the crucial role
played by constructions of female identity in articulating the relationship between Britain and its West Indian colonies, and the innovative
role that female domestic virtue played in deciding the nature of
Britain's involvement with Caribbean slavery. To understand how an
idea of female virtue, specifically compassion and sympathy, could
assume such an important part in the abolitionist campaign, however,
we first need to understand how that campaign played these disembodied virtues off against the threats of bodily contamination that were suggested in the abolitionist rhetoric surrounding Britain's investment in
the slave economies of the Caribbean.[1]

  Although refined cane sugar was all but unknown in England before
the seventeenth century, by the beginning of the eighteenth century, a
supporter of the production of sugarcane in the Caribbean could
declare that "Sugar has been called a superfluity. Undoubtedly at its
first introduction it was so. But the constitution, from long habits of
luxury, becomes so much changed as to render that at last necessary,

which originally owed its introduction to caprice and effeminacy."[2] In this formulation, the fruits of colonial expansion have a direct effect on the bodies of consumers; transatlantic trade has altered the British "constitution." Supporters of the trade in slave-grown sugar described it not as a sensuous luxury, but as a physical necessity; one such writer says, "my reason tells me, and experience tells me, and medical authority assures me, that sugar is not a luxury; but has become, by constant use, a necessary of life; and great injury have many persons done to their constitutions by totally abstaining from it."[3] For advocates of mercantile trade, sugar is needed by those bodies whose nutritional intake is regulated by the market. Thus, the individual bodies inhabiting the domestic space become important indices of the status of international trade; they register sugar's shift from luxury to necessity not as a change in the purchasing power of the consumer, but as a developing biological need. The necessity of sugar to what one might then call the domestic body was promoted by such writers as Dr. Frederick Slare, who, in a treatise on the value of sugar "dedicated to the Ladies," proposes "a strong and home argument to recommend the use of sugar to infants." He says, "The argument I bring from Nature's first kind tribute, or intended food for children, as soon as they are born; which is, that fine juice or liquor prepared in the mother's breasts, called breast milk, of a fine, delicate, sweet taste. This sweet is somewhat analogous, or a taste agreeable, to sugar; and in want of this milk, it is well known, sugar is brought to supply it."[4]

Through the force of Slare's comparison, the products of England's successful colonial expansion penetrate the most intimate spaces of English domestic life. Slare naturalizes sugar consumption by associating it with the biological processes of the female body; the child who can have sugar substituted for its mother's milk is as dependent on international trade for sustenance as it is on her breast. That breast becomes the site of an "agreement of taste" between colonial production and domestic consumption.

In 1791 and 1792, antislavery advocates, hoping to undermine the institution of Caribbean slavery by abstaining from "slave-grown" produce, attempted to de-naturalize the consumption of sugar in the home. Those who advocated the continuation of the slave trade focused on the domestic consumption of sugar as a seemingly natural exchange of liquids between two bodies, as a breast-feeding mother and her child, an analogy that participates in the common eighteenth-century trope of comparing economic structures to the human circulatory system.[5] In contrast, antislavery rhetoric associated the colonial production of sugar with a physically aggressive transfer of such liquids. Take, for example, this description of the horrors of slavery:

> [The slave] cannot think why . . . the wretches who have laden him with chains are desirous that he should eat; he cannot account for their brutal kindness; he concludes that they mean to fatten him, in order to feast upon him at a convenient season. He resolves to circumvent their designs; he refuses food: he is whipt to make him eat; but the indignant firmness of his mind is not to be subdued by the lash. The speculum oris is resorted to; a broken tooth gives an opportunity for its introduction; his mouth is forced open, rice is crammed down his throat, and he is compelled to live.[6]

Here, forced feeding is logically connected to cannibalism; why would slave owners compel a worker to eat, unless they meant to eat him themselves? Thus, eating becomes a kind of violence: the slave's mouth is forced open, nourishment is "crammed" into it, a tooth is broken in the process, and a particular instrument of torture is even called into use to force open his mouth.[7] The slave's refusal to consume, though doomed, is a method of resistance, and the pamphlet argues that the British consumer can make this method work. It urges, "let us loose sight of the interest of tyrants, and not continue to be cannibals from motives of compassion." The compassion to which it ironically refers is the misguided compassion slavery advocates argued that consumers should feel for slaves who would be put out of work by declining sugar consumption. But the logic of the slave is borne out in the antislavery argument; he is indeed being fattened up, to be magically transformed into the sugar he produces, and to be force fed by tyrannical West Indian planters to British consumers, making the latter unwilling cannibals. What initially seems to be the slave's mistaken "savage" superstition is ultimately validated by supposedly civilized patterns of consumption.[8]

Thus, abolitionists retaliated against the proponents of the Caribbean sugar trade precisely by problematizing the association between sugar and a necessary exchange between bodies. Like such advocates, however, they deployed a certain idea of the domestic body to underlie their political tenets. While supporters of the West Indian sugar trade imagined a British constitution that could expand to incorporate any product of the colonial arena, abolitionists envisioned a domestic body in constant danger from a poisonous world; in order to make their moral point, they mobilized fears of bodily pollution. The anthropologist Mary Douglas argues that we must be "prepared to see in the body a symbol of society, and to see the powers and dangers credited to social structure reproduced in small on the human body."[9] She claims that

> all margins are dangerous. If they are pulled this way or that the shape of fundamental experience is altered. Any structure of ideas is vulnerable at its margins. We should expect the orifices of the body to symbolise its specially vulnerable points. Matter issuing from them is marginal stuff of the most obvious kind. Spittle, blood, milk, urine, faeces or tears by simply issuing forth have traversed the boundary of the body. So also have bodily parings, skin, nail, hair clippings and sweat. The mistake is to treat bodily margins in isolation from all other margins.[10]

These ideas have some relevance to the rhetoric of the campaign to abstain from slave-grown sugar. The substances around which abolitionist writers locate the danger to English consumers are indeed substances, like blood, sweat, pus, and even flesh, that may travel improperly from one body to another, from pores and wounds to mouths. In order to invest those substances with the potential to threaten British culture, however, they had to represent boundaries around the domestic body, where supporters of the sugar trade had seen none.

Most supporters of abolition were from the metropolitan middle classes; associated with industrialization—as workers, owners, or beneficiaries of urban culture—they generally advocated free trade.[11] They saw proponents of slavery as mercantilists whose economic philosophy put up barriers to a more competitive and efficient market economy. Indeed, later in the nineteenth century, the principal argument against slave-grown sugar (and cotton) was that, without mercantile manipulation, produce grown by "free labor" in the East Indies would be better and cheaper. Thus, the cultural barriers abolitionists saw as threatened by the consumption of slave-grown sugar should not be confused with the barriers to *trade* they associated with mercantilism and slavery.

Instead, antislavery activists claimed that consumption of slave-grown sugar breached the boundaries between the colonial arena and the domestic space. When they claimed that this breach compromised national identity, they had, in a sense, reconfigured certain cultural boundaries. The idea of national identity mobilized by this campaign rests on two assumptions: first, that a circumscribed domestic space is more representative of an authentic British identity than are the powerful, international networks of commerce; and second, that this space, in order to remain purely British, must somehow be separable from, and superior to, those networks. The creation of this separate, private sphere, may, in fact, be a reaction to the myriad social changes inaugurated by the entrepreneurial middle classes with which abolition was associated.[12] The opposition between a body that can accommodate the products of colonial trade and a body that needs to guard itself against those products can be seen, in this context, as one of a number of oppositions through which the idea of a national culture was being redefined. While pro-slavery mercantilists imagined an expansive, encompassing nation, in which trade and culture were continuous, abolitionists saw a culture that needed to rework its domestic boundaries, even as unregulated trade expanded its economic power.

In 1791, William Fox published a pamphlet entitled "An Address to the People of Great Britain, on the utility of refraining from the use of West India Sugar and Rum." This pamphlet may have been as popular as the first part of Thomas Paine's *Rights of Man*, which sold fifty thousand copies in 1791.[13] Fox's imagery and argumentation were widely known, and they were widely imitated during the period. Even an opponent notes "the rapid and extraordinary manner in which it has been circulated in all parts of the kingdom."[14] Fox describes slavery as a threat to a bodily orifice, as pollution that might enter through the mouth. "The laws of our country may indeed prohibit us the sugar cane, unless we receive it through the medium of slavery. They may hold it to our lips, steeped in the blood of our fellow creatures; but They cannot compel us to accept the loathsome portion."[15]

This passage articulates a concept of consumer rights; Fox figures the regulated sugar trade as an attempt to dictate not only the economic choices of British consumers but also their ethical choices. His insistence that consumers have such choices—that they cannot be "compelled" by producers—implicitly replaces a mercantilist concept of the market with a "free" market controlled by consumer demand. Explicitly, Fox focuses on the moral framework of consumer behavior; implicitly, however, he relies on a rhetoric of pollution. He describes the "forced" consumption of sugar as an interdicted exchange of nutriments: as cannibalism. "So necessarily connected are our consumption of the commodity, and the misery arising from it," Fox argues, "that in every pound of sugar used, (the produce of slaves imported from Africa) we may be considered as consuming two ounces of human flesh."[16] These images transform the slave into the commodity he produces; each two ounces of his flesh is eventually used up and replaced by a pound of sugar.

This metaphoric equivalence between the producer and the thing produced is not unique to abolitionist rhetoric. A tendency to imagine laboring bodies as the food they labored to produce, or as the food whose consumption fueled their labor, was widespread in the social and economic philosophy of the later eighteenth and early nineteenth century. Dr. Benjamin Mosely, for instance, in the course of a discussion of sugar, claims that: "The formation of the body, and more of the inclination of the mind than is generally imagined, depend on the nature and quality of our food. . . . This is indeed so strongly distinguishable among the lower classes, in some countries, that one would almost conclude, a man is but a walking vegetable—or a hieroglyphic—importing the food, of which he is compounded."[17]

For Mosely, working-class bodies are signs—hieroglyphics—of the food they consume; laboring body and digested food are tied together in the relationship between signifier and signified. Thomas Malthus, whose *Essay on Population* was published in 1798, makes a similar move on a broader scale, collapsing national identity into nutritional paradigms. He claims that "Countries are populous according to the quantity of human food that they produce, and happy according to the liberality with which that food is divided, or the quantity which a day's labour will purchase. Corn countries are more populous than pasture countries, and rice countries more populous than corn countries."[18]

Catherine Gallagher has proposed that this equivalency between food, labor, and national identity provided one basis for theories of value at the end of the eighteenth century. For Malthus and thinkers like him, "the value of bodies is not absolute, but is rather based on their ability to create a commodity whose value is only defined in relationship to its ability to replenish the body. Food and the body, commodity and labor, thus constantly indicate each other as the source and gauge of their value."[19] Yet, such formulations seem shadowed by the hint of cannibalism; if bodies are simply compounded of the food they eat, and all food is just one step away from conversion to laboring bodies, what is to prevent us from simply eating bodies?[20]

Proponents of the campaign to boycott slave-grown sugar turned these ideas about the interconnectedness of the value of laboring bodies and the value of the food substances they labored to produce, as well as the corresponding hint of cannibalism, to their own advantage. I would like to suggest, however, that the accusation of cannibalism took on an added charge when it was associated with Britain's relationship with Afro-Caribbean slave economies. Peter Hulme has argued that the word cannibal, with its connotations of bloodthirsty savagery, "gained its entire meaning from within the discourse of European colonialism," particularly the European expansion into the Caribbean.[21] Cannibals, he claims, were a sort of shadowy double to the native Caribs. Although we might want to emend Hulme's thesis with regard to perceptions of the native Irish in the seventeenth century, it seems clear that a persistent dread of flesh-eating savages lurking always just out of sight of the colonial eye haunted European expansionism.[22] The abolitionist accusation of English cannibalism enacts a kind of paranoid reversal of this fantasy; as a result of their improper consumption of colonial products, British consumers are themselves transformed into the savage cannibals they had once fantasized about as existing only on the colonial periphery.[23] When Fox claims that in eating sugar, British consumers "may be considered" to be eating the flesh of slaves, that metaphor most probably conjured up for his readers the purported practices of the Afro-Caribbean world. That is, his rhetorical strategy of equating the consumption of sugar with the consumption of Afro-Caribbean flesh would have pointed the eighteenth-century reader to the Caribbean anecdotes that substantiated his or her horror of colonial cannibalism. We might see his rhetoric, then, as an intersection between a late eighteenth-century method of evaluating the laboring body, whether slave or free, an age-old horror of eating human flesh, and specific images of abomination associated with the colonial periphery during the later eighteenth century. Such references were meant to shock the consuming public into abstaining from sugar, but, in doing so, they imply that metaphors equating the sugar trade with physical exchange are no longer proper, no longer adequate. According to the opponents of slavery, those metaphors must be reconfigured to represent the ethical dangers of the physicality of that exchange.

In this way, abolitionists played on the power of metaphorical equivalences to suggest the possible reality of physical acts. Descriptions of the process by which the body or the blood of the slave is made indistinguishable, through metaphor, from the produce for which he labors crop up consistently in antislavery literature, although not always with reference to the consumption of flesh. Often, as in William Cowper's poem, "The Negro's Complaint," which might be called the motto of the abolitionist campaign of the 1790s, bodily fluids become metonymies for the bodies of the slaves:

> Why did all-creating Nature
> Make the plant for which we toil?
> Sighs must fan it, Tears must water,
> Sweat of ours must dress the soil.[24]

In this rhetorical move, a collection of fluids, rather than a coordinated body, becomes the active agent in the production of sugarcane. Sugar thus seems to result from the physical excretions of the slave—his tears, his sweat—rather than from his agricultural labor. This strategy, of replacing the body of the slave with his constitutive fluids, was common in abolitionist discourse. One abolitionist writer declares: "[The consumption of sugar] is a chain of wretchedness, every link of which is stained with blood!. . . . It becomes us to say of every part of this system, and of everything connected with it—here's the smell of blood *on the hand still, and all the perfumes of Arabia* cannot sweeten it."

Echoing Fox, a writer for the *Manchester Herald* declares: "Though you say that we shall not take the luxury of the sugar cane, unless it is polluted with slavery and steeped in blood; yet you cannot compel us to swallow the loathsome portion." Another pamphlet writer inquires: "Does it not behove all professors of Christianity well to consider how far they encourage the oppressor, by purchasing their commodities, thus defiled with blood?" And Samuel Taylor Coleridge wonders: "Will the Father of all men bless the Food of Cannibals—the Food which is polluted with the blood of his own innocent children?"[25]

This association between blood and sugar occasionally intersected with religious metaphor, as this later poem of Cowper's demonstrates:

> To purify their wine some people bleed
> A *Lamb* into the Barrel, and succeed;
> No Nostrum, Planters say, is half so good
> To make fine sugar, as a *Negro's* blood.
> Now lambs and negroes both are harmless things,
> And thence, perhaps, this wond'rous Virtue springs,
> 'Tis in the blood of Innocence alone—
> Good cause why Planters never try their own.[26]

The explicit irony of these verses runs along the lines of religious metaphor; the negro, like the lamb, is a figure of Christlike innocence misunderstood by the planters to be a mere animal. Yet, this imagery has strange effects; the spilling of this innocent blood contaminates the sugar. The poem's insistent metonymical transformation of laboring slaves into bodily fluids that may pollute colonial produce draws its reader's attention away from the exploitation of labor and toward the suggestion of physical contamination.[27] While the blood mentioned in these passages is not polluting by virtue of being African, but rather comes from "our fellow creatures" and "[God's] own innocent children," it nonetheless "defiles" English food. Another example of this rhetorical twist appeared in the *Gentleman's Magazine* in March 1792, in a poem describing a slave throwing himself into a vat of boiling sugar:

> Thus tormented, wild, despairing,
>     Every hour my bosom wrung,
> T'escape worse torture, blindly daring.
>     O'er the cauldron's verge I sprung.
> In the boiling sugar sinking
>     Cruel man! thou dids't me see;
> But the cup thy slaves are drinking
>     After death awaits for thee.[28]

Here, too, the suffering of the slaves is equated with Christ's suffering; they are "drinking the cup" of martyrdom. Yet, the example that confirms that suffering—the slave's body dissolving into boiling sugar—inevitably calls to mind not just the metaphorical cup of punishment the slave owners will eventually drink, but also the actual cup of tea sweetened by polluted sugar.

Perhaps the most explicit attempt to capitalize on the political power of the equation between the body of the slave and the sugar he produces occurs in a pamphlet that might be described as the paranoid double of Fox's "Address." The author of "A second address to the people of Great Britain: containing a new and most powerful argument to abstain from the use of West India sugar, by an Eye Witness to the facts related" notes that while Fox roused "those sentiments of humanity, which it is to be hoped, are more or less implanted in every breast" it is "difficult to persuade some, that when they eat Sugar, they figuratively eat the Blood of the Negro."[29] In other words, he admits that the chain of metaphorical associations on which Fox and others rely may not be strong enough to effect political change. In contrast, he hopes to make an argument that will "affect the senses" rather than one that is "only sentimental," occasion "some very uneasy and disagreeable sensations," and convince "the inhabitants of Great Britain, who use soft sugar, either in Puddings, Pies, Tarts, Tea, or otherwise, that they literally and most certainly in so doing, eat large quantities of that last mentioned Fluid, as it flows copiously from the Body of the laborious Slave, toiling under the scorching rays of a vertical Sun, mixed with many other savory ingredients."[30] While this pamphlet explicitly rejects metaphor in favor of concrete examples, it may also be said to reveal the workings of the metaphor it literalizes. That is, it assures its readers that the images of bodily contamination, which they thought might lie at the end of a chain of metonymic associations, are in fact literally true; but, in doing so, it, like its more metaphoric relations, relies on the plausibility of those images.

The "Second address" proceeds, along Swiftian lines, to make literal every figure used by the campaign to abstain from slave-grown sugar. While, in Cowper's poetry, sweat is a metonymy for labor, in this text it is a "nauceous effluvia emitted from [slaves] by excessive Perspiration" and is "almost insupportable"; furthermore, "every Hogshead of Sugar, imported into England from the West Indies, is more or less impregnated with this liquid from the human body."[31] The slave's body is thus a porous body, perforated by many small openings, and streaming with "torrents of Blood and Sweat." The "Second address . . ." even discusses the emission of pus, in connection with jiggers, insects that are

> first perceived by a violent itching; and when that part is closely examined, a small bag, about the size of a garden pea, filled with a whitish liquor, in which the insect swims, is found under the skin; and if this bag is not carefully extracted, without breaking, every toe on the foot will become a perfect honeycomb; and as this operation cannot be performed without occasioning little oozing sores, they become for a time very troublesome to the poor Negro; few of whom are exempt from the plague.[32]

The body of the slave is on the verge of becoming a "honeycomb," threatening to erupt with substances that are not poisonous in the ordinary sense, but taboo, interdicted. In contrast to antislavery discourse that underlines the innocence and universality of blood spilled in sugar production, this pamphlet emphasizes the specific, disgusting excrescence of the African slave laboring in the tropical sun. The slave's body has been made dangerous in this way by the conditions of Caribbean labor: burning sun, exotic insects. By rejecting contaminated sugar, then, consumers are not only rejecting slavery but also separating themselves from the foreign environment in which slave labor occurs. In this literalization of the widespread metaphor, sugar is the medium by which the body of the African slave penetrates English domestic intimacy through the mouths of unsuspecting consumers. To isolate themselves from the perforated body of the slave, which exudes an excess of bodily fluids, British consumers are asked to make themselves impenetrable, to refuse to swallow unknown substances. The potential cannibalism that sugar consumption suggests implies the dangerous possibility of reversal; the difference between that enslaved laborer and British consumers verges on erasure. Britons will be able to distinguish themselves from these colonial bodies only by maintaining impermeable corporeal boundaries. In the end, the only way British consumers can prevent their enslaved colonial laborers from entering the domestic space is by refusing to consume cane sugar, rendered indissociable from the bodily fluids of the slave by abolitionist rhetoric.

Yet, the insistence on the literal possibility of consuming the bodily fluids of slaves we find in the "Second Address" is unusual, if not unique, in antislavery rhetoric. Most writers on the subject reserve physical ingestion as a threat for those who cannot feel the force of the metaphorical connection. In other words, opponents of slavery often argue that domestic subjects ingest (morally if not physically polluted) sugar only because they cannot identify with the sufferings of colonial slaves. For example, in order to convince his readers to abstain from slave-grown produce, William Fox asks them to imagine that England itself was a sugar plantation and to "suppose our wives, our husbands, our children, our brethren swept away, and the fruit of their labour, produced with agonizing hearts and trembling limbs, landed at the port of London. What would be our conduct? Should we say, sugar is a necessary of life, I cannot do without it?"[33] He implies that domestic consumers only continue to purchase sugar because they cannot forcefully enough envision themselves in the place of captive Africans. Samuel Taylor Coleridge, in an essay in *The Watchman* entitled, "On the Slave Trade," declares that

> Surely if the inspired Philanthropist of Galilee were to revisit Earth, and be among the Feasters at Cana, he would not now change water into wine, but convert the produce into the things producing, the occasion into the things occasioned. Then, with our fleshly eye should we behold what even now Imagination ought to paint to us; instead of conserves, tears and blood, and for music, groanings and the loud peals of the lash![34]

In this nightmare image, the too "fleshly" consumer is threatened with the possibility of drinking tears and blood, instead of jam: digesting the "things producing." Such taboo exchanges of bodily fluids are represented as the result of the domestic consumer's inability to imagine far-away sufferings; in order to avoid this grisly passage from the metaphorical association between jam and colonial suffering to the horror of drinking blood, the consumer must recognize the power of imagination, and with it the power of metaphor.

This line of argumentation persisted after parliamentary measures to abolish the slave trade were defeated in 1792. In "The British Slave,"

Robert Southey berates those, "who at [their] ease / sip the blood-sweetened beverage."[35] The author of "The Rights of Man in the West Indies" asks that the feelings produced by metaphorical associations turn to physical action. He requests that every man,

> [a]s he sweetens his tea, let him reflect on the bitterness at the bottom of his cup. Let him bring the subject home to his heart, and say as he truly may, this lump cost the poor slave a groan, and this a bloody stroke with the cartwhip; and this, perhaps worn down by fatigue and wretchedness and despair, he sunk under his misery and died! And then let him swallow his beverage with what appetite he may.[36]

Occasionally, as in Coleridge, the enjoinder to "bring the subject home to one's heart" and recognize the connection between actual suffering and metaphorical "bitterness" is accompanied by the threat of actual pollution. In an 1826 pamphlet entitled "What does your sugar cost," the narrator relays this anecdote:

> A gentleman that I know very well, who came from the West Indies, told me he was once helping to pack some puncheons of rum. A negro who helped him happened to hurt his hand, and it bled, and he washed his hand in one of the puncheons of rum. The gentleman reproved him it, and said, "Your blood will be drunk in England." The Negro answered, "You no think, Massa, *when you eat our sugar, you drink our blood*."[37]

Here, the circumstances that allow the slave to literally bleed in the rum (a sugar product) seem to be made possible by the gentleman's, and by extension the British people's, inability to see that to drink rum is already to metaphorically drink the blood of slaves. The pamphlet urges its readers to forestall that possibility of physical contamination by heeding the power of metaphor, the power of its own language, to conjure up the horrors of slavery, and to take political action on the strength of those images.[38]

Emphasizing the idea that powerful sentimental reactions to written texts are necessary to forestall physical abominations, abolitionists argue that the relationship between England and her Caribbean colonies should no longer be organized around the consumption of colonial products, but rather around the compassionate observation of colonial suffering; they urge consumers to imagine British colonial slaves, instead of eating them. And it is here that antislavery rhetoric intersects with late eighteenth-century constructions of female identity, deploying such formulations toward political ends.

Recently, English literary studies have devoted considerable attention to the evolution of the category of the domestic and its growing importance in the organization of English society. Nancy Armstrong, in *Desire and Domestic Fiction*, has perhaps most fully developed the idea that the invention of the domestic sphere in the middle of the eighteenth century revolutionized the status of women in English culture. The discourse of domesticity created a space in which individual thoughts and emotions were separable from and superior to the economic and political world. She argues that this new concept of "the most basic qualities of human identity" gave rise to a peculiar kind of female subjectivity, one which depended on the discursive construction of domestic virtue.[39] In other words, a woman was no longer valued for her physical attributes, but for her ability to articulate a kind of emotional authority. As Lenore Davidoff and Catherine Hall have argued, by the end of the eighteenth century, "power was for men, influence for women. Through their example in life women could hope to make those around them, in their family circles, better people. It was *moral influence* which was to allow a reassertion of self for women."[40] In *Desire and Domestic Fiction*, Armstrong never takes up the relation between the reorganization of the domestic space around moral influence and emotional authority and changing attitudes toward the colonial arena, but her theories enable such an investigation. Turning her arguments to that use, however, requires an expansion of her idea of the female domestic gaze. This feminine "eye of power" must be understood not merely as a force disciplining the interior of the home, but as an organizing structure that brought the supposedly feminine qualities of compassion and sympathy to bear on the colonial world.

Abolitionists took seriously the efficacy of moral influence, and emphasized its conjunction with the female capacity for compassion; they explicitly attempted to harness these qualities as tools for changing the colonial world. As one pamphlet declares, "the peculiar texture of [a woman's] mind, her strong feelings and quick sensibilities, especially qualify her, not only to sympathise with suffering, but also to plead for the oppressed, and there is no calculating the extent and importance of the moral reformations that might be effected through the combined exertion of her gentle influence and steady resolution."[41] Thus, such naturalized feminine characteristics were appropriated as political tools. The author of "An Address to Her Royal Highness the Duchess of York, against the use of sugar,"

> cannot suppose there exists a female, possessing a heart of sensibility, who can consider at length the detail of the facts [about the slave trade] . . . without many a deep sigh, without many an earnest wish, that the world may be fairly rid of a traffic which involves it in such complicated villainy; without feeling the deepest anxiety that the guilt of it may no longer belong to the land of her nativity or the country of her residence.[42]

This text represents the relationship between England and her colonies not in terms of the female breast but rather with regard to the female "heart of sensibility"; it shifts the emphasis from simply her capacity to consume to her capacity to feel something about what she consumes. Even an opponent of the campaign to abstain from slave-grown sugar theorized that women supported it for sentimental reasons:

> The English ladies have patronized it; to their kind and fostering protection it is much indebted. The heaven-born daughters of our isle, with all the delicate sensibility which is their distinguishing characteristic, were pierced to the heart with the sufferings of the oppressed African; and with a fortitude which does them the highest honour, refused to enjoy those sweets, which they supposed to be the price of blood.[43]

According to this author, women enact the abolitionist ideal: "pierced to the heart" by images of suffering, they take political action.

This feminine capacity to visualize and feel the sufferings of others had to be carefully distinguished from a frivolous susceptibility to fictional scenes, a quality to which women were also supposedly prone. Coleridge claims "the fine lady's nerves are not shattered by the shrieks! She sips a beverage sweetened with human blood, even while she is weeping over the refined sorrows of Werter [sic] or of Clementina. Sensibility is not Benevolence."[44] This "fine lady" cannot connect the feelings aroused by her reading with her material surroundings: her sympathy with the heroes and heroines of novels is a kind of false compassion, because it blinds her to the scene of suffering that has been enacted to sweeten her tea. Again, Coleridge's imagery suggests that the horror of bodily pollution, of drinking blood, is the result of a failure in imagination. Thus, it is not the psychological structure of sympathetic identification that he objects to, but rather the way it is misused by the "fine lady." Coleridge contrasts her futile sensibility with "benevolence," which "may be defined [as] Natural Sympathy made permanent by an acquired conviction, that the interests of all are one and the same."[45] The distinction between a false "sensibility" and "Natural Sympathy" seems slight, since both qualities rely on the ability to see oneself in another. The difference between them lies in their outcome; seeing oneself in the place of a suffering novel heroine produces no action in the world, while seeing oneself in the place of a suffering West Indian slave urges one to political action. For Coleridge, "there is one criterion by which we may always distinguish benevolence from mere sensibility—Benevolence impels to action, and is accompanied by self-denial."[46] The structure of sympathetic identification goes unchallenged by Coleridge; he criticizes only its object.

The political radicals of the 1790s had to modify definitions of femininity somewhat to accommodate this active sensibility. Mary Wollstonecraft, like Coleridge, connects a kind of false femininity with the continued subjugation of Caribbean slaves in a complicated analogy: a correspondence similarly anchored by the image of the bodily pollution of drinking blood.

> Why subject [woman] to propriety—blind propriety—if she be capable of acting from a nobler spring, if she be the heir to immortality? Is sugar always to be produced by vital blood? Is one half of the human species, like the poor African slaves, to be subjected to prejudices which brutalize them, when principles would be a surer guard, only to sweeten the cup of man? Is this not indirectly to deny woman reason?[47]

The *Vindication of the Rights of Woman* was published in 1792, at the height of the movement to abstain from slave-grown sugar, and this analogy resonates with the fears of the contamination of the domestic space that that campaign mobilized. Femininity based simply on "propriety" "sweetens" man's domestic space in the same poisonous way that the labor of African slaves sweetens his cup of tea. Wollstonecraft links the oppression of women by man's desire for the metaphorical "sweetness" of femininity with the oppression of

Africans by man's desire for the literal sweetness of sugar. The connection implies that a feminine virtue based on reason rather than propriety would rid the home of both forms of pollution—false sweetness and colonial produce.

In abolitionist pamphlets, such active female virtue is conjoined to a kind of national sensibility, a female anxiety over the virtue of the "land of her nativity." The compassion of British women symbolizes a specific national identity—a quality that distinguishes England from the rest of the world. This association is often repeated in antislavery discourse; for example, William Allen concludes his attack on the consumption of West Indian produce by asking, "Is it possible, Sir, that the ladies of England, possessing a sense of *Virtue*, of *Honour*, and of *Sympathy* beyond those of any other nation—is it possible for them to encourage the slave trade?!"[48] Gender identity and national identity are linked here, anchored by the quality of sympathy. Abolitionist rhetoric thus consciously calls on female sensibility to safeguard the home from colonial contamination, to preserve that home as a symbol of a purified English identity, and thus to ensure that the domestic sphere remains distinct from the colonial arena.

This particular characteristic of femininity, women's susceptibility to compassion, to sympathetic identification with faraway sufferers, is called on to mediate and reorganize England's relationship to its Caribbean colonies. Women were supposed to anchor a chain of identifications between British subjects and West Indian slaves, an imaginative connection that was to replace the dangers of incorporation posed by physical consumption. Allen continues by arguing that "[women] are universally considered as the Models of every just and virtuous sentiment—and we naturally look up to them as Patterns in all the softer virtues. Their example, therefore, in abstaining from the use of West India produce—must refute every objection—and render the performance of the Duty as universal as their Influence."[49] If a woman, reading an abolitionist pamphlet, can so strongly sympathize with the sufferings of colonial slaves, that she refuses to consume sugar, then she can act as a "pattern," an "example," to the men who observe her. There seems to be a connection between her ability to alter her own feelings in terms of the feelings of racial others, that is, to sympathize, and her capacity to "model" those feelings for the English men who will be persuaded to imitate her.

The role that the female modeling of virtue played in the abolitionist movement is made explicit in the case of the distribution of the famous emblem of a kneeling slave, asking "Am I not a man and a brother?" Created by Josiah Wedgwood in 1788, these ceramic ornaments, according to Thomas Clarkson,

> were soon . . . in different parts of the kingdom. Some had them inlaid in gold on the lid of their snuff boxes. Of the ladies, several wore them in bracelets, and others had them fitted up in an ornamental manner as pins for their hair. At length, the taste for wearing them became general; and thus fashion, which usually confines itself to worthless things, was seen for once in the honorable office of promoting the cause of justice, humanity and freedom.[50]

Here, one kind of consumption is used to oppose another. Wedgwood's ceramics, domestically produced and sometimes seen as the seeds of England's industrial revolution, replace colonial products. But, more to the point, the consumption of images designed to evoke feelings of compassion replaces the consumption of foodstuffs destined to be digested. In this description of the efficacy of feminine fashions in the political arena, we can see that the role played by the female body in the relationship between England and her colonies has changed. Instead of functioning as a site of congruence between the domestic space and the colonial arena, its fluids analogous to colonial products, the female body has become both a kind of screen for identification and an active agent of consumption; bearing the emblems of sympathy, it is an exemplary model of compassion imagined as an ethics of consumption. The passivity of "taste" and "fashion" have been replaced by a new attention to the moral process of choosing and displaying commodities; these women are active agents in the market, "promoting" a "cause." In other words, the solution to the problem of sugar consumption is not a retreat from consumerism, but rather a reconfiguration of consumer behavior, in which, paradoxically, the affective charge of commodities—their capacity to suggest emotion—increases.

The connection drawn by the abolitionist movement between the purchasing of colonial goods and the international political system gave women a new and crucial place in the political arena, not only as compassionate observers, but also as wielders of a material, though circumscribed, power. The abolitionist movement of the 1790s was one of a number of eighteenth-century social actions that acknowledged the political power of consumer activity.[51] It worked on the assumption that the consumer's discretionary power to buy or not to buy certain commodities could in fact be used to transform ethical assumptions and social conditions. For example, an "Appeal to the hearts and consciences of British Women" asks "to whom can we appeal with such propriety as to our enlightened and patriotic countrywomen? In the domestic department, they are the chief controllers; they, for the most part, provide the articles for family consumption."[52] And perhaps the strongest formulation of the domestic power of women comes from a pamphlet that claims that by "refusing to use any articles which have been cultivated by Slaves, woman, feeble as she is, may do more for the suppression of the inhuman Slave Trade, than all the ships of war that have ever ranged the coast of Africa."[53] The feminine capacity to sympathize with the sufferings of others thus leads to two sorts of political activity. First, women are themselves convinced, through the structure of sympathetic identification, to abstain from purchasing colonial products for the home. Second, their compassion acts as a model, or pattern, for the men who observe them. These political moves put domestic virtue in the service of the eradication of the brutal institution of Caribbean slavery; domestic management is seen to have a direct impact on colonial management.

The sympathetic identification called for by abolitionist discourse differs from the unlimited consumption proposed by mercantilist sugar producers not because it calls for an end to foreign trade—most abolitionists supported the movement toward fewer barriers to free trade—but rather because it demands some form of mediation between the compassionate observer and the suffering slave. Female sympathy depends on the distance reestablished between consumer and producer by images, either pictorial, as in the case of Wedgwood's medallion, or textual, as in the case of the proliferation of abolitionist pamphlets, poems, and histories. Yet, the corporeal does not entirely disappear from this discourse; on the contrary, nightmarish images of the British consumer literally eating the body of the slave are consistently associated with the consumption of slave-grown sugar. One might read this strain of abolitionist rhetoric as suggesting that unchecked domestic consumption of colonial produce brought colonial bodies too close to domestic bodies by bringing the blood of colonial slaves to domestic lips. This reading suggests that abstention from colonial products might work to purify the domestic space by purging the domestic body of the implicitly racial contamination of African blood, sweat, and tears. In a way, this rhetoric of the antislavery movement constructs physical incorporation and sympathetic identification as each other's opposites. If the savage cannibalism of British consumers is only occasioned by a lack of compassionate imagination, an inability to put themselves in the place of suffering others, then only by strengthening that capacity can slavery be eradicated. For this reason, a certain assumption about female identity anchors the campaign to abstain from slave-grown sugar. Women's capacity for compassion was to inspire their male companions to follow their model, and to join the women in undermining the institution of slavery by abstaining from its products. Women's political power, in this struggle to redefine and uphold the national honor of Britain, lay in their ability to regulate the domestic space, keeping its contents separate from the economic dynamics of colonial trade.

Thus, the British antislavery movement of the 1790s, while it struggled to force a social recognition of the humanity of cultural others, also worked to renegotiate British cultural identities and gender roles. Women were accorded an innovative and influential form of political agency by the antislavery movement, which often worked in harmony with a particular formulation of domestic ideology. By examining abolitionist rhetoric in relation to that contemporaneous development of domestic ideology, we can begin to understand how those two discourses complemented and supported each other, and, in understanding this, we may gain a critical purchase on the way they have combined to structure our idea of cultural difference.

## Chapter 5

# "Reading Before Praying"

*Ladies' Antislavery Societies, Textuality, Political Action, and* The History of Mary Prince

In 1831, the former slave Mary Prince, relating the contempt showered on her family as they were sold, exclaimed: "Oh those white people have small hearts who can only feel for themselves."[1] Prince here voices an imperative of the antislavery movement: that the hearts of white people be made to grow through an understanding of the suffering of slaves. Yet, how was this enlargement to be accomplished? One of the most appealing strategies for British abolitionists was the dissemination of affecting texts, the dual benefits of which are visible in the following passage from Sancho's *Letters*. Upon receiving an abolitionist book from an American Quaker in 1778, he writes:

> [T]he illegality—the horrible wickedness of the traffic—the cruel carnage and depopulation of the human species—is painted in such strong colours—that I should think would (if duly attended to) flash conviction—and produce remorse in every enlightened and candid reader.— The perusal affected me more than I can express;—indeed I felt a double or mixt sensation—for while my heart was torn for the sufferings—which, for aught I know—some of my nearest kin might have undergone—my bosom, at the same time, glowed with gratitude—and praise toward the humane—the Christian—the friendly and learned Author of that most valuable book.[2]

Sancho, a former slave himself, models here the perfect readerly experience; he identifies with the slaves' suffering, experiences a flash of abolitionist conviction, and understands the moral generosity and legitimacy of antislavery activism.

It was exactly this kind of response that ladies' antislavery societies hoped to foster in readers with less material connection to the horrors of slavery than Sancho. These groups focused their energies on the dissemination of affecting information about the true nature of slavery, perhaps most strikingly found in Mary Prince's autobiography—the first such document by a female slave. Because of their close relationship to print capitalism and to the market in texts, the efforts of ladies' antislavery societies were as embedded in consumer culture as were those of the campaign to abstain from slave-grown sugar. But, as Prince's words demonstrate, the politics of these groups were also imbricated with a theory of sentiment; the groups were deeply committed to the idea that a heart of the proper size would never allow the horrors of slavery to continue. This belief in the importance of sentiment to social change also forced them to confront the problem of women's place in the public sphere. Sandra Pouchet Paquet has argued that Prince's description converts a degrading form of female publicity—the slave market—into a kind of morally sanctioned public speech—her published testimony.[3] The white, British women of ladies' antislavery societies also transformed the potential scandal of their involvement in public affairs into a legitimate activity, sanctioned by a morality emanating from the "private" sphere of domesticity. The situations of Caribbean slaves and metropolitan British women were not commensurate by any means. Still, it is important to note that for both black and white women, entrance into the public sphere took place most easily when their bodies were rendered inconsequential by print.

## PRINT AND POLITICS

Recently, a number of critics in various disciplines have begun to investigate the effects of print culture on political activity at the turn of the eighteenth century. Both Olivia Smith and Thomas Laqueur have argued that the education of working-class men and women, and the resulting rise in literacy, made possible the radical political movements that flourished in England between the French Revolution and the ascent of Napoleon; Laqueur claims that "the history of literacy, and the history of political culture are profoundly interconnected."[4] This history in England dates back to at least the mid-seventeenth century. During the Civil Wars, the number of newspapers and broadsheets skyrocketed, and political and religious questions were debated by a growing public.[5] Women, as well as men, participated in this new sphere of political debate, as female literacy rates climbed.[6] The resulting development of print culture, too complicated to be more than gestured at here, led to new forms of political community—particularly the nation. Benedict Anderson has argued that we need to see "the novel and the newspaper" as helping to organize "the *kind* of imagined community that is the nation." He claims that "print capitalism" "made it possible for rapidly growing numbers of people to think about themselves, and to relate themselves to others in profoundly new ways."[7] David Turley connects these developments to the abolitionist movement, noting its ability to exploit "technical developments and geographical expansion in printing, tendencies to specialisation in publishing and the establishment of a coherent national distribution network for books and pamphlets."[8]

At the same time, however, critics have identified another understanding of eighteenth-century print culture. The texts that characterize this trend are mostly fictional, and are designed to evoke individual emotions rather than to pass on useful information. Furthermore, these emotional responses were often seen to be in the service of selfish or solipsistic pleasure, rather than of national or political feeling; they were thought to cause readers to turn inward rather than outward. Such texts and reading practices are usually labeled sentimental, and by the end of the eighteenth century and the beginning of the nineteenth, they were most often associated with women. Although earlier in the eighteenth century the capacity for sentimentality to engage political questions had been taken for granted, by this period that discourse had become suspect. Coleridge, as we have seen, was incensed by "the fine lady" who "sips a beverage sweetened with human blood, even while she is weeping over the refined sorrows of Werter [*sic*] or of Clemetina."[9] Here, the woman's enjoyment of the novels of Goethe and Richardson is disassociated from an ethical understanding of the equally sad events that have sweetened her tea with the metaphorical blood of slaves. Her pleasure is private and individualized, qualities that arguably epitomize the appeal of sentimental literature in general.[10] Furthermore, the disjunction between her emotional investment in novels and her attitude toward the exploitation of slave labor may itself be part of the structure of an expanding capitalist society. Catherine Gallagher has argued that "this deliberate creation of emotional discontinuity allowed for a separate dimension of affective life, one in which emotions were only 'practiced,'" teaching readers "the necessary discontinuities of feeling that must be suffered so that larger continuities (of property and family) might be built."[11] Coleridge's "fine lady" thus participates in a form of leisure activity that helps consolidate the same economic structure that exploited slave labor. Indeed, as Terry Lovell has noted, the activity of reading came to symbolize the leisure that the domestic woman's removal from the scene of labor enabled. It placed her firmly in the role of consumer rather than producer.[12]

Thus, on the one hand, the spread of print culture, in the form of newspapers, cheap pamphlets, and chapbooks, and of certain kinds of allegorically nationalist fiction, made possible a new kind of political community—a public space primarily accessible to men. On the other hand, sentimental fiction seemed to elicit emotional investments from its readers that could become solipsistic, self-indulgent, and privatized, concentrating such readers on their own individualized fantasies, rather than on the group struggles going on around them; this form of reading was primarily associated with women. Of course, the line between these two kinds of reading was, and is, difficult to draw. That may be because, according to Jürgen Habermas, the two kinds of reading—"private" and "public"—initially were connected:

> The sphere of the public arose in the broader strata of the bourgeoisie as an expansion and at the same time completion of the intimate sphere of the conjugal family. Living room and salon were under the same roof; just as the privacy of the one was oriented to the public nature of the other, and as the subjectivity of the privatized individual was related from the very start to publicity, so both were conjoined in literature that had become "fiction." . . . The privatized individuals coming together to form a [reading] public also reflected critically and in public on what they had read.[13]

Later in the eighteenth century, as a public sphere of extra-governmental debate became more organized, it seemed to consolidate a private sphere in its wake. Women were defined increasingly as private, sentimental readers, and were excluded from the debate over public affairs.[14] Abolitionists, however, particularly women, seemed able to resurrect and reconfigure those foundational relationships between private and public, sentiment and reason. The rhetoric of antislavery texts depended as heavily on emotionally affecting sentimental images as it did on the factual accounts disseminated by newspapers.

The abolitionist movement consistently found political uses for the habits of textual consumption formed by sentimental literature and art. Thomas Clarkson, for example, describes the efficacy of Cowper's poem "The Negro's Complaint" for converting possible sympathizers:

> This little piece Cowper presented to some of his friends in London; and these, conceiving it to contain a powerful appeal on the behalf of injured Africans, joined in printing it. Having ordered it on the finest hot pressed paper, and folded it into a small and neat form, they gave it the printed title of "a subject for conversation at the tea table." After this, they sent many thousand copies of it in franks into the country. From one it spread to another, till it travelled almost over the whole island. Falling into the hands of the musicians, it was set to music; and it then found its way into the streets, both of the metropolis and of the country, where it was sung as a ballad; and where it gave a plain account of the subject, with an appropriate feeling, to those who heard it.[15]

Like the Wedgwood medallion, the poem's distribution is tied to other practices of consumption; note the care that Cowper's friends expend on its "small and neat form." Clarkson is interested not only in the number of copies that eventually pervaded the country but also in the form of the information so disseminated. It must be "plain" enough to be understood, as well as powerful enough to provoke an "appropriate feeling." In this respect, it is important that Cowper's poem is so easily translated into a ballad, the "major musical idiom of industrial workers."[16] Cowper's poem, and the antislavery message it carried, was both an object of mass consumption and part of new reading practices;[17] the patterns of consumption implied by Clarkson's careful description of the poem's packaging are harnessed for a political end. Clearly, the sentiment engendered by a fiction is an important part of achieving a popular abolitionist consensus.

This relationship between information and affect in antislavery texts facilitated women's increasingly active role in the abolitionist movement, primarily under the aegis of ladies' antislavery societies. In the previous chapter, we saw that the abolitionist movement created innovative forms of political power for women, forms based on their ability to sympathize with, even identify with, the sufferings of African slaves in the Caribbean. This chapter examines the concerted attempt by ladies' antislavery associations to harness women's reading practices, even those associated with sentimentality, for moral and political ends. These organizations often saw their primary purpose in the abolitionist movement to be the distribution of texts delineating the horrors of slavery, in order to educate their primarily female readers and to sway them toward the cause of abolition. Through such activities, they expanded both the purview of women's reading habits and the content of what women read. Furthermore, in their search for truthful but affecting texts about slavery, these groups also made possible *The History of Mary Prince*. They reconfigured the affective investment women supposedly brought to textual representations of suffering as a form of useful political energy.

Yet, the kinds of political activity fostered by ladies' antislavery societies would have been impossible without the placement of sentimental reading within a consumer culture—a connection Anderson makes visible in the phrase "print capitalism." Antislavery writers did not always sell their pamphlets—indeed, ladies' antislavery societies were more likely to distribute tracts subsidized by charitable contributions than to use texts themselves to raise money. Nevertheless, the place of these female activists in a gendered discourse of consumerism can be deduced from their reluctance to figure themselves as the authors or producers of these artifacts. Instead, members of ladies' antislavery societies are more likely to represent themselves as mediums through which information passes, or even as exemplary receivers of "true pictures" of slavery. Thus, even as they entered into political debate, these activists remained within a bourgeois paradigm that idealized the leisured consumerism of middle-class white women.

## DOMESTICITY AND POLITICS

As we have seen in the rhetoric surrounding the campaign to abstain from slave-grown sugar, the domestic woman, because she was uniquely capable of sympathetic identification with the suffering of slaves, became a central figure in abolitionist campaigns. Her capacity for compassion opened up an area of political agency peculiarly accessible to white, middle-class, British women. In the early nineteenth century, these assumptions helped consolidate the social influence of ladies' antislavery societies. These groups, along with a number of other women's philanthropic associations formed at the turn of the century, turned a growing cultural reliance on middle-class women's moral rectitude into a vehicle for political activities outside the home.[18]

F. K. Prochaska has found that "approximately 160 religious, moral, educational and philanthropic associations were founded in England between 1700 and 1830. About 130 of these were established in the years 1790–1830."[19] By the 1830s, women's longtime involvement in the antislavery movement had led them to form their own philanthropical associations to focus on this issue; "in 1825, three women's antislavery societies were formed, at Birmingham, Sheffield and at Calne in Wiltshire: by the end of the decade there were forty others."[20] The membership of such associations was made up primarily of middle-class religious women and "evolved out of their already accepted roles in religious philanthropy and the religious societies aimed at the expansion of evangelical Christianity. Philanthropy and religious work were accommodated as extensions of women's caring and domestic functions, part of the *status quo* of gender relationships."[21] In a full-length study of women's involvement in the abolitionist movement in Britain, Clare Midgley concludes that it was "the first large-scale political campaign by middle-class women, and the first movement in which women aroused the opinion of the female public in order to put pressure on Parliament," making important "interconnections between domestic and political life and between public and private activities."[22]

But that line between the privacy of the domestic sphere and the publicity of political engagement had to be negotiated carefully by these groups. By and large, women confined even their political activities to the domestic sphere; "in most [philanthropic groups], women worked only with women. If they addressed mixed-sex meetings, they did not speak in public but at 'drawing room' or 'parlour' meetings of invited guests."[23] Yet, even these activities sometimes seemed too openly political for their male colleagues. Wilberforce, for example, once told Macauley that "all private exertions for such an object become their character, but for ladies to meet, to publish, to go from house to house stirring up petitions — these appear to me proceedings unsuited to the female character as delineated in scripture. I fear its tendency would be to mix them in all the multiform warfare of political life."[24] Interestingly, Wilberforce does not question women's ability to inform themselves, or to influence those close to them. Their right to participate in the public sphere as readers seems incontrovertible. What bothers him is their physical participation in politics — going door to door, attending meetings; even publishing seems too public an activity. Thus, he emphasizes two crucial limitations for women's involvement in the public sphere during this period: that they are welcome as readers, but not as writers; and that the proper positioning of their bodies is vital to any legitimate intervention.

Yet, were the lines between suitable public and private behavior for women really as clearly drawn as Wilberforce asserts here? If the late eighteenth and early nineteenth centuries saw an increasing sensitivity to female immodesty, the period also witnessed a pronounced rise in the level of organized female intervention into cultural affairs. In retrospect, these activities often look quite "public." Wilberforce's "broadcasting of the language of separate spheres," might be read, as Amanda Vickery suggests, as a "conservative response to the opportunities, ambitions and experiences of late Georgian and Victorian women."[25] Indeed, the rhetoric of separate spheres was a double-edged sword — used by some to caution women against public behavior, and by others to render such behavior appropriate. The ability of female abolitionists to defeat "the opposition with its own weapons" emerges, for example, in the following exchange from an abolitionist pamphlet entitled "A Dialogue on West Indian Slavery":[26]

> B: But I really think women ought not to interfere in this business, on account of its being a political question: for women have nothing to do with such subjects; they are quite out of their province, and I think it is not consistent with propriety and hardly with feminine modesty, that they should put themselves forward on this occasion.
>
> A: I own I have never been able to affix any clear meaning to the expres-

sion you have just used, and which I have often heard before, that this is a political question. It appears to me to be peculiarly a religious and moral question.[27]

In order for antislavery feelings to conform with "propriety" and "feminine modesty," they had to be coded as part of the feminine realm of religion and morality, rather than as part of the masculine sphere of politics. Women were thus assigned a kind of agency in the world outside the home that had more to do with the cultural force of private domestic practices than with overtly public political actions. Yet, Elizabeth Heyrick, in her "Apology for Ladies' Anti-Slavery Associations" (1828), proposes that the exclusion of women from the political arena gives them an influence over colonial production equal to that of the military:

> Though *we* have no voice in the senate, no influence in public meetings,—though no signatures of ours are attached to anti-slavery petitions to the legislature,—yet we have a voice and an influence in a sphere, which, though restricted, is no narrow one. To the hearts and consciences of our own sex, at least, we have unlimited access. By dispelling their ignorance, by disseminating among them correct information on the nature and consequences of West Indian slavery, and dissuading them from all participation in its guilt, by a conscientious rejection of its produce, we may withdraw its resources and undermine its foundations.[28]

After elaborating upon the ways in which women cannot exercise political power, Heyrick argues that the "hearts and consciences" of women are a powerful tool in the destruction of the slave trade. Like the campaigners of the 1790s, she proposes that the nexus of colonial exchange is the bourgeois household, where sugar is bought and consumed.

More typically, however, ladies' antislavery societies emphasized the power women's moral sense might exert over men's political decisions. The descriptions given by ladies' antislavery societies of their own activities often underline the potential force and efficacy of influence, rather than the necessity for public argument. As the author of "Appeal to the Hearts and Consciences of British Women"(1828) explains,

> [a woman] may . . . exert a powerful influence over public opinion and practice without violating that retiring delicacy which constitutes one of her loveliest ornaments. The peculiar texture of her mind, her strong feel-

ings and quick sensibilities, especially qualify her, not only to sympathise with suffering, but also to plead for the oppressed, and there is no calculating the extent and importance of the moral reformations which might be effected through the combined exertion of her gentle influence and steady resolution.[29]

This statement makes a woman's femininity contingent on her abolitionist sentiment. Her qualities of "strong feelings," "quick sensibilities," "gentle influence," and "steady resolution"—in short, the qualities that define her gender—demand her involvement in the antislavery campaign. Even her lack of actual political power is mobilized as a moral asset; she thus qualifies to "plead for the oppressed." The author is careful to deploy domestic sentiments toward the public good, while showing women to be uninterested in manipulating actual political decisions. The woman lending her voice to the cause of the suffering slaves has no stake in the economic or political consequences of her actions; her only concern is with moral rectitude. An "Appeal to the Christian Women of Sheffield" also argues for the powerful, though apolitical, force of moral influence:

> We are met with the question, what can *women* do in this cause? We are happily excluded from the great theater of public business, from the strife of debate, and the cares of legislation; but this privilege does not exempt us from the duty of exerting our influence, in our own appropriate and retired sphere, over the public opinion, without which no important moral reformation can be accomplished. . . . It is ours to shew what can be effected by the combined exertion of gentle influence and steady resolution. Is it assuming too much to say, that no cruel institutions, or ferocious practices could long withstand the avowed and persevering censure of the women of England?[30]

Statements such as this avow both the value and the power of the domestic sphere. Such retirement is not a relief from civic duties, but requires its own activities—influence and censure.

Male antislavery activists usually courted and relied upon the strength of feminine influence.[31] Sir James McKintosh "observed, that in proportion as they possessed the retiring virtues of *delicacy* and *modesty*, those chief ornaments of women, in that proportion had they come forward to defend the still higher objects of humanity and jus-

tice." More crudely, a Bristol handbill of the 1820s exploits the popular
belief in the power of women's influence to promote a particular can-
didate for parliament. Ventriloquizing the voice of a Caribbean slave
woman appealing to those of her sex in Bristol, it reads:

> Missy, Missy, tink on we
> Toder side of the big blue sea—
> How we flogged and how we cry—
> How we sometimes wish to die.
> . . .
>
> When de Buckra 'peaker sent
> To de house call Parliament,
> Send *such* Bukra 'peaker dere
> As regard poor Neger prayer.
>
> Massa Proderoe—*he* good man!
> Send *him*, Missy—SURE YOU CAN
> Den you fill poor Neger eye
> Wid de tear brimful of joy!
>
> Toder man—call Massa *Baillie*
> He no care what Neger ail'e!
> Massa Proderoe—He de man!
> Send him Missy—sure you can![32]

This appeal makes visible the cultural force attributed to the sentimental bond between English women and captive women in the Caribbean. The poem describes this bond in terms of shared tears; English
women thinking about the tears and suffering of slave women presumably are supposed to cry themselves. The actions motivated by these
English tears—the election to parliament of "Massa Proderoe" by
"fathers, husbands, brothers and sons" influenced by female compassion—then produce tears of joy in the grateful slave women. Of course,
the poet's expression of this appeal to sisterhood in crude dialect works
against the poem's call for sentimental solidarity; the words make the
slave women's exclusion from standard English strikingly evident. The
two groups of women are also separated by their different physical relationships to publicity; while the white women's agency is expressed in
terms of a private physicality—tears—the bodies of the slave women
are exposed publicly in brutal flogging. These differences work to

remind the reader that the two groups of women are separated by more than geographical distance; sympathy does not necessarily lead to equality. Nevertheless, the poem's author seems very sure of the powerful effort middle-class metropolitan women might exert in the service of a specific political cause.

### READING BEFORE PRAYING

If women's role in the political arena was to influence the men around them, one of the primary methods of influence they used was the dissemination of texts. Ladies' antislavery societies often saw the production and distribution of antislavery tracts as their chief responsibility. In 1828, the Dublin Ladies' Anti-Slavery Society noted in its "Rules and Resolutions" that "the primary objects of the Ladies of the society be, to procure and to circulate universally, throughout Ireland, copies of all such documents, as show the great evils of slavery."[33] And the Birmingham Society, which served as a kind of central organizer of many local groups, recorded in its first report that:

> The mode pursued for awakening attention, circulating information, and introducing to the notice of the affluent and influential classes of the community a knowledge of the real state of suffering and humiliation under which British slaves yet groan, experience has proved to be one of the most eligible that could be devised, *viz*, the dissemination of current information through the medium of the societies workbags and albums, of the former of which about 2,000 have been disposed in England, Wales and Ireland.[34]

Such activity seems most "eligible" for women because it is mediated both by the anonymity of print and by the familiar domesticity of such objects as workbags and albums. The dissemination of information "through the medium" of these items informed the public of these women's ethical and political views about slavery, but did not involve them in public speaking or petition signing. Indeed, the language of this passage, which is representative of most such appeals, highlights the role of women as transmitters of neutral information, rather than as creators or shapers of a pointed political message; the group "introduces information," and "awakens attention," rather than emphasizing their own abilities as writers or rhetoricians. Thus, these women negotiate a particular discourse of gender and class that asserts that middle-class white women should be consumers rather than producers—modeling rather than sculpting emotion. They also reinforce that discourse by emphasizing the natural quality of female compassion, which only needs to be awakened, rather than fostered or produced.

Although these groups were themselves sometimes defensive about the efficacy of their chosen method of overthrowing slavery, they were proud of the sheer quantity of textual artifacts they distributed. In 1825, the Society in Sheffield explained:

> In reporting the proceedings of the first year of our infant society, we are aware that it may appear that little has been done to aid the labors of the various associations for the great cause of the abolition of slavery, but it will be recollected, that the principle object to which our efforts are directed, was the dissemination of the facts connected with the evils of slavery. . . . In compliance with this resolution, upwards of fourteen hundred pamphlets, tracts, etc., have been distributed, in addition to the Monthly Reporters given to the Committee for circulation every three months, besides the sale of two hundred and seventy eight work bags, filled with tracts, with an engraving suited to the subject.[35]

Again, this group figures itself as "disseminating facts" and "distributing" pamphlets, rather than writing descriptions, or even assembling information. If the members see themselves as producers of anything, it is as creators of domestic objects: workbags that contain poems and engravings as well as tracts. Yet, the doubleness of this representation, in which women are both mediums for the dissemination of texts and agents of a certain kind of commodified exchange, functions to bridge the ideological gap between political activity and the leisured domesticity of middle-class British women. Political texts, in this context, become domestic objects for exchange among women, and domestic objects carry a political charge. This interpenetration of seemingly private, consumerist activities—like reading—with a public agenda—the abolition of slavery—could produce new uses for seemingly private objects, such as personal correspondence. One of the most radical abolitionist women, the Quaker Anne Knight, affixed brightly colored stickers to the outside of her private letters carrying bits of prose or poetry, in order to advertise her cause more widely.[36] Knight's friends often did not appreciate her gesture, but it seems to symbolize the way that private communication between women and political agitation for a cause could simply become two parts of the same package, just two sides of the same piece of paper.

For these reasons, reading, rather than writing, figures as the primary political activity of ladies' antislavery societies. It assumed such importance among these groups that in 1837, the Sheffield Association of the Universal Abolition of Slavery could declare in their "Appeal to the Christian Women of Sheffield" that

> We place reading before praying, not because we regard it as more important, but because, in order to pray aright, we must understand what we are praying for; it is only then we can pray with the *understanding* and with the *spirit* also. We lay great stress upon reading—torturing to the feelings, as the dreadful evils produced by slavery must often prove;—for when you read these accounts you cannot help making them known to others; and the great thing wanted is, that the real nature of the system should become *known*;—it would then seem impossible that its continuance should be longer endured.[37]

This statement makes a number of interesting connections between reading and political action. It assumes that once readers gain knowledge of the "real nature" of slavery through antislavery texts, they will no longer be able to "endure" its existence, and presumably will be compelled to increased agitation against it—or at least to prayer. Furthermore, it claims that such knowledge cannot remain individualized or private—"when you read these accounts you cannot help making them known to others." Textual dissemination is characterized here as the key to the growth of abolitionist consensus in Britain. The writers also make certain assumptions about the activity of reading, itself. Reading produces an "understanding" of slavery despite the fact that the "details of the dreadful evils produced by slavery" often prove "torturing to the feelings." These campaigners resist the dissociation of reading from social action that Catherine Gallagher claims as one of the functions of sentimentality; for them, the sympathetic pain produced by textual representations of suffering is seen to be indissociable from, even necessary to, an understanding of slavery.

Thus, while ladies' antislavery associations saw their purpose to be educating others about the realities of slave culture, they also relied on sentimental reading practices to make those texts politically effective, at least among women. As a "Picture of Colonial Slavery in the Year 1828, Addressed Especially to the Ladies of Great Britain" explains: "The object appears particularly worthy of the attention of the female sex, and to have peculiar claims on their best sympathies. Their susceptibilities naturally enlist them on the side of suffering humanity in all cases; but in the present case, where the cruelly demoralizing effects of slavery on the female character are so strongly marked, their cordial concurrence may be confidently expected."[38] The supposedly natural and often ridiculed susceptibility of women to representations of suffering assumes a political context here. If, as Gayatri Spivak has argued, one characteristic of nineteenth-century colonial ideology is the trope of "white men saving brown women from brown men," this passage insists that white men will be motivated to that task by the sympathetic identification between white women and brown women—a sympathy constructed by the sentimental reading of affecting texts.[39]

Women's understanding of slavery through antislavery texts was never presumed to be a passive or inactive knowledge. For example, the report for the Sheffield Female Anti-Slavery Society for 1827 recorded that "This meeting . . . [is] persuaded that the progress hitherto made towards removing from this Nation the foul reproach and deep sin of African slavery, by abolishing the detestable traffic in Negroes, is to be ascribed, in great measure, to the diffusion throughout the country of the knowledge of its real horror, and to the general sentiment of abhorrence which followed."[40] In this description of the root causes of political change, "knowledge" produces a "sentiment" that leads to "progress." Textually produced knowledge is enmeshed with emotional response—and with moral action. The mechanism of that action is made clear by a "Ladies' Petition for the Abolition of Slavery" from 1838—a period when women were allowed to sign petitions. "Imagine your *own* mother on the treadmill—your *own* innocent daughter chained to a vile wretch, sweeping the streets, for the alleged crime of *indolence*—your own cherished infant left to die unattended. Cannot you bear the *thought*? Then sign this petition on behalf of your Negro sisters, who experience the sad *reality*."[41] Twenty-five thousand women signed this parliamentary petition, presumably heeding the passage's call for sentiment through imaginative identification—and found themselves enough moved by the emotional pain to put pen to paper.

This model of political action has some of its roots in literary conventions. While many of the passages I have cited seem to rely implicitly on paradigms drawn from sentimental novels, in at least one instance, this kind of appropriation becomes even more explicit, as a passage by Laurence Sterne migrates from its literary context into the political sphere. In his history of the abolitionist movement of the 1780s and 90s, Thomas Clarkson claims that "Sterne, in his account of the Negro girl in his *Life of Tristram Shandy*, took decidedly the part of the oppressed Africans. The pathetic, witty and sentimental manner, in which he handled the subject, occasioned many to remember it, and procured a certain portion of feeling in their favor."[42] Clarkson here makes several assumptions about British reading habits: first, he emphasizes the episodic nature of Sterne's novel, assuming that a single scene will stand out in memory, along with, or even more than, the plot of the novel, or its characters; second, he imagines that the "pathetic and sentimental" feelings produced by that scene are transferable—they can be applied to matters outside the text.

Markman Ellis has argued recently that Sterne's composition of this scene was motivated by his correspondence with Ignatius Sancho—a former slave living in England—and that the scene thus represents one of the first intimations of antislavery feeling in British culture. But, as Ellis also notes, that context is carefully occluded in the episode itself.[43] It occupies only a page in Sterne's novel and has nothing much to do with the conditions of slaves in the British West Indies, as it concerns a Negro girl whom Corporal Trim's brother Tom sees in a shop window in Portugal; it is a very Sternian digression within a digression within a digression. Moved by his recollection of his brother's description of the girl's mercy in sparing the flies she is sweeping away, Trim asks Toby:

> Why then, an' it please your honour, is a black wench to be used worse than a white one?
>
> I can give no reason, said my uncle Toby—
>
> —Only, cried the corporal, shaking his head, because she has no one to stand up for her—
>
> —'Tis that very thing, Trim, quoth my uncle Toby,—which recommends her to protection, and her brethren with her.[44]

By the 1820s, this statement had dislodged itself from Sterne's novel, and become part of a discursive construction used to describe the specific horrors of Caribbean slavery. In a pamphlet entitled "A Cottage Conversation on the Subject of British Negro Slavery," a female anti-slavery organizer, probably a member of a ladies' antislavery society, comes to a house canvassing for support. After listening to her argument, the lady of the house exclaims:

> "Why madam, is a black woman used worse than a white one?"
> Daughter weeps: "I can tell you mother—because, because mother, *she has no one to stand up for her.* Father would not let you be used so—nor William neither."[45]

The quotation from Sterne is unattributed, but the anonymous author of the pamphlet assumes, like Clarkson, that possible converts to the antislavery movement will react to scenes of suffering in the same way as do Uncle Toby and Trim. Because of their sex, however, the woman and her daughter are able to compare themselves to the female slave in a way that Toby and Trim cannot; they can assure themselves that they will never be placed in her position, as they have "Father and William" to protect them. Tellingly, the male relatives of the slave women are assumed to be absent or ineffectual; their "standing up" for their own families would involve actual rebellion, a possibility the ladies' antislavery societies hoped to avert by ending slavery by peaceful means.

This example casts an interesting light on the differences between sentimental novels and sentimental political appeals. The pamphlet locates the source of feeling not in a sentimental male observer but in a susceptible female. Furthermore, the text imagines these women not as passive observers but as allies who will begin to "stand up" for the slave woman, or at least influence "father and William" to do so. It is as if the gendered identificatory bond between black and white women both makes the motivational force of the scene more powerful, and renders transparent the representational devices making that identification possible. In other words, part of what produces sentimental affect for Uncle Toby—and presumably for the reader of *Tristram Shandy*—is the pleasurable framing of the scene not only by the shop window but also by Trim's narrative reframing of the story he has heard from his brother Tom. In the 1828 pamphlet, such devices implicitly remain in place, but are not foregrounded in the same way. Sterne's scene hints at the voyeuristic pleasure of men looking at women through shop windows; the abolitionist appeal entirely subordinates voyeurism to an active and morally righteous sympathy. In the movement from the literary to the political, then, sympathy replaces sexuality, and charity replaces the implicitly commodified exchange of the shop. Most important, however, a strong claim for truth and centrality replaces the semi-fanciful and digressionary nature of Sterne's scene. The production of sentimental affect in the female residents of the cottage is presumed to be unmediated by the mannered rhetoric of sentimentality; through the descriptions of the female organizer, they are viewing the "true nature" of the system of slavery as directly as possible. Turning these literary conventions to explicitly political ends naturalizes the cultural practices on which they rely—and a gendered, emotional response to texts is explained as a natural and unavoidable reaction. If part of the sentimental affect in novels such as *Tristram Shandy* is produced by how well Trim tells his story, in abolitionist texts these same conventions are represented as the only way such a story can be told.

Yet, reimagining the relation between a sentimental scene and a sympathetic reader as catalyzing the reader's energy for social action was particularly useful to female activists for several reasons. Printed political texts, conjoined with, or transformed into, more conventional domestic objects, potentially mediated between the privacy and modesty of the domestic sphere, and the publicity of the political arena. Furthermore, the emphasis abolitionists placed on compassionate response as a motivation for abolitionism gave a form of reading beginning to be exclusively associated with women—sentimentality—a political valence. Finally, their representation of themselves as readers, rather than as writers, allowed these women to remain inside the role of leisured consumers assigned to white middle-class women by domestic ideology. Like the campaign to abstain from slave-grown sugar, ladies' antislavery societies represented a certain kind of consumer behavior as an active and ethical pursuit; their reliance on textual dissemination transformed an aspect of consumer culture into an effective form of political protest.

### POLITICAL LIMITS, POLITICAL POTENTIAL

Since their inception, the activities of ladies' antislavery societies have been seen in the context of a history of emancipation—first of men and women of African descent, then of white middle-class British women themselves. By the end of the nineteenth century, the *Westminster Review* could look back and note that

> [t]he Reign of Queen Victoria and the progress of the emancipation of women began together, and have flourished side by side. It was inevitable, when a woman sat on the throne, that the thoughts of other women should turn towards a wider sphere of usefulness than that previously known; while the spread of education, the development of railways, and the increase of wealth all tended in the same direction. The public work of women began appropriately with the antislavery agitation, when William Wilberforce then prophesied that the step thus taken by them would lead to their own emancipation.[46]

This author's conviction that the "public work" of white middle-class women in the antislavery cause led to political action on their own behalf has been confirmed by a number of recent historians of women's involvement in abolitionist activities. Many of these authors, however, focus on the way abolitionist activity fostered the administrative skills and political self-awareness crucial to British middle-class women's fight for their own rights later in the nineteenth century, rather than emphasizing any necessary link between abolition and feminism. Kenneth Corfield points out that despite the practical knowledge they gained, the members of ladies' antislavery societies "made no explicit claims for their sex's rights."[47] Nevertheless, Louis and Rosamund Billington conclude that "feminism [drew] upon the more radical elements of abolitionist ideology and the experience of a network of women working within the reform milieu. In this sense, as later feminists recognized, the activities of their mothers, grandmothers and aunts in the antislavery movement laid the foundations of feminism."[48] These explanations highlight the political utility of the connections white middle-class women were able to forge among themselves within the framework of the antislavery movement: geographically distanced connections often fostered by textual production and consumption. In other words, the distribution of antislavery texts worked to organize and cement political community among women; the Dublin association advised other Irish organizations "that, if possible, a monthly meeting [should] be held by those ladies who are willing to attend (perhaps) alternately at each other's houses, when the Anti-Slavery reporters may be read, and other works perused, which will convey information, and excite interest for the oppressed African Race."[49] Thus, the privacy of the domestic space was converted into a new site for political involvement. In this context, it is perhaps significant that the writer in the *Westminster Review* highlights the connection between the thoughts of politically minded women and the ascension of Queen Victoria; the empowerment of middle-class women may have been enabled in part by their identification with the most politically powerful British woman of the period.

Yet, while the practical activities of ladies' antislavery societies may have laid the groundwork for women's political self-realization in the later nineteenth century, the rhetoric of these groups focused much of its energy, as we have seen, on developing the potential for sympathetic bonds between white middle-class English women and enslaved women in the Caribbean. Furthermore, the emphasis this discourse placed on compassionate feminine response to suffering demanded that the suffering to which sympathetic women were exposed be comprehensible. If British women were to plead for an oppressed figure, that figure was often enough a domestic woman like herself, who had been deprived of domestic happiness.

Frequently, that deprivation was evidenced by the slave woman's separation from her children, as it is in "A Dialogue on West Indian Slavery." The woman narrating this pamphlet challenges her female interlocutor to put herself in the place of an African slave:

> If you were liable, at any hour to have those children . . . torn from you and sent away where you would never see them more, what would you think of her who should say that she was too much engaged to try and save you from such a dreadful fate? Bring such a heart-rending separation from all your beloved children strongly to your mind, and will you then say that you have not time to save other women from it?[50]

This passage directly appeals to the dynamic of sympathetic identification; the British woman must bring the suffering of a captive mother "strongly to [her] mind" by imagining that her own position is interchangeable with an African slave's. That appeal is predicated on the assumption that a similar situation would produce identical feelings in both mothers. This congruence of feeling was supposed to motivate political action against slavery. Yet, at the same time, the outrage evoked by this woman deprived of familial happiness worked to cement the value of the domestic sphere for the white middle-class English women who inhabited it, by assuring them that in agitating against slavery they were helping slave women to attain what they themselves were fortunate in already having. As Clare Midgley notes, the members of ladies' antislavery associations "constantly expressed not dissatisfaction with their own social position, but rather a desire to extend to enslaved women the privileges and protection that they themselves claimed to enjoy."[51] Thus, an idealized image of domestic virtue organizes the sympathy that such appeals hoped to generate, in this case a universalized and idealized conception of maternal love that denies the possibility that historical and cultural definitions of motherhood might be different in slave communities.[52] Assimilating captive African women entirely into the categories of English domesticity made them accessible to abolitionist sentiments, even as it erased the cultural specificity of their condition.

For these reasons, to contemporary eyes, the textually mediated identifications that were supposed to motivate women's involvement in the antislavery cause seem relatively static and circumscribed. British women were asked to identify with suffering slaves, but only through images of themselves as compassionate, domestic women, content to exert a moral influence within the family. Constrained by this version of domestic ideology, such women could identify with female Caribbean slaves only when the latter were described as victims excluded from domestic life. As the following passage illustrates, the very idea of emancipation in abolitionist discourse is tied to a particular valuation of the domestic space:

> [The female slave] cannot obey the wishes of her husband; her body, strength and time, are the property of another, whom she is compelled, at her peril, to obey. The concerns of her family must be, to her, matters of very inferior moment, compared with the work of her owner. He insists on all the prime of her strength being devoted to his business; it is only after the toils, the indecencies, the insults and miseries of a day spent in the gang, that she can think of doing anything to promote the comfort of

her household. . . . Domestic enjoyment is, therefore, I must maintain, totally impossible.[53]

This passage ties the reader's sympathy for the suffering of the female slave to a particular conception of the kind of labor proper to women. According to this text, the slave woman's misery results from the way she is kept from domestic labor by agricultural labor as much as from the brutal physical conditions of captivity. This image of a woman forced to labor for the wrong man was designed to elicit the sympathies of those English readers who believed that a "free" woman would want to "promote the comfort of her household."

Such pleas for identificatory sympathy consolidate an ideal of female domesticity for African slaves, as well as for British women. Karen Sanchez-Eppler remarks about similar dynamics in American antislavery discourse that "the enlightening and empowering moments of identification that connect feminism and abolition come inextricably bound to a process of absorption. . . . [They] obliterate the particularity of black and female experience. . . . The difficulty of preventing moments of identification from becoming acts of appropriation constitutes the essential dilemma of feminist-abolitionist rhetoric."[54] The structure of sympathetic identification, and the power of the sentiments it evoked, created a new kind of political agency for women and broadened the range of the abolitionist campaign, but, because these dynamics carried with them the cultural formations of the era in which they were formed, they sharply restricted representations of the aspects of women's lives that fell outside the boundaries of domestic ideology—including nondomestic labor. An inability to account for such labor as anything other than the deprivation of "domestic enjoyment" curtailed any understanding the members of ladies' antislavery societies could have of the conditions of Caribbean slave women, not to mention the condition of female wage laborers at home.[55] Even as ladies' antislavery societies broadened the possibilities for middle-class British women's involvement in political change, they foreclosed representations of the particularity of slave women's experience in the Caribbean.

Yet, the emphasis this movement placed on reading as a necessary prelude to political action demanded a supply of ever-more-persuasive texts that told the "truth" about slavery; thus, on at least one occasion, the dynamics of women's antislavery activity produced a representation of slavery that could not be contained by the definitions of women's political roles that initially generated it. In its search for such texts, the antislavery movement fostered what may be the only printed autobiography of a female slave from early nineteenth-century England, the *History of Mary Prince*, published in 1831. Autobiographies, polemics, and other kinds of texts by African writers had appeared in Britain previously—including works by Ukawsaw Gronniosaw (1772), Ignatius Sancho (1782), and Olaudah Equiano (1789). But although Phillis Wheatley's poems were published in 1773, Prince's narrative was the first female autobiographical text available to the reading public.[56] An Antiguan slave who escaped from her owners while in England, Prince made her way to the London Anti-Slavery Society, where "her narrative was taken down from Mary's own lips by a lady" resident with the Pringle family, leading antislavery activists with whom she took refuge (45).[57] Her story was told within the framework of the antislavery movement and distributed to a readership of antislavery activists.

In dictating her story, Prince seems aware of the conventions of sentimentality that would structure the response of her readership; she inserts herself as a retrospective observer of her own former sufferings, and demonstrates the compassion such episodes merit. After describing being separated from her family, she exclaims "Oh, the trials!, the trials! they make the salt water come into my eyes when I think of the days in which I was afflicted—the times that are gone; when I mourned and grieved with a young heart for those whom I loved" (54). We have seen the importance of shared tears for the identificatory bonds between British women and their enslaved Caribbean counterparts; this passage, too, relies on the conditions of reading set up by ladies' antislavery societies, which dictate that the reader will duplicate the tears Prince sheds in recalling her suffering.

Yet, Prince's description of her own tears seems to exceed the social and literary conventions of that domestic scene. It is hard, when reading her later description of her labor in the salt flats of Turk's Island, not to be reminded of Prince's non-idiomatic description of the way recalling her experiences as a slave "make[s] the salt water come into [her] eyes":[58]

When we were ill, let our complaint be what it might, the only medicine given to us was a great bowl of hot salt water, with salt mixed with it, which made us very sick. — Sometimes we had to work all night, measuring salt to load a vessel; or turning a machine to draw water out of the sea for salt-making. Then we had no sleep — no rest — but were forced to work as fast as we could, and go on again all the next day the same as usual. Work — work — work — Oh that Turk's Island was a horrible place! The people of England, I am sure, have never found out what was carried on there. (63–64)

This passage implicitly relies on an assumption about representation fostered by ladies' antislavery societies: that reading about the true conditions of chattel slavery will motivate readers to campaign against it. Prince suggests that such places exist in part because the readers of England have never found out about them.[59] This belief in the efficacy of printed accounts motivates her own narration; as she later explains: "what my eyes have seen, I feel it is my duty to relate; for few people in England know what slavery is. I have been a slave — I have felt what a slave feels, and I know what a slave knows; and I would have all the good people of England know it too, that they may break our chains, and set us free" (64).

Prince's description of the salt flats certainly reinforces the ideas about what made slavery horrible, especially for women, that we have seen expressed by other abolitionist appeals for female support; relentless physical labor destroyed all chance of "domestic enjoyment." Nevertheless, despite the similarities between Prince's narrative and other antislavery propaganda, the former also disrupts the representational conventions that both enabled its production and structured its content. Prince's rhetorical connections between the way sentimental recollections "make salt water come into her eyes," the physical labor involved in producing salt, and the physical pain of being made to drink saltwater, presume a much closer connection between sentimental affect and the material conditions of Caribbean slave women than that ordinarily found in abolitionist texts. The salt, which both causes misery and supposedly alleviates it, might be seen as a concrete figure for the sentimental pain upon which abolitionists relied. Of course, in Prince's story, that substance is also the motivation for slavery, a means of capital accumulation, a destructive pharmakon, and even an allusion to the salt waters of the Atlantic slave-trading routes—a series of overdeterminations undercutting the solidarity of shared tears.

Indeed, Prince's descriptions of the emotional effects of slavery often suggest the very particularities of slave life in the Caribbean occluded by English representations of the suffering of female slaves. Of her own reaction to the callousness of white slave owners while she and her family are being sold, for example, Prince says "their light words fell like cayenne on the fresh wounds of our hearts" (52). While images of physical wounds are conventional sentimental metaphors for emotional pain, Prince also transforms that convention with a new language made possible only by knowledge of the Americas: cayenne is grown along the Caribbean rim. The material implications of sentimental language haunt Prince's narrative, and she later describes the physical enactment of this metaphor. The owner of the salt flats tortures an "old slave called Daniel" by having him

> beaten with a rod of rough briar until his skin was quite red and raw. He would then call for a bucket of salt, and fling [it] upon the raw flesh till the man writhed on the ground like a worm and screamed aloud with agony. This poor man's wounds were never healed, and I have often seen them full of maggots, which increased his torments to an intolerable degree. (64)

While such graphic descriptions were commonly used by white abolitionists to elicit sympathy for the suffering of slaves, in Prince's text this description becomes, on one level, an implicit commentary on sentimental discourse itself; by literalizing its metaphors, she hints at what lies beyond its margins. The correspondence between her metaphorical descriptions of emotional pain and her graphic descriptions of the brutal working conditions slaves were forced to endure insists that substances such as salt or cayenne have meanings for Caribbean laborers that cannot be assimilated to domestic ideology. These rhetorical connections imbue the language of emotional affect with a knowledge of the particularities of Afro-Caribbean experience not often available in the discourse of ladies' antislavery societies.

It is significant that Prince's narrative invokes the scene of manual labor even at its most sentimentalized moments, and in its most conventional language, since it is the issue of the proper labor for black women for which female abolitionism found it most difficult to account. As Clare Midgley points out, abolitionists "envisioned a society in which women would have largely withdrawn from the plantation field labour that was their primary occupation under slavery. . . . Emancipation would mark the end of the sexual exploitation of women, and of the disruption of family life, and the creation of a society in which the black woman was able 'to occupy her proper station as a Daughter, a Wife and a Mother.'"[60] Yet, it is worth remembering that although Mary Prince certainly presents herself as eligible for this idealized existence, the conditions of her life as a slave have already excluded her from it. She married only in the face of great difficulty, late in life, and could remain free in England only by being separated from her husband in Antigua; she had no children, and she became a domestic servant in the house of her benefactors, the Pringles. As Midgley trenchantly concludes, "for black women in Britain, freedom did not in practice lead to the acquisition of the 'privileges' enjoyed by middle-class women, but rather to facing the problems of working-class women."[61] In this context, the rhetorical connection Prince makes between sentimental appeals for sympathy and her material experience of manual labor works to disrupt the identification between the readers of abolitionist texts, and the black women who were the objects of their sympathies. The social distance between an Afro-Caribbean woman in England and her middle-class white benefactors turns out to be almost as daunting and unbridgeable as the geographical distance between England and the West Indies. Prince reveals the disjunction between idealized images of the domestic sphere, where tearful reading is the only means of producing saltwater, and the realities of labor conditions for women in the Caribbean, where saltwater had other sources, and other uses.

### TEXTS AND BODIES

The new centrality of textual production and consumption in abolitionist activities in early nineteenth-century Britain had important implications both for white middle-class women, and for the Caribbean women to whom they pledged their aid. For female participants in antislavery societies, printed materials helped bridge the gap between a private, domesticated space, and the public arena of colonial politics. The reading practices urged by ladies' antislavery societies, which turned sentimental conventions to overt political use, also transformed the suspiciously solipsistic pleasure of emotionally engaged private reading into a political force. By representing themselves as primarily mediums for the dissemination of proper reading material, and as exemplary readers of it, members of these groups also avoided the stigma of professional writing, obscuring their own agency in shaping the ways that colonial scenes were viewed. Mary Prince's own agency in shaping the scenes of slavery in her narrative is, of course, even more vexed than that of the white members of ladies' antislavery societies. Like those women, she speaks through the conventions of sentimental femininity, conventions that position her primarily as a passive victim of slavery, and a resonant medium for the emotional truth of suffering. We need to remember, however, that those conventions may have exerted a greater material restraint on Prince's narrative than on the other products of women's involvement in abolition, as her illiteracy forced her to dictate her story to an amanuensis with the power to alter her printed words. Thus, the literary and rhetorical conventions that characterized representations of Caribbean slavery were naturalized, along with the emotional responses of white middle-class women. On the one hand, this strategy allowed white middle-class women to enter political debate without abandoning the gender identities defined by bourgeois, metropolitan, consumerist culture. On the other hand, of course, it worked to consolidate the limitations of those very roles.

For former slaves, such as Mary Prince, abolitionism's reliance on print culture may have mediated the distance between the colonial arena and domestic space in a different way. While for many middle-class white women, reading and writing abolitionist literature was far less domestic than the activities they would otherwise perform, for Prince, describing her experiences in the conventions of a sentimental appeal was an activity far more assimilable to early nineteenth-century standards of middle-class femininity than was her manual labor in the West Indies.[62] The terms in which she narrates her experience provide, at least on one level, a point of commonality between Prince and her benefactors, cementing shared political goals. On another level, however, the way she revises those conventions to refer more specifically to the conditions of colonial labor subverts and enlarges the beliefs about femininity held by her nineteenth-century middle-class readers. Yet, at times, the assumptions that Prince and her abolitionist audience seem to share about both the experience of reading and the potency of that experience in political struggle override the differences between the leisured lives led by most members of ladies' antislavery societies, and the arduous labor Prince had to perform to survive.

Several aspects of this new form of political activity for women were made possible by the growth of print culture, and by the commodification of print itself. For Mary Prince, authorship made possible a kind of financial support unavailable to her as a slave, or as a domestic servant. Thomas Pringle, in publishing her story, makes clear its status as a moneymaking venture, noting that he has "published the tract not as [the Secretary of the Anti-Slavery Society], but in my private capacity; and any profits that may arise from the sale will be exclusively appropriated to the benefit of Mary Prince herself" (186). Pringle distinguishes between the abolitionist cause and Prince herself, establishing her as an individual economic agent. Crucially, in this transformation, Prince exchanges physical publicity for the incorporeality of print. Paradoxically, she benefits, as a producer, from a market in which, by virtue of her illiteracy, she cannot participate as a consumer.

Yet, if the commodification of texts helps to enable Prince's independence by allowing her to possess her own story and the profits accruing from it, it may have been the anonymity of political literature that made it attractive to white, middle-class female activists. While some female antislavery activists, like Elizabeth Heyrick, wrote under their own names, most of the publications of ladies' antislavery societies were written either anonymously, or by groups of women who gave the name of their organization as author. It is possible that the capacity of printed materials to carry messages unattached to specific bodies offered some escape from the feminine conditions to which they would otherwise be confined; it gave the members of ladies' antislavery societies a public voice, without turning their bodies into public spectacles.

In some ways, the anonymity of print also released Mary Prince from the physical conditions into which she was born. Telling her story in written form in England saved her from returning to the brutal working conditions she had endured in the West Indies. Yet, the body of a

Caribbean slave did not disappear as easily from abolitionist discourse as did the increasingly occluded body of the middle-class female sympathizer, already transformed from an enthusiastic consumer of Caribbean products to a sentimental consumer of images of Caribbean suffering. The narration of her experience in print did not allow Prince to transcend or elide the limitations of her physical experience in quite the same way as it allowed her British "sisters" to do so. Not all abolitionist women were prepared to accept Prince's written account of her suffering, and she was called upon to display her body as proof of the truth of her words, after Lucy Townsend, an officer of the Birmingham Ladies' Society for the Relief of Negro Slaves, asked "to be furnished with some description of the marks of former ill-usage of Mary Prince's person."[63] In response to this request, Prince allowed Margaret Pringle and three other women to examine the scars on her back, and Pringle sent a description to Townsend. Moira Ferguson argues that this display "offer[ed] [Prince] a rare opportunity to speak her history—and the history of other slaves—corporeally to the world,"[64] but I would suggest that the event presents a more troubling instance of the ambiguous place of representations of slave bodies in abolitionist discourse. Evidence of the suffering of these bodies, particularly when they were female, was central to the sentimental appeal mounted by the antislavery movement, but this incident implies that such evidence was less than legitimate when it was written by the sufferers themselves; intimate inspection of these bodies by "reliable" white observers seemed necessary to verify the truth of printed texts. Although it functions, eerily enough, as a private, charitable inversion of the commodified publicity of the slave market, such inspection still seems relatively benevolent in the context of the sympathetic participants of abolitionist London society. In the Caribbean, however, that dynamic took on a more disturbing dimension; there, the intimacy of black female sufferers and white female observers triggered a powerful set of cultural anxieties, including the threatened reembodiment of the sentimental, middle-class white woman.

Chapter 6

# Overseeing Violence

## *Sentimental Vision and Slave Labor*

An ideal of feminine virtue based in sentiment rather than physical attributes was central to the abolitionist cause in Britain. Both the campaign to abstain from consuming slave-grown sugar and the increasing number of ladies' antislavery societies attempted to reorganize ideas of feminine consumer habits around the sentimental consumption of images, instead of around the physical consumption of colonial products. In this way, they hoped to align emotional engagement with consumer choice. As we have seen, this idealized congruence helped structure the politicization of metropolitan consumerism that the antislavery movement hoped to enact. At the same time, however, it also inflected representations of the labor that took place in the colonies themselves. Paradoxically, even as such images helped politicize consumer practices, they also obscured the conditions of production for the commodities in question, transforming questions of labor into questions of moral and sexual conduct.

Representations of colonial labor became more conventionally sentimental during the late eighteenth and early nineteenth centuries, as they sought to signal their affective engagement with the moral problems of colonial production. As we saw in the previous chapter, depictions of colonial slavery had to be viewed through a moral framework accessible to virtuous women, the better to elicit their sympathy. Yet, the degree to which the conventions of sentimentality were able to make images of colonial labor comprehensible for metropolitan observers was limited. These limits are most easily seen in representations of sexual behavior in the colonies. This chapter analyzes the way certain ideas about female sexuality were used by both sides of the debate over the legitimacy of slavery in the West Indies to deflect and absorb the problems posed by miscegenation to the smooth running of a slave economy. It also investigates the way that the codes of feminine sexuality operative in Britain itself were brought into confrontation with the economic structures governing sexual reproduction in the West Indies, taking as examples three novels by English women written at the end of the eighteenth century: Sophia Lee's *The Recess* (1785), Charlotte Smith's *Wanderings of Warwick* (1794), and her *Letters of a Solitary Wanderer* (1800).[1]

Although none of these narratives are centrally concerned with the running of a slave society, all set important segments of their narrative in the West Indies, and thus take up the problems of direct interaction between white and black women intimated by the physical examination of Mary Prince. These Caribbean settings pose a particular problem for middle-class British women, however; the sentimental gaze such women were supposed to direct toward the scenes of brutality confronting them verges dangerously on the controlling gaze of the plantation manager, supervising brutal labor conditions. Because of the intimacy of black and white bodies in colonial households, the role of disembodied, sympathetic observer proves difficult to maintain. Although the British abolitionist movement used emerging codes of femininity to deemphasize the bodies and physical desires of the white, middle-class women who were among its primary constituents, the bodies of similar women living in the Caribbean became a crucial index of the status of slavery for both sides of the slavery debate. If, in England, the body of Mary Prince must furnish the evidence for her white sympathizers, in these novels, and in the nonfiction prose I discuss in conjunction to them, the white woman's body itself becomes contested evidence of the viability or inviability of slave production.

## WRITING THE WHITE FEMALE BODY

Ideally, white British women living in the Caribbean were supposed to be defined by the same moral engagement with and physical disengagement from economic production as were women in England. For example, the historian John Stewart proudly describes the white women of Jamaica in these terms: "The females of this country (the white females are of course meant) may truly be said to be the most decorous, amiable and virtuous of the West Indies."[2] The parenthetical break in his sentence, in which he assures his readers that the word female stands for white females, and thus excludes women of other races from the sex, reveals a crucial element in the ideology of Jamaican slavocracy. In order for the hierarchies of plantation society to remain in place, women of African descent and women of European descent had to remain polar opposites. If Afro-Caribbean women, slaves, and free coloured women deserved their oppressed status because of their sexual promiscuity and lack of domestic virtue, as advocates of slavery claimed, then white women had to prove the existence of another kind of femininity, and were represented as passive, asexual, and pious. As Barbara Bush points out, white women's "superiority and sexual untouchability were emphasized in order to reinforce the cultural and racial distinctions necessary for the preservation of slavery."[3] Racially inflected gender definitions were therefore a cornerstone of slave culture: white women were "decorous, amiable and virtuous," while black women were usually represented as uncivilized, violent, and immoral.[4]

Black women's bodies were a political spectacle; abolitionists and planters alike debated their promiscuity, their failure to reproduce, their continual physical distress. By the late eighteenth century, however, white women did not perform plantation labor, and they inspired no parliamentary debates about the number of children to which they gave birth. Yet, as the awkward syntax of Stewart's description demonstrates, stabilizing the distinctions between categories of women proved difficult. Although white women were supposed to be the disembodied, domesticized opposite of embodied, eroticized, black female laborers, fears of contamination by African blood called forth a multitude of attempts to define the unchanging attributes of white female bodies by writers of the period. Contemporary historians, such as plantation owner Bryan Edwards, were careful to note that

> the ladies of the Creoles are sober, temperate, and possessed of great self-denial. Except the exercise of dancing, they have no other amusements to excite the spirits to a volatile gaity . . . [but] it cannot be denied that in many respects they are infinitely inferior in attraction of person to our country women; for though their figures are fine, there is not much spirit of animation in either their feature or manners. They want, too, that indispensable requisite of complete beauty, the glow of youthful vermillion, which heightens the graces of the English fair.[5]

According to Edwards, English women cannot truly flourish away from their native land. Nevertheless, the very marks of their oppression by the West Indian climate intensify their gendered racial identity; Creole women become even less active, even more pale, even more restrained, than their British counterparts, as if better to preserve the former's claim to racial purity.

The transplantation of English bodies to tropical climes gave rise to fears for the fixed racial identity of those bodies among the observers of Caribbean society. Edward Long, a West Indian proprietor like Edwards, and one of the first proponents of a pseudo-scientific racism, addresses this issue directly: "Many of the good folks in England have entertained the strange opinion that the children born in Jamaica of white parents turn swarthy, through the effects of the climate; nay, some have not scrupled to suppose that they are converted into black-a-moors. The truth is, that the children born in England have not, in general, lovelier or more transparent skins than the offspring of white parents in Jamaica."[6] Signifiers of racial purity had to be carefully guarded against the possibility that race might be environmentally produced: complexions needed to be protected from the climate, and bodies from the telltale signs of labor. Even seemingly conventional maternal advice assumed a different valence in the racially charged atmosphere of the colonies, where not only skin color but also the shape and motion of the body became signifiers of economic power. As Lady Broadbelt tells her daughter, "let me entreat you to be particularly careful in holding yourself, in Walking [sic], sitting and standing, for otherwise you will get crooked, and was that to be the result, I should be miserable, as I think, with the Generality of the World, that a *well-formed shape* is far preferable to the beauties of the face."[7] Despite the ideological imperative to define white women according to interior qualities such as amiability and sobriety, finally, in a culture based on racial hierarchy, only physical attributes distinguished the oppressor from the oppressed. Thus, although domestic virtue was supposed to be divorced from physical characteristics, the pressures of social relations in the slave colonies of the Caribbean gave rise to numerous attempts to describe and define the domesticized white female body.

Around the beginning the nineteenth century, advocates as well as opponents of slavery became increasingly concerned about the status of both black and white female virtue in the Caribbean slave colonies. This concern was directly related to a growing anxiety about biological reproduction, which peaked when the British slave trade was abolished in 1807. Since no new slaves could be legally imported, the labor force had to be made to reproduce itself. Enslaved women, who by that point outnumbered enslaved men, had to be convinced to have children. Therefore, many of the new laws the colonies passed in order to ameliorate the condition of slaves related to the protection of pregnant and nursing women.[8] Extra-legal measures were applied also; in 1816, Matthew Lewis, a Jamaican proprietor as well as the author of *The Monk*, was willing to offer the women on his estate a dollar for each child "which should be brought to the overseer alive and well on the fourteenth day," but no such measures seemed to increase the slave population, and concern over sexuality and reproduction in the slave colonies escalated during the period.[9] "Monk" Lewis was sure that slaves controlled their own rates of reproduction: "I really believe that the negresses can produce children at pleasure; and where they are barren, it is just as hens will frequently not lay eggs on shipboard, because they do not like their situation."[10] But Marietta Morrissey insists that, according to her study of surviving materials, "inconsistencies and omissions in the historical record suggest that Europeans might have overstated efforts by slaves to prevent childbearing and rearing."[11] Female slaves were themselves workers, brutalized by an economic system that kept them exhausted, malnourished, and often separate from their husbands or partners. If they did not bear children into captivity, it may have had as much to do with their physical condition as with their capacity to thwart their owners' desires.

The drive to distinguish white femininity from black femininity, even while extending the benefits of domestic virtue across racial lines, therefore, did not involve abandoning concern over the capacity of the female body to support colonial production. While pro-slavery writers claimed that only the enforcement of a British version of domestic virtue in both the black and the white populations would stabilize the plantation economy, abolitionists argued that the exposure of white women's sensibilities and black women's bodies to the brutalities of slave culture was a permanent and mortal threat to domestic virtue. Thus, oddly enough, both sides of the debate found themselves defending the same ideal: a sympathetic, sentimental, virtuous woman. Both positions also acknowledged that this female identity was not innate, but needed to be protected, nurtured, and deployed along proper political paths. How to best absorb both the plantation mistress and her slave into a single ideal of domesticity, without disrupting the racialized division of labor that structured production in the Caribbean, became a crucial battleground in the debate over slavery.

## THE ARGUMENT FOR DOMESTICATED SLAVERY

Defenders of plantation society argued that the presence of virtuous women was necessary to the stability of the slave economy. Indeed, most eighteenth-century historians included descriptions of Creole women creating domestic happiness in their descriptions of the islands. In the hands of pro-slavery writers, the discourse of domesticity, as applied to both black and white subjects, seems to spring directly from concerns over economic production. In their eyes, the enforcement of domestic virtue among British settlers, and the exportation of that virtue to slaves, would cement a profitable division of labor based on race. Newly domestic black women would reproduce a captive labor force, while virtuous white women would keep their men from straying beyond the domestic scene to create an ungovernable class of mixed-race children.

Rather than seeing the continual decrease of the slave population as the result of brutal labor conditions, observers of the colonial scene often proposed that unusual sexual practices were the cause. Even the relatively mild Bryan Edwards notes "that the practice of polygamy, which subsists among the blacks, operates as . . . a very powerful cause of decreasing population. . . . The natural consequence of [the] superiority of numbers in the males, is abandoned profligacy in the other sex, whose irregular habits expose them to continual abortions."[12] Edwards, like most proponents of such theories, offers no biological explanation for how polygamy or promiscuity would fail to produce children. Indeed, the self-evident nature of the idea that reproduction can best occur within a conjugal union seems to signal its centrality to domestic ideology.[13] The fact that this idea remains unquestioned, however, transforms a problem of economic production into a problem of sexual reproduction. The effects of coercion, from malnutrition to brutalizing labor to rape by their white owners, on black female bodies, are transmuted, by means of the discourse of domesticity, into the effects of willfully perverse sexual activity.[14]

But the lack of domestic virtue among the slaves themselves was only half the problem. To curb sexual relations between white men and black women, relations that failed to replenish the labor force, pro-slavery writers wanted to organize Jamaican society as two separate and unequal domestic groups; the plantation labor force could only be maintained by slaves producing children with other slaves. Furthermore, it was agreed that slave women would not submit to producing children to be slaves unless their white owners stopped taking them as mistresses, and white men would never stop taking black mistresses until they saw the attractions of virtuous white women.[15] In 1774, Edward Long described the relationship between the social structure and white domestic virtue quite baldly:

> Can the wisdom of legislature be more usefully applied, than to the attainment of these ends [promoting morality]; which, by making the women more desirable partners in marriage, would render the island more populous, and residence in it more eligible; which would banish ignorance from the rising generation, restrain numbers from seeking these improvements, at hazard of life, in other countries; and from unnaturally reviling a place which they would love and prefer, if they could enjoy in it that necessary culture, without which life and property lose their relish to those who are born, not only to inherit, but to adorn, a fortune.[16]

In Long's account, the responsibilities of the white domestic woman are manifold: in economic terms, she must increase the population of Jamaica by attracting a man, having his children, and preventing him from leaving the island; in social terms, she must also make the colony a place where the benefits of "property" and "fortune" are complemented by a "necessary culture" of domesticity. If these conditions were to be met, a certain ideal of femininity would work to hold the social structure of slave owners firmly in place.

The stability of marriage among the white settlers was of particular concern to writers in Jamaica, because of widespread alliances between white men and black or mulatto women. This sexual configuration threatened to create an alternate society in which racial barriers collapsed. Stewart, for example, points out the degree to which free coloured and white society mirrored one another: "the man who tonight leads out as partner the fair Creolian, may to-morrow give his hand, on a similar occasion, to the olive beauty of a darker shade, who dresses as well, and thinks herself as lovely and attractive as the other."[17] In the face of such unions, miscegenation seemed a rising tide that would overwhelm the slavocracy: "It may, without exaggeration, be said, that the annual white births are not more than one to fifteen of colour . . . the same attentions, the same education, is bestowed on children of colour, if the offspring of men of fortune, as if they were not of an illegitimate race."[18] Only a virtuous, attractive white woman could stem the flow of mixed blood: "To allure men from these illicit connexions, we ought to remove the principal obstacles which deter them from marriage. This will be chiefly effected by rendering women of their own complexion more agreeable companions, more frugal, trusty, and faithful friends, than can be met with among the African ladies."[19] Here, Long urges planters not only to exchange dark complexions for fair, but also to defuse the power of misdirected sexuality to disrupt social structures by substituting a relationship based on frugality and trust for one seemingly rooted in physical appetite. In the ideal colony, according to these writers, sexual relations would be based on cultural similarity: men of European descent would marry women of European descent, men of African descent would marry women of African descent. The exportation of domestic virtue to slaves was thus designed to solidify rather than to dissolve the racial divide. Proprietors argued that the assimilation of such values, including the desirability of monogamy and fidelity, by slaves would ensure the continuation of slave culture by producing a new generation of laborers.

Lady Maria Nugent, a resident of Jamaica from 1801 to 1806 as wife of the governor, outlines these concerns quite clearly. She writes:

> it appears to me, there would be certainly no necessity for the Slave Trade, if religion, decency and good order, were established among the negroes; if they could be prevailed upon to marry; and if our white men would but set them a little better example . . . white men of all descriptions, married or single, live in a state of licentiousness with their female slaves; and until a great reformation takes place on their part, neither religion, decency nor morality, can be established among the negroes.[20]

In Lady Nugent's words, the language of domestic virtue works to articulate a solution to an economic problem. She argues that an economic
practice, the trade in slaves, would be made unnecessary by a social
practice, "decent marriages." If, as she wishes, "religion, decency and
morality" are established in the slave community, the concrete result
will be more slave children—children who will save plantation owners
the expense of importing new slaves from Africa. Thus, instead of producing the greater equality between the races that one might expect in
a community of shared values, the hoped-for conversion of slaves to
domestic virtue works to cement the racial hierarchy. The disruption of
social and economic relations by miscegenation is recuperated through
an appeal to "decency and morality" for both races.

### JAMAICA AND THE DOMESTIC IMAGINATION

Extended examples of this deployment of domestic ideology to establish separate and unequal communities appear often in representations
of the slave colonies of Jamaica in the fictional writing of British
women at the end of the eighteenth century. Characters from or plot
developments concerning the Caribbean appear in the work of Maria
Edgeworth, Sarah Scott, and Jane Austen, among others. In the novels
discussed here, the West Indies figure as a place where the distinction
between domestic virtue and economic interest, the division that
defines a separate domestic space, collapses. This collapse illustrates
the precarious position of English femininity in the colonial world;
more specifically, however, it reveals the way codes of domestic femininity were used not to erase but to solidify the divisions between black
and white women in the eighteenth-century Caribbean. In this section,
I will examine two such novels, Sophia Lee's *The Recess* (1785) and
Charlotte Smith's *Letters from a Solitary Wanderer* (1800). Neither
novel overtly takes sides in the slavery debate, but despite being written
on opposite sides of the French Revolution and the first large-scale
debates about slavery in England, the episodes each sets in Jamaica
demonstrate the crucial role divisions between black and white women
played in the smooth functioning of a slave economy in very similar
ways. The first contains an allegory about how the rhetoric of domesticity legitimates racial inequality for the purpose of maintaining a divi-

sion of labor, while the second provides a more detailed examination of the dangers that miscegenation posed to that division.

Sophia Lee's novel, *The Recess* (1785), has claims on being both one of the first Gothic novels and on being one of the first English historical novels.[21] It concerns the different fates of two daughters of Mary, Queen of Scots, produced by a secret fourth marriage, who are raised in an underground monastery, the recess of the title. Well received and widely read in its own day, but only now coming back into print, *The Recess* both connects and contrasts sentimental private histories with the public history of Elizabethan England.[22] These interconnections between sentiment and social structure play out in various contexts in the course of the narrative, including in one episode concerning slave culture. Midway through the novel, one of the sisters, Matilda, is kidnapped and taken to Jamaica. Through the vicissitudes of a complicated plot, she is first abducted by rebellious slaves, then imprisoned by the Spanish governor for his own gain.[23] Matilda's only occupation in this colonial prison is the education of her daughter, Mary, the product of her secret marriage to the Earl of Leicester, and she finds a kind of happiness in this domestic enterprise: "engrossed by, and devoted to this sole object of my eyes and heart, which the gracious author of universal being permitted her to fill, I no longer repined at my unmerited captivity."[24]

One day, while Matilda is occupied by this circumscribed maternity, she "suddenly perceive[s] a black woman, apparently of distinction, leaning under an awning, raised at no great distance; and while she talked busily to the slaves who were fanning her, the eyes of all were turned intently on [Matilda's] infant."[25] Unlike Matilda, this woman, Anana, has the ability to enter and leave the prison. Her observation of the maternal scene leads to her demand for Matilda's child; for Matilda, this is a horrifying example of the loss of maternal jurisdiction to the whims of the colonial world. Yet, that threat disappears when it becomes apparent that Anana only wants to benefit the child. Mary returns: "in the arms of her sable conductor, she appeared to me like new-born light, reposing on the bosom of chaos."[26] Seemingly, the subversion of the maternal possession by this colonial "bosom of chaos" is negated by the universal sentiment of maternal concern that the two women, one black and one white, appear to share. After this confirmation of mutual feeling, Matilda and Anana are united in a sort of maternal sisterhood, sharing Mary's care between them.

When the cruel governor, who turns out to be Anana's lover and benefactor, dies, Anana decides to complete her ascent into domestic womanhood. With the wealth her protector has willed her, she intends to free Matilda and transport her back to England, "for which voyage her friendship would amply supply me with means, company and attendance, as it was her purpose to quit forever a country, where she had lost her only connection, and seek in another, protection, religion, and peace."[27] Matilda is disturbed by the prospect of taking a woman with such a sordid past back to England, but overcomes her prejudice:

> The state in which she had lived with Don Pedro, supplied an objection at which my pride revolted, but that almost instantaneously gave way to principle. I resolved to be above sacrificing the duties of gratitude and benevolence to opinion, and remembering her untaught mind knew no tie in wedlock but constancy, and perhaps in that instance might vie with myself, I sought, by cultivating the wild but solid virtues of her soul, to bury the remembrance of her former error, and fortify her against any future one. Open to the pure impressions of religion and morality, the amiable Anana promised to become an ornament to human nature.[28]

The novel endorses the possibility that domestic virtue can be produced, even in an Afro-Caribbean woman. In the proper environment, Anana's black body, and the degradations to which it has been subject, will cease to matter in comparison to her interior qualities: she will be effectively disembodied by her new status as a domestic woman. Furthermore, Matilda admits that Anana might already possess some domestic virtues, constancy, for instance, although they have gone unrecognized by "opinion." Thus, in *The Recess*, domestic virtue, which promises an identity of sentiment between black slaves and their white owners, seems to create a bridge between the races. Matilda, passive and confined to her maternal duties, and Anana, sexually free and powerful in her restricted world, represent the polarized positions of black and white women in the colonies. Yet, they combine their resources for their mutual benefit; with Anana's wealth, and Matilda's "pure religion and morality," they will both be able to enjoy the privileges of the domestic sphere in England.

But, before the two women leave Jamaica, Anana dies of smallpox;

Matilda inherits the governor's wealth from her friend, and sails to England alone. Wylie Sypher has noted that "[tragic death] is one of the few acts common to both the ideal and the actual Negro,"[29] and with Anana's death, the implications of this episode change dramatically. Instead of a story of female community, it becomes both an allegory and a metonymy for the way that the sexual double standard of the Caribbean worked in conjunction with the exploitation of slave labor. Allegorically, the wealth Anana gains through her illicit sexual activity passes, at her too-convenient death, to her white "sister," just as the labor of black slaves was transformed into the material possessions of their white owners.[30] Metonymically, Anana's sexual service to the governor is another instance of the coerced labor of captive workers; in this context, her death can be seen as just one of a series of physical destructions that transform the labor power of slaves into metropolitan wealth. In both scenarios, however, domestic discourse naturalizes and legitimates this transaction; the wealth the cruel governor extorted from the island, and passed on to his sexual favorite, ultimately upholds the domestic ideology for which Matilda is a placeholder. Anana's conversion to domestic virtue, like the planters' vision of happily married slaves, simply enables the passage of capital along the proper channels, rather than challenging the assumptions of the economic system. Domestic ideology constructs an ideal to which the black woman is expected to conform, even though she is materially excluded from the privileged domestic space.[31]

*The Recess* illustrates the way domestic ideology absorbs both black and white women into an ideal femininity that disguises the material inequality between the races; the community of sentiment Matilda and Anana hope to found camouflages the economic structure that makes any interracial community in the slave cultures of the Caribbean impossible. Charlotte Smith's novel *Letters of a Solitary Wanderer* (1800), however, demonstrates the dangers that arise when this racial hierarchy is challenged. The novel is divided into three parts—a gothic tale, a historical romance, and a story about the West Indies—each featuring, like many of Smith's novels, a heroine in distress. When it comes to describing the Caribbean, Smith's novel, like *The Recess*, figures problems of material empowerment in terms of domestic relations. The section entitled "The Story of Henrietta" describes what happens to a young girl raised in England when she returns to her father's plantation in Jamaica. From the moment Henrietta arrives on the island, her secure identity as a civilized English woman begins to collapse. She finds her "sisters of the half-blood"[32] living comfortably in her father's house:

> The youngest of them, who is a quadroon—a mestize—I do not know what—is nearly as fair as I am; but she has the small eye, the prominent brow, and something particular in the form of the cheek, which is, I have understood, usual with Creoles even who have not any of the Negro blood in their veins. As I am a native of the island, perhaps I have the same cast of countenance without being conscious of it, and I will be woman enough to acknowledge that the supposition is not flattering.[33]

Whereas Smith's earlier novel of the French Revolution, *Desmond* (1792), in a passing discussion of slavery, makes an argument for racial equality based on sexual compatibility, this post-revolutionary novel sets about constructing gendered differences between the races.[34] Unfamiliar with the ethnic mixture of the colonies, Henrietta is unsure of the racial categories around her. Racial distinctions are unstable, ultimately unrelated to physical appearance; her sister is as fair as Henrietta herself, and Creoles resemble mulattos even if they "have not any of the Negro blood in their veins." Henrietta's own features become unfamiliar to her, seen in relation to these shifting categories; to her horror, she realizes that she might resemble her mixed-race sisters. She is "woman enough" to compare herself physically to these women, and concerned enough about her status as a privileged European woman to find the comparison disturbing. Her white body is foregrounded in this passage, as it provides potential evidence of her kinship with the mixed-race women; yet, it is also devalued as a signifier of racial superiority, as physical characteristics prove unstable markers of racial difference. Henrietta's possible similarity to her sisters undermines the capacity of physical, moral, or cultural differentials to legitimate the racial divisions that uphold the slavocracy.

Henrietta's reliance on her white body and domestic virtue to separate her from the brutality of a slave economy is further undermined when her father proposes to marry her to a man of his own choice in order to increase his property. When Henrietta protests, he locks her in a room until she submits:

> He has been used to purchase slaves, and feels no repugnance in selling his own daughter to the most dreadful of all slavery! . . . Would I could believe that an alteration in my appearance would change the intentions of the purchaser whom my father has chosen! for then I should rejoice at these pallid looks, and this emaciated form; which I now only consider as symptoms of decline,—that though not rapid enough to save me from the tyranny so immediately meditated, will yet perhaps so enervate me as to prevent my escape; for to escape I will attempt if I am able.[35]

Henrietta's own subjugation to corporeal force prompts her analogy between an unwanted marriage and chattel slavery, although, in her version, forced marriage is the worse fate of the two. In her transition from the disembodied precepts of domestic virtue to the violence of physical coercion, Henrietta's body, rather than her feelings, again becomes the primary signifier of cultural meaning. Yet, the meaning of her physical state remains unclear; the alterations in Henrietta's appearance may be evidence of the only form of agency left to her, or they may be the marks of her oppression. In other words, if her body is too "emaciated" to appeal to her "purchaser," her suffering is a form of resistance to her status as property, but if she is simply too "enervated" to escape, but too well taken care of to die, she remains the prisoner of her father's superior power. This unreadable physical condition, which is only a more extreme version of her position in her father's household, places Henrietta, like the female slaves to whom she compares herself, outside the domestic sphere, and its community of shared sentiment.

The conventions of the eighteenth-century novel heroine, the conflict between her fragile body and her indomitable desire for virtuous love, perhaps most exemplarily delineated in Richardson's *Clarissa*, assume a different valence when set in colonial Jamaica. Henrietta's lament seems to construct an unavoidable equality between herself and enslaved women—an equality based not, as abolitionists would claim, on shared domestic sentiments, but rather on their similarly disempowered positions in a patriarchal culture. As Henrietta's words make clear, if a white woman becomes the subject of physical force, her body becomes virtually indistinguishable from a slave's. Yet, Henrietta's analogy is itself part of a discourse of domesticity that absorbs and defuses economic problems; her assumption of the equality between black and white women is figured in terms of sexual relations. Henrietta is threatened by sexual force, after all, and she hopes that through her psychological suffering, her body will cease to be sexually attractive. Although slave women certainly experienced sexual oppression, the most startling connection that Smith's novel suggests, but does not elaborate, is that between the bourgeois marriage and the more physically punishing varieties of forced labor, which also produced "emaciated and enervated" bodies. Unlike *The Recess*, the possible connection "The Story of Henrietta" imagines between black and white women has less to do with domestic virtue than with the material similarity of their powerless position in a male-dominated world.

In such a world, only mutually desired marriages can erase the threat of female suffering. Ultimately, Smith's novel, like Lee's, resurrects the barriers against racial confusion through the production of segregated domestic happiness, and thus defuses the possibly radical implications of Henrietta's imprisonment. Henrietta eventually escapes from Maynard, her father's choice, but immediately falls into the hands of Maroons, runaway slaves "always terrible in their passions, and to whom the fierce inclination for European women was now likely to be exalted by the desire for revenge on a man so detested as the father of [the] unhappy Henrietta."[36] Thus, the sexual threat that Maynard represents, the fall from domestic virtue, is replaced by one even more horrible in Henrietta's eyes, miscegenation through rape.

The Maroon chief brings his prize back to his camp, and seems ready to make her one of his wives. Henrietta, terrified, is thrown into a position of equality with black women she finds difficult to confront. "The oldest of the [Maroon] women turned and came towards me. I never beheld so hideous, so disgusting a creature; and such was the dread with which I was inspired as she hung over me, that I was once more on the point of losing my misery in insensibility."[37] The dread the Maroon woman produces in Henrietta springs, at least in part, from the realization that the power structure has been reversed, and she, Henrietta, is now subject to the sexual whims of her black captors. This situation inspires, not the analogical equality Henrietta earlier imagined, but rather the resurrection of the crudely physical markers of racial difference that she had found so disturbingly absent in her father's household. When Henrietta recovers her powers of description, she records an absolute, physical incompatibility between European codes of femininity and black female bodies. She says of the chief Maroon wife, "This negress was a fat and heavy creature, her arms and neck ornamented with beads, strung seeds, and pieces of mother of pearl; and though there was an affectation of European dress, she was half naked, and her frightful bosom loaded with finery was displayed disgustingly."[38] Although this woman might attempt to transform herself into a European woman through costume, the eruption of a black body, impossible to hide beneath her clothes, ensures that racial difference remains insurmountable.

Yet, the supposed universality of domestic sentiment defuses this potentially violent confrontation. Luckily for Henrietta, the Maroon concubines are as eager to preserve the division between the races as she is herself; "the favorite sultana of the Maroon chief . . . had no inclination to have another rival in his favour."[39] Two of the women help her escape, and, soon after, she reunites with her true love, Denbigh, marries, and returns to England. As in *The Recess*, the will to reestablish the privileges of the white, middle-class, English woman is imputed to black women themselves.[40] The Maroon women's jealousy, like Anana's generosity, works to preserve the very divisions that oppress them, and to support the workings of a slave economy. Both novels open up the possibility that black and white women share a powerlessness that places them in a similar position in a male-dominated world. Yet, both Lee and Smith ultimately defuse that possibility by keeping material and domestic divisions intact; at the actual scene of oppression, racial divisions reassert themselves. The rhetoric of domestic virtue is deployed in these texts to construct racial difference, not as the product of economically interested brutality, but as the inherent desire of both the white and the black women who inhabit the colonial structure. If the work of ladies' antislavery societies demonstrated that the discourse of domesticity and separate spheres could increase the range of white women's political activities, these novels reveal the limits of that ideology, and the way it constrained the representation of slaves and former slaves in particular.

The emphasis on correcting disruptive sexual behavior apparent in both of these texts points to the fact that both sexual pleasure and sexual reproduction were integral aspects of the economic ordering of a slavocracy. At the same time, however, these representations of the exploited sexuality of black women can be interpreted as standing in for images of the exploited physical labor of both male and female slaves. In both novels, representations of the brutality of colonial production, the violent coercion described by Mary Prince, are absent; instead, the profitability of the West Indies is presented in sexual terms—in Anana's riches, and in the threat to production posed by the aggressively sexual Maroons.[41]

### COLLIDING BODIES

In practice, however, the ideal of unequal domestic arrangements could not entirely neutralize the brutality of slave culture, nor could it effectively insulate white women from the affronts to their sensibility surrounding them in the Caribbean. For example, touring a sugar plantation, Lady Nugent finds that slaves watched the boiling sugar in twelve-hour shifts: "how dreadful to think of their standing twelve hours over a boiling cauldron; and [the overseer] owned to me that sometimes they did fall asleep, and get their poor fingers in the mill; and he showed me a hatchet, that was always ready to sever the whole limb, as the only means of saving the poor sufferer's life! I would not have a sugar estate for the world!"[42]

Through her description, the violent economic relations of slavery become visible. Faced with an obvious affront to "decency," Lady Nugent expresses sympathy for the "poor sufferers" and disavows any economic interest in sugar production. Yet, while this disavowal accords with the expected reaction of a morally engaged, sympathetic English woman, in the context of colonial society, it rings false, in much the same way as the conventions of eighteenth-century novel heroines change their meaning in the "Story of Henrietta." Lady Nugent's desire to disassociate herself from sugar production is belied by the fact that her husband's position as governor of Jamaica makes him the emblem of the British Crown's control over all sugar production in the Caribbean. Her words erect a barrier between female sentiment and virtue and the world of economic production, yet, the fact that she does not condemn the necessity of amputating slaves' limbs, but merely insists that she could never order such a thing herself, reminds us that the two worlds were mutually dependent. In the West Indies, the dependence of white female privilege on the exploitation of black labor is measurably more visible than it is in metropolitan England. The somewhat awkward nature of Lady Nugent's reaction to this scene, then, can be explained by the proximity of domestic sentiment to economic exploitation in the Caribbean; white, middle-class, English women, no matter how emotionally repulsed they were by violence, could not help becoming intimate with such scenes of brutality.[43]

The fact that such violence was witnessed by the place holders of domestic ideology, white women, worried contemporary commentators on the Caribbean to an extraordinary degree. Abolitionists, as well as advocates of slavery, feared that exposure to such scenes, in which a white woman came face to face with the cruelty imposed on black bodies, would ruin both the female capacity for compassion and the lines between familial and economic relations. Neither group imagined that domestic virtue could withstand the pervasive cruelty of Jamaican slave culture, but proponents of slavery thought the threat could be contained, while abolitionists argued that the danger to femininity was ineradicable and mortal. John Stewart, speaking for the proprietors, outlines the potential consequences:

> It . . . sometimes happens, that [women] contract domineering and harsh ideas with respect to their slaves—ideas ill-suited to the native softness and humanity of the female mind; so that the severe and arbitrary mistress will not infrequently be combined with the affectionate wife, the tender mother, the dear friend and agreeable companion; such is the force and effect of early habits and accustomed prejudices. . . . The tender heart of a lovely woman should weep at a tale of distress, and she should ever be prone to relieve and alleviate, rather than inflict pain. Cruelty and revenge should be far from the female bosom.[44]

Stewart's account is revealing in the way it describes the fragile composition of a virtuous woman. If not protected from ugly scenes, a woman is likely to lose the "native softness" with which she is born. Like the writers for ladies' antislavery societies discussed in the last chapter, Stewart implies that women's contribution to society has to do with their exemplary reactions to emotionally affecting representations, reactions that lead them to "relieve and alleviate" pain. Yet, their capacity for such reactions can be undermined by "early habits and

accustomed prejudices"—by the necessity for direct female involvement in the brutality of colonial production. Stewart suggests that the
only way to ensure that a woman will "weep at a tale of distress" is to
make sure that she is never present when that tale is acted out. If, however, a woman is overexposed to scenes of plantation discipline, the
barriers surrounding the "affectionate wife [and] the tender mother"
break down, and the domestic woman is shown to be complicit in the
colonial exploitation of African labor; she has learned to wield a kind of
power that Stewart calls arbitrary because it is based on nothing but
physical force.

Stewart is convinced that, as a result of proper vigilance, this possibility has been eradicated: "the West Indian females, with a few exceptions, are at the present day as mild, as indulgent, and gentle towards
their slaves, as their relative situation will admit."[45] Abolitionists, however, appropriated the image of a white woman so degraded that she
enjoys watching her slaves being punished as evidence of the inevitable
dissolution of British morals occasioned by Britain's involvement in the
slave economies of the Caribbean. This nightmarish opposite of the
domestic woman appears continually in antislavery texts of the period.
Mary Prince, for example, provides evidence of the cruelty of white
mistresses in the West Indies: "Mrs. Wood told me that if I did not
mind what I was about, she would get my master to strip me and give
me fifty lashes: 'You have been used to the whip' she said, 'and you
shall have it here.' . . . My mistress was always abusing and fretting after
me. It is not possible to tell all her ill language."[46] Prince establishes
herself, rather than her white mistress, as the arbiter of propriety on this
occasion. Mrs. Wood's violence, in Prince's account, has shut her out
of the domain of female reading, and the benefit of female compassion; her "ill language" cannot be included in a respectable text.

Abolitionists were determined to trace the origin of such unfeminine
actions to the conditions of a slave culture. One pamphlet, for
instance, entitled "West-Indian sketches drawn from authentic sources:
anecdotes tending to elucidate the nature of our colonial bondage,"
includes a section on "The effects produced by slavery on the character
of white women." Inside, the author recounts a scene from his travels:

> The lady I have above alluded to appears of good natural disposition, and
> in no degree disposed to general cruelty: but the frequency of the sight

has rendered her callous to its usual influence upon the feelings. Being one morning at her house, while sitting in conversation, we suddenly heard the loud cries of a Negro smarting under the whip. Mrs. ——— expressed surprise on observing me shudder at his shrieks; and you will believe that I was in utter astonishment to find her treat his sufferings as a matter of amusement.[47]

This writer expresses the same tension Stewart records between the "usual" or "natural" composition of the female character, and the disintegration of that character under the pressures of colonial society. Unwilling to admit that women might be just as "naturally" unfeeling as sympathetic, abolitionist writers find themselves simultaneously defending an essential feminine identity and deploring the effects of environment on character.[48]

Perhaps more disturbing than the challenge this scene presents to the idea of innate female identity is the way in which it disrupts the divisions between a disembodied female virtue and the physically brutal world of slave culture; such scenes show the damage done by the violent labor relations of slavery to the ideal of a home as a site of domestic enjoyment propounded by the abolitionist movement. The image of a woman physically involved in the coercive violence of slave labor illustrates the ways in which no aspect of British settlers' lives was entirely removed from slavery. John Riland, a planter converted to abolitionist sentiment, notes that he has "a vivid remembrance . . . that a female cousin of mine, who in her childhood lived in the family, and enjoyed all the privileges of a daughter, had a little Negress of her own age pointed out to her as one destined to be her future waiting maid; and who, in consequence, became the victim of the young lady's first efforts at tyranny."[49] Even within the intimate space of the family, femininity can become contaminated by the economic system that supports its innocence. The ambiguity as to which girl has become the victim of tyranny in Riland's final clause points to the dangerous slippage in female roles that the presence of slaves within the family occasioned; the white woman's use of violence takes her outside the borders of domestic virtue, positioning her in the same exterior relation to that ideology as the black servant she punishes. In other words, when domestic values dissolve, the power differential between the races, and the coercive violence that supports it, becomes visible.

Such intrusions of the material structure of exploitation into the immaterial precepts of domesticity threatened to reembody the white woman by granting her an unfeminine physical force. In 1824, the fervent abolitionist Thomas Cooper complained that "white women, who are the owners of slaves, will, in general, without any scruple, order their slaves to be flogged, and some of them will even stand by to see them stripped bare and punished in the usual disgusting manner."[50] At least part of what Cooper expects to disgust his readers about this scene is these brutal women's interest in bare flesh. A kind of voyeurism that registers its power over its victim by stripping that victim naked is entirely opposed to the kind of sentimental female vision deemed proper by writers like Stewart, who says that "the tender heart of lovely woman should weep at a tale of distress, and she should ever be prone to relieve and alleviate, rather than inflict pain."[51] The scene of reading Stewart imagines resembles the reading habits propounded by ladies' antislavery societies; power resides in the spectacle described by the tale, which moves the woman to tears. In the scenario of punishment Cooper deplores, however, power resides in the gaze of the torturer; an ideal of sentimental identification and compassion stands opposed to a nightmare image of physical confrontation.

Yet, according to abolitionists, slave culture perverted even this opposition between reading and watching, destroying the female capacity for compassion. Mary Wollstonecraft, in her "Vindication of the Rights of Men," writes: "Where is the dignity, the infallibility of the fair ladies, whom, if the voice of rumour is to be credited, the captive negroes curse in all the agony of bodily pain, for the unheard of tortures they invent? It is probable that some of them, after the sight of a flagellation, compose their ruffled spirits and exercise their tender feelings by the perusal of the last imported novel."[52]

Wollstonecraft believes that an extreme version of the disjunction Catherine Gallagher describes reigns in the West Indies, and the feelings aroused by reading may be entirely misdirected; "imported novels" become both the source and object of any "tender feelings" they elicit. Instead of inciting their readers to "alleviate distress," such novels absorb the emotion provoked by the "sight of a flagellation" into a solipsistic exercise in relaxation. The reading practices of the women who indulge in such novels are entirely separated from their active lives; their "tender feelings" are divorced from their cold "invention" of punishments. In the context of day-to-day life in the Caribbean, this divorce betrays not a simple lack of Coleridgian benevolence, but also an active interest in the mechanisms of colonial production; these women reveal an awareness that violence is necessary to make slavery a profitable mode of production. This discontinuity between reading and action marks the failure of an ideology of feminine, disembodied sympathy to overcome, or transcend, women's own economic interest in a slave-powered economy. For white women in the West Indies, a privatized act of reading potentially stands as the complement to the unmediated spectatorship of physical violence, rather than as an antidote. The belief in the subversive political potential of a naturalized female sympathy we have seen propounded by the campaign to abstain from slave-grown sugar and ladies' antislavery societies is undermined in this context by the involvement of white, middle-class British women themselves in the efficient running of a slave economy.

An elaborate exploration of this failure of sentimental identification occurs in Charlotte Smith's novel, *The Wanderings of Warwick* (1794), which narrates the further adventures of one of the secondary characters in her novel *The Old Manor House* (1793). While *The Wanderings of Warwick* follows its hero and his wife through many lands, the section set in Jamaica contains an inflammatory image of the vicissitudes of slave culture. A friend of the narrator's is engaged to a beautiful Creole girl. While paying her an unexpected visit one morning, he discovers in her apartment the perfect scene of domestic happiness: "it was elegantly dressed with flowers;—her toilet was tastefully set out;—her music book was open at a pathetic song;—everything round seemed to breath tenderness and love;—and I reflected with delight that that fair form—the elegant mind that made these arrangements was soon to be mine."[53] Only the mistress of these surroundings is missing, and the young man soon finds her in an unexpected scene: "My fair, my gentle Marianne, whom I have seen weep over the fictitious distress of a novel, and shrink from the imaginary sorrows of an imaginary heroine, walked with cool but stately steps before two old Negro women who dragged before them a mulatto girl of ten or eleven years old. . . . I saw her back almost flayed; and Miss Shaftesbury seemed to enjoy the spectacle."[54] The young man flees the scene in horror, reduced to tears, never sees his fiancée again, and leaves the colonies. Clearly, Marianne, having abdicated the domestic space, is no longer, in the novel's terms, a marriageable woman. She has, unforgivably, demonstrated the discontinuous nature of "pathetic songs" and the "imaginary sorrows of an imaginary heroine" and the position of a leisured white women in the Caribbean.

The episode illustrates the problems posed to an ideal of sympathetic femininity when sentimental vision, the "fictitious distress" and "imaginary sorrows," produced by emotionally engaging songs and novels, does not lead to benevolence but rather supplements the economically interested gaze that accompanies physical violence. There was surely something horrifying for Smith's readers, as well as for the young man, about the proximity of the women's bodies themselves in this scene of punishment. The meeting between the old Negro women, the young white woman, and the mulatto girl reveals not the feminine capacity for sentimental identification and sympathy, but, rather, the material inequalities that lie between the women. The marks on the young girl's back denote not only her own subjugated status, but also Marianne's participation in an economy that recognizes such physical marks as the most powerful signifiers of social position. Thus, by creating this scene, and by deploying the power of her own gaze, Marianne signals that she, as well as the captive girl, stands outside the disembodied virtues of domestic ideology, outside the compassion that springs from the feminine imagination. Her spectatorship of these punishing blows breaks down the barriers between the incorporeal virtues of the domestic sphere and the coercive violence necessary to colonial production. Marianne's transgression lies in her knowledge and manipulation of that violence, the economic proceeds of which support her own privileged position as a domestic woman. This transgression is not accidentally associated with the sexual pleasure of sadistic voyeurism; the alliance of economic production and nonreproductive sexuality here, as in *The Recess*, signals the role played by sexual pleasure in a slave economy. In other words, Marianne's choice of violence over sentiment not only sexualizes the scene of colonial labor but also suggests the ways in which certain kinds of pleasure helped generate the profits of colonial production.

The dynamics of voyeurism, pleasure, and profit bring us back to the authors' role in producing these representations of the colonial arena. As professional writers rather than philanthropists, popular novelists characterize the activity of writing not as a moral imperative, but as an economic necessity. For this reason, they address the problem of their own agency in creating scenes of colonial suffering in a more self-conscious way than do the female writers of the antislavery societies. This self-consciousness has a great deal to do with their defensiveness about transgressing the boundary between the market and the domestic sphere through writing for profit; yet, such responses also work to de-naturalize the role of representational conventions in shaping colonial ideologies.

The necessity for a certain distance between a compassionate female observer and the scene of colonial violence she observes had serious implications for the female author who presumed to represent such scenes. The women who wrote under the aegis of ladies' antislavery societies were aware of this issue, and they devised specific strategies to avoid any taint of impropriety. Their writing, they consistently claimed, was motivated by a moral imperative to make the horrors of colonial slavery known to the British public. They insisted that they wrote out of a disinterested virtue, and that any profits accruing to their venture would immediately benefit Caribbean slaves. Furthermore, their focus on the political efficacy of emotionally engaged reading foregrounded the consumption of images; even the pamphlet writers themselves seem more like witnesses to the scenes they describe than like the creators of them. The scandal of the transgressive images produced by ladies' antislavery societies, then, was contained by a sense of their moral mission, and by their authors' representation of themselves as consumers rather than as producers of these images.

For Mary Prince, as we have seen, the scandal of writing about the horrors of slavery is also mitigated by her moral obligation to tell her story. She claims to speak not only on her own behalf but also on the behalf of others, saying that "in telling my own sorrows, I cannot pass by those of my fellow slaves—for when I think of my own griefs I remember theirs" (p. 65). Prince certainly profited from her venture into print, but that profit became a mark of her freedom from the degradation of slavery; her authorship was acceptable in the antislavery circles in which her narrative circulated, if only because it improved on the kinds of labor she had performed as a slave. Thus, although Prince stood in an asymmetrical relation of power to her abolitionist benefactors, she also used the strictures of domestic ideology to code her writing as both feminine and respectable.

Commercial novelists such as Charlotte Smith, however, were faced by the scandal of their own labor. Indeed, the eleven novels Smith wrote can be seen in direct relationship to the West Indian slave economy. Married to an abusive spendthrift at an early age, from whom she separated after bearing many children, she wrote novels to compensate for the money she expected to receive from her father-in-law's will, including revenues from his estate in Barbados.[55] Writing about colonial violence, then, Smith profited economically from her capacity to textually recreate the brutality that accompanied slavery in the Caribbean.[56] In the preface to *Desmond*, Smith herself describes her position as an author as similar to that of the too-knowledgeable female spectator of colonial violence:

> Knowledge, which qualifies women to speak or to write on any other than the most common and trivial subjects, is supposed to be of so difficult attainment, that it cannot be acquired but by the sacrifice of domestic virtues, or the neglect of domestic duties.—I however may safely say, that it was in the *observance*, not in the *breach* of duty, I became an author; and it has happened, that the circumstance which have compelled me to write, have introduced me to those scenes of life, and those varieties of character which I should otherwise never have seen.[57]

Paradoxically, in her attempt to carry out her domestic duties toward her children, Smith is forced into a kind of labor that undermines her domestic virtue. Her sense of her own indecent exposure to the "varieties of character" lurking outside the domestic space suggests the scandal of female spectatorship of coercion. In a letter, Smith even describes her legal efforts on her own behalf as a "public flogging" of the executors of her father-in-law's will.[58] Thus, her literary vision of colonial violence, unlike that of the writers for ladies' antislavery societies, exposes the economic structures that underlie and uphold a domestic space free of labor.

According to the precepts of domestic ideology, the expulsion of white women writers like Charlotte Smith from the domestic space constitutes their oppression. William Cowper once wrote of her: "I know not a more pitiable case. Chain'd to her desk like a slave to his oar, with no other means of subsistence for herself and her numerous children, with a broken constitution, unequal to the severe labor enjoin'd her by necessity, she is indeed to be pitied."[59] Since Cowper was himself a fervent abolitionist, this is probably no light analogy; there is a way in which Smith's professional writing is associated not only with the illicit spectatorship of colonial violence but also with the coerced labor of slavery. Despite the fact that Cowper, and Smith herself, coded her labor as being in the service of her family, professional writing takes her outside eighteenth-century definitions of middle-class femininity; she is analogous to a male slave in Cowper's example, as if gender has ceased to matter outside the boundaries of the domestic space. Furthermore, Cowper notes the physical marks her labor has made upon her body; her expulsion from the domestic space is signaled by her "broken constitution."[60] The position of the professional female writer with regard to the representation of colonial violence is highly unstable; she both suffers because of the nature of her labor, because she is cast out of domestic space, and scandalously profits by her own transgression, through her knowledge of the "varieties of experience." Ironically, this scandal, this transgression, may only be recuperated through the propagation by female writers like Smith of the discourse of domesticity that their very practice undermines. At the same time, however, the role of white women themselves in producing the affect they were supposed to involuntarily feel foregrounds the relationship of representational conventions to colonial ideology. Smith's self-consciousness about her own role in generating such pleasure works against the natural quality of readerly affect described by ladies' antislavery societies.

### LABOR, PLEASURE, AND POLITICS

The rapid decline of feminine virtue in the West Indies indicated to both sides of the slavery debate that certain aspects of femininity had to be carefully nurtured and enforced. The barriers intended to keep the domestic woman intact, the walls that separated her from the physical disruptions of sexuality and violence, were drawn with extreme care by all observers of the slave economies of the West Indies. Strangely enough, the existence of a domestic sphere inhabited by women, where virtue was always economically disinterested, was as necessary to the continuation of plantation society as it was to its destruction. The repetition of an inflammatory image of violent white women in literature that falls on both sides of the debate indicates that abolitionists did not so much challenge the terms of pro-slavery arguments, as they deployed the same rhetoric toward different ends. Both sides subscribed to a similar image of what an ideal domestic woman would look like, and both, to a certain extent, agreed that she needed to be protected from the ravages of slave culture. The qualities such a woman possessed included "a proper education," "a modest demeanor," "a very moderate zeal for expensive pleasures," and "a skill in economy," according to Edward Long.[61]

Yet, while advocates of slavery argued that domestic ideology had a necessary organizing function in the Caribbean, antislavery writers contended that slave culture and domestic virtue were incompatible. The shift between these two positions rests on the new preeminence that abolitionists gave to female compassion and sentimental vision in definitions of domestic virtue. While earlier, pro-slavery descriptions of the domestic virtue that was to stabilize the slave colonies centered on female prudence, honesty, and chastity, abolitionists argued that the material conditions of slave culture prevented women such as Marianne from transforming sentimental reading practices into an active, effective compassion. It is this failure that places them outside definitions of virtuous domestic femininity for antislavery writers. Abolitionists demanded that an ideal woman exemplify female sensibility, be sensitive to the pain and suffering of others, and be a good domestic manager. Such a woman would not only be moved to strong feelings by the spectacle of suffering slaves, she would also be urged to work for the abolitionist cause by those feelings.

This structure of sympathetic identification, which emphasized the equality of the sentiments black and white women shared, might be expected to lead to the erasure of racial divisions. Yet, in the case of eighteenth-century Jamaica, it seems to have solidified such divisions further. On the one hand, abolitionists believed that the exposure of white women to the cruelties of slavery left such women degraded and insensible, while, on the other hand, they urged British women to imagine that their feelings were identical to those of captive African women. By necessity, they created a division between sentimental vision and the voyeuristic spectatorship of colonial violence. Thus, paradoxically, the absence of the abolitionist sympathizer from the scene she abhorred was crucial; her sentiments had to be mediated, through reading or other forms of representation, by idealized images of domestic virtue in distress. For this reason, the presence of white, middle-class British women in the Caribbean, and the visibility of their economic interest in the profitability of slave production in that setting, complicates, even undermines, the "natural" status of female compassion, and the inevitability of its political stance.

As we have seen in the narrative of Mary Prince, the question of female labor was particularly troubling to a sentimental abolitionism that derived much of its strength from the rhetoric of separate spheres. Representations of colonial labor found in antislavery writings during this period both illustrate the effects of domestic ideology on perceptions of Britain's colonial possessions, and demonstrate its limits. Along with images of the colonial arena in sentimental literature, they evidence the ways in which problems of colonial labor were consistently sexualized at this time. Both the brutality of slave labor, and any resistance to it, are figured either as sexual violence, like Marianne's punishment of her slaves, and the Maroons' threat of rape, or as sexual exploitation, like Anana's service to the governor of Jamaica. This sexualization of interracial contact may be interpreted as a refiguration of the brutal conditions of colonial production. In many of the repeated scenarios I have described, the violence of the white, middle-class woman seems to stand in for her economic interest in plantation productivity, her reembodiment in this action figuring for the scandal of her labor in keeping such a social structure running. Thus, the repetition of images of violent white women on both sides of the slavery debate may be said to indicate their mutual ideological investment in a disembodied feminine virtue kept separate from economic production. This explains why the debate over slave labor continually returns to the question of whether white middle-class women could inhabit a domestic sphere entirely separated from, and disinterested in, economic production.

The effects of domestic ideology on perceptions of colonial production can be seen as well in the ways the solutions proposed for the

improvement of slave culture were often predicated on the implemen-
tation of certain gender definitions; happy marriages between men and
women of the same race would either ameliorate slavery or lead to its
abolition, depending on one's political persuasion. Nonetheless, even
fervent belief in these idealized definitions of domesticity was not able
to keep the division of labor in Britain's West Indian colonies intact.
The material conditions of the Caribbean often threatened to disrupt
the conventions of domestic or sentimental discourse, in much the
same way as does the narrative of Mary Prince. Depictions of white,
middle-class English women in the Caribbean, in political as well as
fictional texts, threatened to reembody the compassionate, sentimental
virtue that enabled many abolitionist claims for the political efficacy of
women. Such reembodiment, as we have seen, usually occurs at
moments when white women's implication in the economic productivity of slave labor becomes visible, and works to replace sympathy with
an unruly sexuality.

# Conclusion

Sentimental abolitionism reached its apex in 1833, with the emancipation of the slaves in the British West Indies. That momentous act was followed in 1838 by the end of the stopgap measure of "apprenticeship" in the colonies. Judged by these events, the British antislavery movement, in its skillful manipulation of the discourses of sentimentality, domesticity, and consumerism, among others, looks extraordinarily successful. The grassroots coalitions the movement built, between the disenfranchised and the powerful, between public men and private women, between producers and consumers, and between colonized subjects and metropolitan citizens, if not the sole cause of the abolition of British slavery, were justly celebrated then and now. Still, the structure of its altruism remains elusive.

This book has traced one aspect of the history of antislavery back through earlier forms of opposition to British imperial expansion. In Swift's critique of England's mercantilist colonial policies toward Ireland, and in Smollett's outrage at the effects of imperial accumulation and colonial luxury in England itself, we catch our first glimpse of the figure that would become so important for the antislavery movement: the nationalistic, morally careful, sentimental consumer. Although Swift satirizes that figure in "A Modest Proposal" as fiercely as he celebrates it in *The Drapier's Letters*, later writers with more faith in the ameliorative power of free-market capitalism latched onto that persona with great energy. For Smollett, the Drapier becomes the self-sufficient and benevolent landowner, Matthew Bramble. In the texts of ladies' antislavery societies, and in other abolitionist appeals, that figure assumes the form of a domestic woman, her consumer choices shaped by sentiment. Increasingly agonistic, liberated from the traditional guidance of her sovereign, landlord, or husband, the consumer who relies only on her personal morality, along with an abstract idea of the national good, persists in our cultural imagination.

Recognizing this history of consumerist resistance and political critiques seems particularly important now, as citizens of the United States—if not the world—are more involved in such projects than ever before. The individual's purchase or refusal of commodities from tuna to sneakers can signify moral probity or degeneracy to the observing eye. Boycott campaigns are often well aware of their historical precedents. In the pages of *The New Republic*, Michael Kinsley has noted that consumer boycotts are "as American as the Boston Tea Party."[1] And, in an article entitled "Voting With Your Checkbook: What Every Christian Should Know About Boycotts," Esther Byle Bruland reminds her readers of the legacy of the abolitionist sugar and cotton boycotts of the nineteenth century.[2] As in earlier periods, such boycotts are primarily nonviolent, relatively conservative, and anxious about accidentally hurting the wrong person. They question whether they work for social change, or merely preserve personal morality.[3]

Like many of the campaigns described in this book, twentieth-century boycotts have tended to be the weapon of the disenfranchised, making strange historical bedfellows of civil rights protesters and the religious right. The long history of African American abstention movements, for example, dates back to at least the beginning of this century, when the segregated streetcars of the south were boycotted.[4] An ongoing commitment not to buy where African Americans could not work prompted W. E. B. Du Bois to write:

> If we once make a religion of our determination to spend our meagre income so far as possible only in such ways as will bring us employment consideration and opportunity, the possibilities before us are enormous. . . . A nation twice as large as Portugal, Holland or Sweden is not powerless—is not merely a supplicant beggar for crumbs—it is a mighty economic power when it gets vision enough to use its strength.[5]

On the world stage, perhaps the best-known campaign of this kind has been the Indian Swadeshi movement mentioned in the introduction, which began in the first decade of the twentieth century in Bengal, and reached its apogee in Gandhi's campaign for Indian independence.[6]

Furthermore, in the tradition of the American colonists' refusal of tea, and of the anti-saccharite campaigns of the eighteenth and nineteenth centuries, consumerist abstention often has been the particular province of women. The Irish Women's Consumer League, for example, helped organize an Irish-American boycott of British goods during the Irish struggle for independence. In what must have been a striking act of political theater, they reenacted the Boston Tea Party in 1921 to emphasize the continuity between the American and Irish Revolutions.[7] During the next decade, the Housewives' League of Detroit worked to direct the spending power of African American women toward the support of African American businesses. The group could claim ten thousand members in 1934.[8] A history of the mutual concerns and influences of these groups, based in such disparate communities, has yet to be written. Their number, however, points to the persistent appeal of the moral rhetoric of domestic consumer power first developed in the late eighteenth and early nineteenth centuries.

A striking example of the survival of this discourse of refusal comes from the grape boycott movement of the 1960s and 70s. Margaret Rose has recorded the efforts of female organizers in Philadelphia, led by Hope Lopez, to convince middle-class Anglo women to support Chicano farm laborers. Lopez calculated that an "idealized maternalist argument based on family values, moral power, and the female domain of the consumer market [would unite] them at the same time as class differences tested their alliance."[9] This strategy produced rhetorical statements uncannily like the gendered appeals of the campaigns against slave-grown sugar. Lopez informed the supermarket owners who still sold California grapes: "May I remind you, . . . that 99% of your customers are women. The ladies put you in the position of strength that you now hold and these same ladies can knock you right off that pedestal. . . . You are laughing in their faces by flaunting grapes and worse yet by featuring them in some cases . . . 'Hell knows no fury'. . . . Need I say more?"[10]

The grape boycott campaign in Philadelphia was remarkably successful; in the face of such demands, supermarkets removed the offending grapes. Of course, this instance differs from nineteenth-century campaigns in that, in the more recent instance, representatives of oppressed laborers themselves constructed the terms of alliance. Still, the very self-consciousness with which these organizers deployed senti-mental images—such as women carrying their babies into the field to work—reveals the powerful reservoir of feeling present in such discourse.

We should not forget, however, that all of these boycotts represent both a response to and a symptom of the globalization of capital, a phenomenon that shaped and preoccupied eighteenth-century Britain as much as it does twentieth-century America. As a response to the diversification of markets and capital, boycotts resist the idea that socioeconomic injustice now happens too far away for the average consumer to do anything about it. In this context, boycotts offer a utopian vision of the consumer's direct, individualized impact on the means of production; they play the ideology of consumerism in a heroic key. At the same time, however, boycotts admit to the separa-tion of consumption from production; indeed, they would never come about without such alienation. The diffusion of capital across the globe has left many of us no more direct means to register our moral outrage than through consumer choice. For those of us who could not travel to Capetown to demonstrate our disgust for apartheid, for exam-ple, the boycott of companies with investments in South Africa seemed an effective method of protest.

Of course, the issue of consumer choice is more complicated in today's fluid markets than it was in the eighteenth century, and it is cor-respondingly more difficult to pin down responsibility for the injustices inscribed in certain commodities, especially as sites of production become ever more mobile. David Harvey has called this new dynamic "flexible accumulation," but he notes that "what is most interesting about the current situation is the way in which capitalism is becoming ever more tightly organized *through* dispersal, geographical mobility, and flexible responses in labour markets, labour processes, and con-sumer markets."[11] The persistence of boycott strategies in the contem-porary world perhaps registers consumers' recognition of and response to such global organization. Boycotts themselves may have become more indirect; for example, recently, one might have chosen to boycott the products of a company that advertised itself during a television sitcom that showed sexual behavior of which one did not approve. Nevertheless, the evidence suggests that an ideal of moral consciousness for the consumer and the expansion of capitalism developed in tandem. We continue to use methods perhaps originally generated by the shock of geographical distance to deal with moral problems as far away as South Africa and as close as our television set, yet, whether local or international, boycotts remain inside the historical structure of global capitalism. Even as consumer practices seem to invent themselves anew in an ever-changing market, we shouldn't lose sight of how oddly stable they have remained over the past three hundred years.

The physical separation of modes of production from modes of consumption has tended to displace the burden of inciting social criticism onto representational forms. Implicit in the argument of this book has been the suggestion that, over the course of the eighteenth century, Britons became more and more reliant on textual representations — both political and literary — to shape their ideas of colonial policy. Whereas Swift wrote for the circumscribed audience of Protestant Dublin in the 1720s, abolitionist writers at the end of the eighteenth century expected that their tracts would be read throughout Britain by people in many walks of life. As the actual products of the colonial periphery became more and more suspect, anxiously, though addictively, consumed, the British turned to pictures, poems, dialogues, and printed speeches to define the bonds between colony and government. Indeed, one could say that two important, though implicit, tenets of the antislavery movement were "don't buy goods, buy texts" and "don't eat, feel." Julie Ellison connects this parallel development of technologies of representation and a sense of moral obligation to the contemporary notion of "liberal guilt." She asks:

> If we obtain detailed knowledge of the suffering of persons on another continent . . . that is, if they come to be reproducible — what happens to the over-zealous sympathizer? How fast should our sympathies outrun our agency? Would liberal guilt proliferate under expanded representational conditions? Does our changing understanding of our role in a global system of interdependence increase the legitimate range of duty? Are the Age of Sensibility and the Age of Mechanical Reproduction the same thing?[12]

## Conclusion

If we think of mechanical reproduction in terms of information and imagery, the combined multiplication of texts, and the increased political reliance upon them in late eighteenth- and early nineteenth-century Britain seems to answer this question in the affirmative.[13] As the relationship between the British public and the life of the colonies became thus mediated, political writers put more and more faith in a paradoxical combination of readerly susceptibility and consumer probity.

Despite its important legacy to consumer politics, however, the triumph of sentimental antislavery was brief. After 1838, appeals to a universal sensibility—mutual emotions discovered in sympathy and tears across vast distances—began to disappear from British conceptions of cultural difference, to be replaced by a more essentialist and "scientific" understanding of "race." During the nineteenth century, "polygenist" theories of difference, which held that people with different skin colors actually belonged to different species, gradually came to replace the older, "monogenist," idea that all varieties of mankind descended from a single ancestor.[14] As Nancy Stepan writes, this new perspective

> involved a change from an emphasis on the fundamental physical and moral homogeneity of man, despite superficial differences, to an emphasis on the essential heterogeneity of mankind, despite superficial similarities. It was a shift from a sense of man as primarily a social being, governed by social laws and standing apart from nature, to a sense of man as primarily a biological being, embedded in nature and governed by biological laws.[15]

Antislavery activists were convinced that Africans and their descendants in captivity suffered from a lack of maturity and civilization, a view often called "cultural racism." They believed that, with philanthropic guidance, these people could achieve levels of Christian domestic happiness and capitalist industriousness equal to the level enjoyed by Europeans. But by the mid-nineteenth century, those views had given way to a more pessimistic, deterministic belief in the ineradicable savagery of inferior nations.

Victorian attitudes toward race remained heterogeneous, as the racism unleashed by the Governor Eyre controversy in the 1860s coexisted with the adulation showered on Harriet Beecher Stowe.[16] Yet, belief in biological determinism as an explanatory force grew. Science was called upon not only to distinguish between "white" and "black," but also to differentiate among the newly encountered inhabitants of India, the South Pacific, New Zealand, Australia, and the Americas. Racial thinking during the nineteenth century became at once more particularizing, as minute biological differences were given ever greater significance, and more encompassing, as the division between "us" and "them" became more sharply defined and harshly enforced. Historians have suggested recently that such beliefs did not arise simply, or even primarily, from England's attempts to subdue and manage the diverse peoples of its far-flung empire. Instead, scientific racism developed in conjunction with beliefs about the natural quality of all social divisions. Kenan Malik, for example, argues that "racial theories . . . as they unfolded in the nineteenth century were part of a broader development—the use of natural explanations for social phenomena."[17] Daniel Pick points out that evolutionary anthropology, one of the methodologies contributing to racial theory, "functioned not only to differentiate the colonised overseas from the imperial race, but also to scrutinize portions of the population at home."[18] The Irish were considered in such a light, but so were criminals and hysterical women.

Certainly, racial, ethnic and social distinctions had been intertwined in British thinking for a long time—as the structural closeness of miscegenation and class mobility in *Humphry Clinker*, for example, tells us—but as social stratification became more rigid in the nineteenth century, so too did ideas of racial difference. In retrospect, this ideological shift suggests that the antislavery sentiment of the urban bourgeoisie in the late eighteenth and early nineteenth centuries was connected intimately to their optimism about class mobility and individual progress. When those middle classes felt themselves more firmly in place, when their class status became a way of life to be maintained and defended from interlopers and upstarts, the grand narrative of abolition lost some of its appeal.

There is a sense, too, in which the very terms with which antislavery

activists framed their arguments left them vulnerable to the racist conclusions drawn by Victorian England. Abolitionists had promised that,
once freed, Caribbean slaves would embrace Christianity, European
domestic norms, and capitalist endeavor. They expected the transition
from slavery to wage labor to be clearcut and exhilarating.[19] When the
former slave colonies of the West Indies did not follow that model,
philanthropic thought, which had always emphasized the individual
moral potential of slaves, had no alternative explanation for the continuing social and economic misery of former slaves. As Douglas Lorimer
points out, "the British rarely found that their schemes for black
advancement fulfilled their exaggerated expectations, and rather than
question their own vision, they revived the question of the Negro's
racial inheritance and often found it wanting."[20]

This disjunction, between abolitionists' projection of English ideals
and expectations onto slaves and the economic realities facing those
freed from slavery, had always been a tension in antislavery discourse.
Most abolitionists, however, enthusiastically put their faith in the market, as did many freed slaves themselves. Ignatius Sancho, a merchant
himself, explains the horrors of the slave trade as a misuse of economic
relations:

> Commerce was meant by the goodness of the Diety [*sic*] to diffuse the
> various goods of the earth into every part — to unite mankind in the
> blessed chains of brotherly love, society and mutual dependence. . . . —
> Commerce attended with strict honesty, and with Religion for its com-
> panion, would be a blessing to every shore it touched at. — In Africa, the
> poor wretched natives — blessed with the most fertile and luxuriant soil —
> are rendered so much the more miserable for what Providence meant as a
> blessing.[21]

And although Olaudah Equiano recounts the racism he experienced
after buying his freedom from slavery, he concludes his narrative with
just the kind of utopian hopes for free-market capitalism on which
much of the abolitionist appeal in England was based:[22] "In a short
time one sentiment alone will prevail, from motives of interest as well
as justice and humanity. Europe contains one hundred and twenty millions of inhabitants. Query. — How many millions doth Africa contain?
Supposing the Africans, collectively and individually, to expend 5 l. a

head in raiment and furniture yearly when civilized, &c. an immensity beyond the realms of imagination!"[23] In these passages, we see again the assumption that humanitarian sentiment and capitalism are essentially complementary. Rather than being a source for human commodities, Africa will become a market for European goods. After the failure of the Sierra Leone venture, however, such utopian appeals to the humanitarian potential of capitalism carried less weight.[24]

Furthermore, the limits of this idealized economic solution for colonial and racial injustice were drawn particularly sharply for women. As we can see from her autobiography, written in the 1830s, Mary Prince has significantly less access to the utopian capitalism that sustained Equiano. Released from slavery, she still labored for others, in discomfort and isolation. The middle-class women who had supported her resistance to captivity did so out of a sincere belief in the moral good of domestic happiness, but this was a condition to which Mary Prince herself could never gain full access. Indeed, the ideological contradictions posed by female labor were built into the very structure of British emancipation. Diana Paton has demonstrated that antislavery discourse, which insisted that women needed to be saved from the moral degradations of slavery, while men deserved the right to work for wages to support their families, occluded the consequences of this gendered division of labor for the West Indian economy. "At this time, at least fifty percent of field laborers in Britain's Caribbean colonies were women. Despite this, those who anticipated that wage work would be done by freed *men* seemed not to realize that this implied that the labor force would be cut in half."[25] Many emancipated women did withdraw from field labor, and the colonial economy suffered as a result. Thus, even when abolitionist moral expectations were met, the results did not produce the happy capitalist families the abolitionists had predicted.

The evidence of women's differential relationship to capitalism still troubles contemporary feminist thought, although the place of domestic ideology has shifted somewhat. In the mid nineteenth century, Sojourner Truth had to explain forcefully that the experience of manual labor she shared with Mary Prince did not exclude her from definitions of femininity: "Look at me! Look at my arm! I have plowed, and planted, and gathered into barns, and no man could head me! And aint I a woman? I could work as much and eat as much as a man—when I could get it—and bear the lash as well! And aint I a woman?"[26] In twentieth-century versions of this raced, classed struggle over definitions of femininity, however, less privileged women are seen to be trapped inside the "traditional home" and kept from the liberation of the marketplace. Chandra Talpade Mohanty points out that contemporary white bourgeois feminism tends to bring the image of an "average third world woman" to this debate:

> This average third world woman leads an essentially truncated life, based on her feminine gender (read: sexually constrained) and being "third world" (read: ignorant, poor, uneducated, tradition-bound, religious, domesticated, family-oriented, victimized, etc.). This, I suggest, is in contrast to the (implicit) self-representation of western women as educated, modern, as having control over their own bodies, and sexualities, and the freedom to make their own decisions.[27]

Ironically, aside from the sad fact that she is victimized and poor, this "third world woman" has become everything abolitionists had hoped for: chaste, religious, domesticated, family-oriented. Yet, this shifting of terms does not mean that the structural divide between white middle-class women and the other women of the world has fundamentally altered. This "average third world woman" is still pitied because she performs an "improper" kind of labor, carried out in "improper" circumstances. As Hazel Carby argues in her influential article, "White woman listen! Black feminism and the boundaries of sisterhood": "much feminist work suffers from the assumption that it is only through the development of a Western-style industrial capitalism and the resultant entry of women into waged labour that the potential for the liberation of women can increase."[28] We might say that one legacy of the abolitionist struggle for emancipation is this continued entanglement of gender and race relations in the history of free-market capitalism.

*

> I am black—I am black!
>   And yet God made me, they say;
> But *if* He did so, smiling, back
>   He must have cast his work away

Under the feet of His white creatures.
With a look of scorn, that the dusky features
   Might be trodden again to clay.

And yet He has made dark things
   To be glad and merry as light:
There's a little dark bird sits and sings;
   There's a dark stream ripples out of sight;
And the dark frogs chant in the safe morass,
And the Sweetest stars are made to pass
   O'er the face of the darkest night.

But *we* who are dark, we are dark!
   O God, we have no stars!
About our souls, in care and cark,
   Our blackness shuts like prison bars:
And crouch our souls so far behind,
That never a comfort can they find
   By reaching through prison bars.

—Elizabeth Barrett Browning,
"The Runaway Slave at Pilgrim's Point"

The pessimism about race relations that grew over the course of the nineteenth century is certainly visible in Elizabeth Barrett Browning's "The Runaway Slave at Pilgrim's Point" (1848), and the poem provides a useful point of comparison to the earlier structures of feeling discussed in this book. Barrett Browning was commissioned to write the poem, and its American setting represents the shift in British antislavery discourse from the criticism of national sin to an exhortation to other nations to emulate British virtue. It was published in the conventional manner of women's antislavery appeals, as part of an anthology called the "Liberty Bell," sold at the Boston National Anti-Slavery Bazaar in 1848.[29] In many other ways as well, this poem resembles the sentimental narratives of earlier abolitionist writers. Barrett Browning, writing in the voice of a female slave, elaborates on the violations to which the woman's status and sex have left her vulnerable: loss of love, rape, bearing the child of her white owner. It goes on to describe her response to these events: flight and infanticide. All of these tropes are present in earlier literary attacks on slavery.

Yet, this poem articulates the slave woman's dilemma in the context of a racialized discourse. The slave woman insistently identifies her color as the cause of her distress. Being black signifies a doom that originated in the moment of creation; she imagines that God made his white and black creatures as different projects. The assumption that color is the most important category of experience permeates the poem. The slave woman measures her own miserable blackness in relation to the "glad" and "merry" "dark things" of the natural world, as if such animalistic, earthy comparisons were more appropriate than those between human conditions. The skin color of slaves becomes a kind of tautological metaphor—they are in the dark, because their skin is dark: "*we* who are dark, we are dark!"

Earlier abolitionist writers had tended to represent the skin of the slave as an illusory and ultimately unimportant characteristic. Hannah More, for example, asks:

> Does th' immortal principle within
> Change with the casual colour of the skin?
> Does matter govern spirit? or is mind
> Degraded by the form to which 'tis joined?[30]

Striking a similar note, Cowper has the slave of the "Negro's Complaint" advise the reader:

> Deem our nation Brutes no longer
> 'Till some reason ye shall find
> Worthier of regard and stronger
> Than the colour of our kind.[31]

Phillis Wheatley admonishes: "Remember Christians, Negros black as Cain / May be refined, and join th'angelic train." William Blake's "The Little Black Boy," perhaps registers a transition, as it represents skin color as a kind of temporary corporeal containment:

> And we are put on earth a little space,
> That we may learn to bear the beams of love,
> And these black bodies and this sun-burnt face
> Is but a cloud and like a shady grove.[32]

For Barrett Browning, however, the black body is no cloud, no "casual colour," but rather a prison that entirely obscures the slave's soul. As if to emphasize the point, later in the poem the slave woman exclaims, "I fall, I swoon! I look at the sky. / The clouds are breaking on my brain" (ll. 246–47). This female slave lives in a world where material forms are brutal and determining. The physical suffering of enslaved bodies grounds slave culture in earthly strife, beyond the possibility of religious redemption. The slave woman ominously declares, "We are too heavy for our cross, / and fall and crush you and your seed" (ll. 244–45). Racial conflict seems permanent, corrosive, and inevitable.

This conviction reminds us that, as Nancy Stepan points out, "just as the battle against slavery was being won by abolitionists, the war against racism in European thought was being lost."[33] Yet, we should remember that sentimental accounts of cultural difference often carried the potential for a kind of essentialized, racialized understanding of the world alongside their more utopian visions of intercultural harmony. The antislavery poems quoted above, like the appeals of ladies' antislavery societies, imply that privileging interior feeling over every outward form will obviate all material differences. This aspect of sentimentality characterizes skin color as just another extraneous condition, far less important than the quality of what lies within. Paradoxically, however, those interior qualities must always be rendered visible on the surface of the body, as tears, blushes, or grimaces of disgust. This characteristic of sentimentality, its reliance on the natural, indexical status of individual emotional responses, has a tendency to reduce the body to an essentialized collection of signs. Matter doesn't exactly govern spirit, to paraphrase Hannah More, but it provides a valuable clue to the spirit's worth. A small shift of emphasis, and the corporeal qualities of the body obscure or imprison any transcendent soul.[34]

The potential for seemingly natural physical reactions to overwhelm more abstract or transcendent moral concerns has been apparent in the various consumerist critiques discussed in this book. Swift, in the person of the Drapier, advises his readers to avoid Wood's halfpence as if it were a threat to the individual body, as well as to the body politic. In *Humphry Clinker*, Smollett relies on the "natural" reaction of revulsion to protect the British consumer from the contaminated substances of the increasingly international marketplace. Abolitionists, in turn, represented slave-grown sugar as an object of disgust, in order to make their philanthropic point. In *Letters of a Solitary Wanderer*, the disgusting body of the maroon slave woman marks the racial division that safe-guards universal domestic happiness. Thus, the spasm of disgust proves the double of sympathetic tears—the former drawing ever sharper lines around national, racial, and sexual distinctions, even as the latter claimed to join souls across vast distances.

As we have seen, the fear that humanitarian sensibility might ulti-mately devolve into a solipsistic fascination with the workings of one's own body haunted philanthropic discourse in the late eighteenth and early nineteenth centuries. But by the mid nineteenth century, con-cern over such seeming hypocrisy was more widespread. As Douglas Lorimer explains, "a sentimentalist became a weak-kneed, impractical individual who, in the words of Carlyle, was particularly associated with the 'rose-pink' 'spoutings, anti-spoutings, and interminable jangle and babble of Exeter Hall.'"[35] Carlyle might be considered biased, but characters like Dickens's Mrs. Jellyby and Wilkie Collins's Miss Clack represent the literary manifestation of the growing contempt for any philanthropy directed too far away from domestic concerns. In this context, the biologism of "The Runaway Slave at Pilgrim's Point" does not necessarily undermine its commitment to the abolitionist cause. Indeed, the poem might be interpreted, like Mary Prince's narrative, as an attempt to reinscribe material differences back into the relation between black and white women, challenging the universal attributes put forward by earlier gendered appeals—particularly with regard to maternity.[36] The poem's most shocking revelation is that the slave woman kills her child not to keep it from the horrors of slavery (as do Behn's Oroonoko and—much later—the heroine of Toni Morrison's *Beloved*), but because she cannot stand to see the white face of her master and rapist replicated in the face of her child.[37]

> Even in that single glance I had
>     Of my child's face,—I tell you all,—
> I saw a look that made me mad!—
>     The *master's* look, that used to fall
> On my soul like his lash . . . or worse!
>                                    —(ll. 141–45)

The poem suggests that racial antagonism can turn even mother love to homicidal rage. No amount of "natural feeling" can make this slave mother forget either the material conditions of her suffering or the racism that is its cause. As she smothers the child with her kerchief, she aggressively revises the conventional "breaking heart" of sentimental convention. In the insistently physical language of the poem, the dying child kicks his feet "against [her] heart to break it through." Not content, like Thomas Day's "Dying Negro," to curse only slave traders and slave owners, the curse of this female captive includes the wives of her trackers:

> I wish you who stand there seven abreast,
> Each for his own wife's joy and gift,
> A little corpse as safely at rest,
> Hid in the mangos!—Yes, but *she*
> May keep live babies on her knee
> And sing the song she liketh best.
> —(ll. 212–17)

Again in contrast to earlier abolitionist appeals, race sharply disrupts gender solidarity, producing an angry difference no mutual feminine sympathy can elide. The poem rejects what Chandra Talpade Mohanty has criticized as "the assumption of women as an already constituted and coherent group with identical interests and desires, regardless of class, ethnic or racial location."[38] In a way, the determining capacity it gives color in slave culture works as a critique of sentimental universalism. Yet, at the same time, that visual difference makes such a deep rift between women of different colors that it seems impossible to imagine a viable basis for solidarity.

In its emphasis on the determining quality of material conditions, the poem reflects its author's more personal feelings about Britain's involvement in slave production. Elizabeth Barrett Browning had a sophisticated sense of her own implication in slavery's history of violence, and of the inevitable antagonism between former slaves and those who had profited from the exploitation of their labor. Much of the Barrett family wealth came from Jamaican sugar plantations, and although both Elizabeth and her father were thrilled by the emancipation of the slaves, she wrote Ruskin in 1855: "I belong to a family of West Indian slaveholders, and if I believed in curses, I should be afraid."[39] The remark reveals a melancholy, post-abolitionist understanding that slavery's legacy of exploitation and violence would not be erased by the humanitarian act of emancipation.

Barrett Browning wrote "The Runaway Slave at Pilgrim's Point" soon after eloping to Italy, and the slave woman's predicament sometimes has been read as an allegory for her own escape from her father's tyranny, and for her anger at the patriarchal establishments that supported that tyranny. In light of Barrett Browning's continuing sense of her own personal connection to slavery, however, we can see that biographical resonance as working in concert with the poem's more public concerns. She wrote in another letter: [I]s it possible that you think a woman has no business with questions like the question of slavery? Then she had better use a pen no more. She had better subside into slavery and concubinage herself, I think, as in the times of old, shut herself up with the Penelopes in the 'women's apartment.'"[40] Here, the poet implies that the futures of black and white women are as bound up in each other as were their pasts. She builds on the same assumptions about women's moral obligation to combat slavery used by ladies' antislavery associations, but her vision of the female role differs from theirs. For Barrett Browning, female liberation is not the right to withdraw into the private sphere, but rather the liberty to use her pen championing political issues.

The connection the poet makes here between physical freedom and freedom of expression perhaps explains the persistent concern with the slave woman's voice in "The Runaway Slave at Pilgrim's Point." Infinitely more cautious about its own ability to ventriloquize the slave than were earlier abolitionist works, the poem makes sure the slave woman reminds us of the social restraints on communication that make it impossible for her to sing even to her own child. She says, "I might have sung like a mother— / But I dared not sing to the white-faced child / The only song I knew" (ll. 131–33).[41] By connecting this complaint to her own act of infanticide, the slave woman suggests that an interdiction of certain narratives contributes to the violence of slave culture, and that an internalized version of such censorship haunts even the escaped slave. In contrast, the privilege of the white wives of slave owners is represented as the freedom to sing songs of their own choosing. Here, the poem returns us to one of the central concerns of this book: the relations between material conditions and the structure of discourse—even the shape of art. Like many of the texts discussed here, Barrett Browning's poem reveals the emphasis placed on literary communication by social critics like the abolitionists during the period. Not only was it written and disseminated as an explicit part of a political movement, but it also imagines that racial reconciliation might come about through art.

Only after she has killed the child, transformed him into "a dark child in the dark" (l. 186), does the woman sing her own song. This moment of artistic freedom and emotional generosity is as close as the poem gets to imagining redemption or racial harmony.

> And thus we two were reconciled,
>   The white child and the black mother, thus;
> For, as I sang it—soft, slow and wild
>   The same song, more melodious,
> Rose from the grave whereon I sat!
> It was the dead child singing that,
>   To join the souls of both of us.
> —(ll. 190–96)

Gothic as this scene is, it does represent the possibility of interracial communication returning in the aftermath of unthinkable violence. Not only can the slave mother now express herself, but the "white-faced child" also seems to recognize and celebrate his mother's culture. Yet, we should remember the conditions under which this reconciliation takes place. The slave woman sings her song in the dark; she is the only living being present. The content and language of the song are hidden even from the sympathetic reader; the poem we read is no mother's lullaby, but a curse for all of those who have condoned slavery, readers included.

It seems right, then, to conclude this book with an image of the inherited occlusions that make it so difficult for us (black and white, male and female) to hear the slave woman's song across the divide of history—and the even greater problems involved with bringing it into the harsh, somewhat sterile light of contemporary academic discourse. The terms of the dialogue between privileged and less-privileged women have been historically constructed; caught between the optimistic universalism of the abolitionists, and the racial pessimism of their descendants, it is hard to know, finally, how to come to terms with the consumerist critiques of colonialism that culminated in the anti-slavery movement. One first step, however, is to recognize that for us, no less than for Elizabeth Barrett Browning, the violent legacy of slavery remains potent. More than that, we must acknowledge that the material and discursive conditions of emancipation—which brought about the end of slavery, but not of racism—lie entombed within us all.

# Notes

## Introduction

1. The credit for inventing the rent strike is usually given to Charles Stewart Parnell. Using the term "boycott" to describe eighteenth-century actions is thus somewhat anachronistic. The movements I will be discussing usually call their strategy "refusal" or "abstention." I will use these terms as often as possible.

2. I understand a discourse to be a field of representation in which "power and knowledge are joined together" (Foucault, 100). Edward Said was the first to apply this concept to the question of colonialism in *Orientalism*. For a discussion of the particular forms of colonial discourse present in the Americas, see Hulme.

3. See Habermas, 27–79. In the later parts of his study, Habermas seems to suggest that consumerism tends to create a kind of "pseudo-privacy" (156–57). Eighteenth-century attempts to create public communities of consumers suggest that the issue may be more complicated.

4. Hunt, 6.

5. Sancho, 271. On the relation between Sancho and Sterne, see Ellis, chapter 2.

6. See Landes; also see Fraser. I return to this issue in Chapter 5.

7. Gates, 5.

8. Gates, 6. The relation of discursive constructions to the realities of colonial violence has been hotly debated. For accounts of how colonial discourse works in collusion with more visible forms of colonial power, see Spivak, "Can the Subaltern Speak," and Bhabha; for a critique of this emphasis on discourse, see Parry.

9. D. Richardson, 106. See also Curtin; Lovejoy.

10. Along with the works discussed below, see Blackburn; Drescher, *Econocide*; Eltis; Eltis and Walvin; and Walvin, *Black Ivory*.

11. For a number of elaborations and critiques of Williams's work, see Solow and Engerman; also Drescher, *"Capitalism and Slavery."*

12. Davis, *The Problem of Slavery*.

13. See also Frankenberg. On the experience of black women in the Caribbean, see Beckles, *Natural Rebels*; Bush, *Slave Women and Caribbean Society*; and Morrissey. On the history of people of African descent in Britain see Fryer; Shyllon; and, more generally, Centre for Contemporary Cultural Studies.

14. Ferguson, *Subject to Others*, 301.

15. Ibid, 6. Ferguson is certainly not the only feminist historian to struggle with this contradiction. I return to this issue in chapter 5.

16. Midgley, *Women Against Slavery*, 203.

17. Armstrong, 95. See also Poovey, *Proper Lady*; Davidoff and Hall.

18. McKendrick, Brewer, and Plumb, 1.

19. Porter, 219.

20. On the relation of women to the development of consumerism, see McKendrick, "Home Demand and Economic Growth"; Weatherill. Kowaleski-Wallace discusses women's interaction with the colonial commodities (including sugar) at the tea table, 19–73.

21. Brown, *Ends of Empire*, 3.

22. Swift, *Gulliver's Travels*, 203.

23. Pope, *The Rape of the Lock*, ll. 29–30. On the ways mercantile accumulation is represented in these lines, see Landa, *Pope's Belinda*; and Brown, *Alexander Pope*.

24. See Mandell. On the way this gendering of consumption interacts with justifications for colonial expansion, see Brown, *Ends of Empire*, chapter 6; and Kaul.

25. S. Richardson, 78.

26. On women and the new activity of shopping in the eighteenth century, see Kowaleski-Wallace, 79–99.

27. See J. Taylor; Lovell; and Uphaus.

28. *Lady's Magazine* 43 (1812): 22. Quoted in Ferris, 39.

29. "Windsor Forest," ll. 397–402. Pope, 76.

30. Day, 19.

31. Brewer, 176.

32. Colley, 105. See also Wilson. For British thinking about excess wealth, see Sekora.

33. For an overview of allegations of cannibalism, see Arens.

34. For the African belief that white people were cannibals, see Cugoano, 9, 19; and Equiano, 55. I return to the questions of cannibalism and colonial dismemberment in Chapters 2, 3, and 4.

35. Hulme, 198. Hulme provides an excellent discussion of the history of representations of cannibalism in the Caribbean, 45–89.

36. This poem also engages in a critique of sentimental reading, an issue I return to in Chapters 4 and 5.

37. The relationship between sentimentality and politics has been discussed by a number of critics. See Johnson; Markley; and Mullan.

## Chapter 1

1. A. Smith, 660.

2. Raymond Williams says that "it was from mC18 that [the word] *consumer* began to emerge in a neutral sense in descriptions of bourgeois political economy. In the new predominance of an organized market, the acts of making and using goods and services were newly defined in the increasingly abstract pairings of *producer* and *consumer*, *production* and *consumption*" (38).

3. McKendrick, Brewer, and Plumb, 1.

4. Ibid., 20.

5. Ibid., 11.

6. Hanway's was not the only voice to object to tea consumption among the laboring classes; he was joined by, among others, Samuel Johnson. Johnson stated that "tea is a liquor not proper for the lower classes of the people, as it supplies no strength to labour, nor relief to disease, but gratifies the taste without nourishing the body" (quoted in Emerson, 8). Kowaleski-Wallace provides an excellent discussion of eighteenth-century representations of tea, including Hanway's (19–37).

7. Hanway, 244–45.  8. Ibid., 243.

9. Ibid.  10. Ibid., 245, 244.

11. Ibid., 213.

12. Wilson demonstrates that "widespread fears of the emasculation and degeneracy of the British body politic" permeated discussions of empire during the 1750s (185). For a more general discussion of eighteenth-century ideas of effeminacy, see Staves; Shapiro.

13. Hanway, 263.

14. Ibid., 273.

15. McKendrick, Brewer, and Plumb, 31.

16. Griffiths, 21.  17. Shammas, 121.

18. Chaudhuri, 385.  19. Griffiths, 12.

20. Mintz, 116.  21. Ibid., 148.

22. Overall, the general population relied less on locally produced foodstuffs and more on comestibles produced outside of England. Clearly, this is a more

complicated process than I will be describing here, and one that had been going on since the sixteenth century. See Wallerstein.

23. Shammas, 147.

24. Over the course of the eighteenth century, England lost her agricultural self-sufficiency and was forced to begin importing grain to support her population. England's growing population, which arguably made possible the industrial revolution, absorbed the grain surpluses of the late seventeenth century. This increased demand transformed England, in the two decades following 1750, from a corn exporter to a corn importer. Although between 1775 and 1792, grain was again exported, the balance shifted again, and between 1792 and 1814, foreign corn was admitted at reduced rates, and the government bounties previously paid on exports were suspended. This new dependence on an international market for basic needs caused "the sharpest, most sudden large change in England's trading situation" in the eighteenth century. See R. Davis, 108.

25. Mintz, 180.

26. Ibid., 182.

27. Swift, *Irish Tracts*, 126. I discuss Swift's involvement in Irish politics at length in Chapter 2.

28. Ibid., 127.

29. Breen, 90. For a critique of these claims, see Agnew, 33. Agnew argues that "when one recalls that Americans promptly rushed back to their British goods after the Revolution, one realizes that the co-ordinates of loyalty and citizenship lay not in the sphere of goods—and certainly not in anything that could be called a consumer culture—but rather in other spheres: religion, ideology and so on" (33). However, I would argue that the discourse surrounding commodities in the Anglo-American world during this period undermines any such distinction between separate "spheres."

30. Breen, 98, 99. 31. Ibid., 93. Also see Young.

32. Breen, 92. 33. Quoted in Emerson, 10.

34. C. Campbell, 34.

35. Ibid., 204, 205. For the female gendering of much of this emotionalism, see Kowaleski-Wallace.

36. Campbell, 89, 203. 37. Wesley, 10.

38. Ibid., 14. 39. Nuermberger, 5.

40. Quoted in ibid., 5–6. 41. Ibid., 4.

42. Ladies' Negro's Friend Society of Birmingham Seventh Annual Report, 25.

43. The British abolitionist movement began in earnest in 1788. This movement, fueled by huge petitions, reached a sort of climax in 1791, when Parliament refused to abolish the trade outright, and instead promised gradual abolition. This defeat did not wipe out popular antislavery agitation, however, but

instead increased the movement's extra-parliamentary activity. Walvin notes the virulence of antislavery feeling in those years: "By the spring of 1792, 519 abolitionist petitions had reached parliament: that from Manchester contained 20,000 names" ("The Rise of British Popular Sentiment," 151). The pamphlets promoting abstention from slave-grown sugar were published mostly in 1791 and 1792, though I will examine a few published in other years.

44. Drescher, *Capitalism and Anti-Slavery*, 79.

45. Ibid., 79.

46. *Northampton Mercury*, December 24, 1791.

47. "Address to Her Royal Highness," 1.

48. This information is taken from the catalog of antislavery material at the Friends House Library in London. Although not the most politically prominent antislavery advocate of his time, Fox (1736–1826), who ran a draper and mercer business, included Granville Sharp and William Wilberforce among his friends. He also founded the Sunday School Society, which was supported by Jonas Hanway.

49. "Strictures on an Address," 3.

50. "Vindication of the use of sugar," 7–8.

51. Mosely, 173.

52. Innes, 9.

53. Pro-slavery advocates could trace minutely the economic relations that made the sugar trade profitable, and, to their eyes, necessary. In 1747, one such writer claimed:

> Many other considerable Branches of the British Trade are, in a great degree, dependent upon the Sugar Colonies, and must partake in their success, or suffer by their Declension. The *African* trade is carried on chiefly to supply them with Negroes; as the African trade itself is furnished by our own Woolen Manufactuory, and by the East India Trade. Our *North American* colonies are enabled to pay for *British* manufactures partly with the produce of the Sugar Islands. And these several parts of Commerce, by the mutual aid of each other, contribute immense Riches to this kingdom, and support together a very extensive navigation. ("Considerations against laying any new duty," 3)

On the importance of mercantile imperialism to English politics in the 1740s, see Wilson, 154–57.

54. "Answer to a pamphlet," 6.

55. Allen, 7–8. Allen (1770–1843) was a Quaker, and the son of a silk manufacturer. He became a chemist, and owned his own laboratory. A friend of Clarkson's and Wilberforce's, he eventually joined Robert Owen in purchasing the New Lanark Mills.

56. "No rum! — No sugar!" 18. This text shares its dialogue form and its attempt at dialect with other popular instructive pamphlets of the period, such as Hannah More's "Village Politics" (1793). For an account of the pamphlet literature of the period, see O. Smith.

57. Fox, 3.

58. Haskell, 550. On the debate surrounding this article, see Bender.

59. Haskell, 555.

60. Ibid., 547.

61. Ibid., 565.

62. The idea that slave economies were creatures of mercantilism, while the dissolution of British slavery was motivated by the growth of industrial capitalism, was first put forward by Eric Williams. The supposed incompatibility between slavery and capitalism has since come under a great deal of scrutiny. Clearly, in many places, slavery continued profitably into the era of free-market capitalism. See Blackburn, 538. And for an overview of the debate, Drescher, "Capitalism and Slavery," 220–21.

63. Blackburn, however, reminds us that, in the abolitionist movement more generally, "it is as well to retain a sense of the discrepancy as well as the overlap between the bourgeois and the capitalist" (534).

64. "Considerations on the slave trade," 1.

65. For the growing importance of the "Rights of Man" in English radical political discourse, growing out of the success of Paine's writings, and supplanting an idea of constitutionalism, or traditional English liberties, see Thompson.

66. Advertisement for William Allen, "The duty of abstaining from the use of West India produce: a speech delivered at Coachmasters Hall, Jan. 12, 1792."

67. Fox, 2.

68. "Address to her Royal Highness," 2; Fox, 12.

69. E. Williams, 154.

70. D. Davis, 458, 456.

71. Drescher, Capitalism and Anti-Slavery, 72.

72. Ibid., 78.

73. Marx, 45.

## Chapter 2

1. Swift, Irish Tracts, 16.        2. Kearney, 113.

3. Canny, "Ideology," 574.        4. Said, The World, 83.

5. Swift was more or less permanently resident in Ireland from 1709. He first wrote on Ireland in "The Story of the Injured Lady" in 1707 but did not

publish the tract (it was printed after his death in 1746). His first public writing on Ireland was "A Proposal for the Universal Use of Irish Manufacture," in 1720. It appeared anonymously, but the printer was prosecuted. Perhaps because of this, Swift didn't re-enter the fray until the controversy over Wood's halfpence in 1724–25. After writing a number of pamphlets about Ireland in the 1720s, he wrote much less on the subject during the 1730s, or before his death in 1746.

6. Swift, *Gulliver's Travels*, 237. All subsequent page numbers for references to this edition will be cited in the text.

7. For an exposition of the way this passage engages contemporaneous debates about imperialist conquest, see Montag, 129–36. The one episode in *Gulliver's Travels* most often taken to refer to imperial aggression is the town of Lindalino's successful resistance of Laputa. This narrative seems to be an allegory for Ireland's resistance to the imposition of Wood's halfpence, but it was never published during Swift's lifetime.

8. Fabricant, "Swift as Irish Historian," 55. Discussions of the relation between *Gulliver's Travels* and Ireland have been many and various. In addition to those cited below, see Deane.

9. For a succinct history of these waves of land appropriation, see Foster. For a suggestion of their effect on Swift, see F. Lock, *The Politics of Gulliver's Travels*, 6–8.

10. In 1691, William Petty wrote, "The last clause of the Explanatory Act, enabled men to put new names on their respective Lands, instead of those uncouth, unintelligible ones yet upon them. And it would not be amiss if the significant part of the *Irish* Names were interpreted, where they are not, or cannot be abolished" (208).

11. For example, by Cromwell at Wexford and Drogheda in 1649.

12. Penal Laws, in full force between 1727 and 1829, but initiated long before, prohibited Catholics from becoming "members of Parliament; bearing arms . . . ; being apprentices to gunsmiths; education abroad; keeping a public school in Ireland; receiving degrees, fellowships, or scholarships at the University of Dublin," and voting (Hechter, 77).

13. I will return to the question of Swift's mixed feelings about Ireland and the Irish below. For an overview of the issues involved, see the somewhat heated exchange between Carole Fabricant and Warren Montag in *Eighteenth-Century Fiction* 8.3, 9.1, and 9.3.

14. Ehrenpreis, *Swift, The Man*, 3: 442–43.

15. Lock, *Swift's Tory Politics*, 179.

16. Lock, *The Politics of Gulliver's Travels*, 117. Examples of allegorical polit-

ical readings are Firth and Case. Critics who urge interpretation based on allusion rather than allegory include Lock and Harth.

17. Hunter, 67–68.

18. Thomas, 123, 125.

19. Pietz, "The Problem of the Fetish, I," 6; Pietz, "The Problem of the Fetish, II," 24. He goes on to say that "the understanding of the Europeans familiar with West Africa was that [fetishes] were not false gods in the traditional sense, but rather were quasi-personal divine powers associated more closely with the materiality of the sacramental object than would be an independent, immaterial demonic spirit" (38).

20. Hechter, 83.

21. Todd, 238. Todd notes references to West Indian Dwarfs, Native American Princes, and cannibals in Swift's texts, but doesn't discuss the context of eighteenth-century colonialism (246, 281). See also A. Taylor.

22. Hawes, 191. On the commodification of leisure in eighteenth-century England, see McKendrick, Brewer, and Plumb.

23. Quoted in Thomas, 128.

24. Thomas, 140, 139.

25. See Brown, *Ends of Empire*, 186; and Pollak.

26. See Kemp, 185–89.

27. This satiric strategy may be said to be typical of Swift's critique of early eighteenth-century European exchange relationships. Swift often reinforces his critique of socioeconomic systems by collapsing the distinction between the human body and the dynamics of the market. Laura Brown has illuminated this process in Swift's bawdy poetry. She argues that in these poems, "through a kind of metonymy, the products of mercantile capitalism with which women surround and adorn themselves come to be implicated with the female body itself. That is, the pernicious corruptions of an expansionist culture are so intimately and inevitably associated with the figure of the woman that they are represented as intrinsic rather than extrinsic to her." See Brown, *Ends of Empire*, 180.

28. See Clifford.

29. Pietz discusses the importance of "the category of the trifling" in "The Problem of the Fetish I," 9, and "The Problem of the Fetish II," 41.

30. Brown, *Ends of Empire*, 195–96. A number of other critics have noted the sources of Swift's descriptions of yahoos in contemporary representations of Africans. See Hawes; A. Kelly; and Rawson, "Gulliver, Marlow and the Flat-Nosed People." Brown, however, is the only one of these writers to expose the connections between racist discourse, colonial expansion, and the growth of mercantile capitalism. I return to the question of the yahoos' relation to the Catholic Irish in the last section of the chapter.

31. Critics have long noted the points of connection between *Gulliver's Travels* and *The Drapier's Letters*, particularly with regard to the Third Voyage, which was written after the controversy over Wood's halfpence. See, for example Firth; Ehrenpreis, "Dr. S***t and the Hibernian Patriot"; Rawson, "Injured Lady and the Drapier."

32. Swift, *The Drapier's Letters*, 7.

33. As Oliver Ferguson explains:

Though in title a kingdom, eighteenth-century Ireland was in fact virtually an English colony. Almost all important government and ecclesiastical positions were held by English appointees. In addition, a number of minor posts, pensions and sinecures held by non-resident Englishmen were a constant drain on the nation's economy. The country had its own parliament, but its powers were so curtailed as to make it little more than a rubber stamp for measures enacted in England. Under the terms of Poyning's Law, an act passed under the reign of Henry VII, the Irish parliament could not convene without the consent of the king, and it could pass no laws without the approval of the King and the English Privy Council. (7)

34. See Landa, "Swift's Economic Views and Mercantilism," 313–14. Also see O. Ferguson, 9, 24.

35. Foster, 161; see also Kelly.

36. On the possible allegorical significance of the floating island, see Firth, 17.

37. See Goodwin. Also see O. Ferguson, 87.

38. Here, Swift is influenced by William Molyneux (O. Ferguson, 139). It is important to realize that for Molyneux, the kingdom of Ireland was made up of Protestant settlers. In "The Case of Ireland's Being Bound by Acts of Parliament in England Stated" (1687), he states that "The Great Body of the present People of Ireland are the Progeny of the English and Britains, what from time to time have come over into this kingdom; and there remains but a mere handful of the Ancient Irish at this day, I must say, not one in a thousand" (quoted in Foster, 161).

39. Swift, *The Drapier's Letters*, 31; see also 61–62.

40. See, for example, ibid, 16–17. The Drapier imagines the multiple ways that Wood will subvert standards of value throughout the letters.

41. Ibid., 6.

42. O. Ferguson, 52.

43. Ehrenpreis, *Swift*, 3: 123; Landa, "Swift's Economic Views and Mercantilism," 331.

44. King to Annesley, September 3, 1722. Quoted in O. Ferguson, 96.

45. Swift, *The Drapier's Letters*, 135.

46. Ibid., 23.

47. Ibid., 4, 46. The endurance of the boycott as a nonviolent protest in Ireland is described in Taatgen.

48. Ibid., 11.

49. Ibid., 12, 88. See also 60. Occasionally, the debased coin has less agency, entering the body like an overdose of medicine mixed with poison (15).

50. Ibid., 63.

51. Ibid., 12.

52. Ibid., 67.

53. Claude Rawson argues that this elaborate scenario reveals that the Drapier himself is something of a projector (Rawson, "Gulliver, Marlow and the Flat-Nosed People," 28).

54. Swift, *The Drapier's Letters*, 127.

55. For an excellent reading of the way the Drapier "forges a new anticolonial rhetoric—albeit in a limited Anglo-Irish context—out of the debased coinage of Roman republicanist rhetoric and venality satire," see Aravamudan.

56. Swift, *The Drapier's Letters*, 61.

57. The relation between Swift and the persona of the Drapier has always been the subject of some debate. For example, Lock sees the Drapier as a strategic mask, allowing Swift to attack the policies of England's Whig government through a member of a typical Whig constituency, urban shopkeepers, as does Rawson (Lock, *Swift's Tory Politics*, 165; Rawson, "Gulliver, Marlow and the Flat-Nosed People," 34). Fabricant, in contrast, argues that "the Drapier who discourses with members of his own and other trades, with city and country gentlemen, with farmers and laborers, like the socially promiscuous Dean himself, emerges as a man for all classes, if not for all seasons" (*Swift's Landscape*, 253); J. C. Beckett also argues that "the Drapier, with no personal or class interest separable from that of the community in general, could speak for everyone" (157). Most critics recognize that the Drapier persona gives rise to contradictions as he writes to different audiences. See Ewald, 100–124.

58. McKeon, 208. According to McKeon, the Drapier's ideal mode of resistance is not consumer power but the "utter refusal to participate in the creation of exchange value"; although the appeal to consumer power is more pervasive, the Drapier does advocate a return to a barter system at one point (See Swift, *The Drapier's Letters*, 7). McKeon calls Swift's critique of the situation "conservative" in the sense that it is not a "negation of capitalist ideology but . . . the expression of a wish to halt the implacable juggernaut of capitalist reform at a stage that preserved, at least for property owners of a certain political and social persuasion, the best of both worlds" (209).

59. Lock, *Swift's Tory Politics*, 168.

60. Swift, *The Drapier's Letters*, 15.

61. Ibid., 24.

62. Although the theme has relatively little importance in the *The Drapier's Letters*, Swift's distrust of the emerging power of autonomous consumers can also be seen in his anger over female purchasing practices. A consuming woman has the ability to subvert the ethics of landowning men; she can destroy "any husband of any fortune in the kingdom" like a "poisonous, devouring serpent in his Bosom" by spending her money on foreign goods (Swift, *Irish Tracts*, 68). See Brown, *Ends of Empire*, 179–80.

63. Swift, *The Drapier's Letters*, 55.

64. Ibid., 64.

65. See Fabricant, *Swift's Landscape*, 35; Firth; A. Kelly; and Torchiana.

66. See Lebow.

67. Swift, "An Answer to a Paper called a Memorial of the Poor Inhabitants, Tradesmen, and Labourers of the Kingdom of Ireland" (*Irish Tracts*, 19). Hechter records similar situations in Scotland and Wales during the same period, as English mercantile policies "led to a situation where the relative value of land surpassed that of labor" (83).

68. Swift, *Irish Tracts*, 178.

69. Ehrenpreis, *Swift*, 3: 630.

70. Swift, *Irish Tracts*, 65.

71. See A. Kelly, 846. The exact nature of Swift's attitude toward the native Irish is the subject of heated debate. I tend to agree with Claude Rawson that "[i]t is not surprising that the targets of Swift's Irish satires cannot always, and are not always meant to, be clearly distinguished from one another, nor that Swift's allegiances as between the English, the Anglo-Irish and the natives are blurred and irrationally fluctuating things, whose very confusions proved the essential energies of his style" ("A Reading of 'A Modest Proposal,'" 129).

72. Swift, *Irish Tracts*, 60.

73. Ibid., 135.

74. Mercantilists believed that a dense population kept wages low and enabled the production of more manufacture for export. Ireland, of course, was prevented by England's mercantile policy from using its population to these ends. See Landa, "A Modest Proposal and Populousness"; and Wittkowsky.

75. Wittkowsky, 83.

76. Petty, 152. For interesting discussions of Petty's effect on colonial policy see, Canny, *Kingdom and Colony*; and Poovey, "Social Constitution of 'Class'."

77. Torchiana notes that the same suggestion later occurs in Bishop Berkeley's *The Querist* (197).

78. Swift, *Irish Tracts*, 174.

79. Wittkowsky, 101.

80. Petty only half-jokingly put forward such a scheme in the late seventeenth century. Swift also elaborates on how the displacement of even larger parts of the Irish population would lead to greater productivity in "An Answer to the Craftsman" (*Irish Tracts*, 175–76).

81. Most critics contend that Swift directed his anger at England's restrictive policies toward Ireland, rather than at mercantilism in general (see Landa, "Swift's Economic Views and Mercantilism"; Rawson, "A Reading of 'A Modest Proposal'"). Laura Brown, in contrast, argues that Swift launches an oblique but powerful critique of mercantilism and colonial expansion in his later writing (see *Ends of Empire*).

82. Swift, *Irish Tracts*, 109.

83. Ibid., 111.

84. It is often remarked that the plan of "A Modest Proposal" is in a way the obvious extension of Swift's ongoing appeal for home consumption. See, for example, O. Ferguson, 171.

85. See Nokes, 171; also Rawson, "Injured Lady and the Drapier," 38.

86. Lestringant, 124.

87. Swift, *The Drapier's Letters*, 103.

88. See, for example, O. Ferguson, 173; Nokes, 172.

89. Swift, *Irish Tracts*, 112.

90. See Rawson, "A Reading of 'A Modest Proposal,'" and "'Indians' and Irish."

91. Cited in Fabricant, "Swift as Irish Historian," 59. For a few earlier examples from the mid-sixteenth century, see Canny, "Ideology," 588.

92. Swift and Sheridan, *Intelligencer* 18, 198.

93. Fabricant, *Swift's Landscape*, 79: Rawson, "'Indians' and Irish," 354.

94. Foster, 34–35.        95. Swift, *Irish Tracts*, 116.

96. Ibid., 58.        97. Swift, *The Drapier's Letters*, 103.

## Chapter 3

1. Copeland, 493; Gassman, 95. Rothstein also concentrates on the novel's "formal ingenuity" in *Systems of Order and Inquiry*, 143. For an interesting recent reading focusing on generic and narratological issues, see Schellenberg, 102–17.

2. See, for example, Gassman, 98.

3. Rothstein, *Systems of Order and Inquiry*, 110. See also Iser.

4. Preston, Introduction to *The Expedition*, xxxvii.

5. On representations of the poor, see Richetti; on agricultural reform, see

Frank, 90–127; on the figure of the castrato, see Carson, "Commodification and the Figure of the Castrato"; on the fashion market, see Kowaleski-Wallace, 1–5.

6. See Crawford; Rothstein, "Scotophilia and *Humphry Clinker*"; Sorensen; and Trumpener, 262–63.

7. Smollett's engagement with colonial problems has also been noted by Giddings, and by Carson, "Britons, 'Hottentots,' Plantation Slavery and Tobias Smollett."

8. Smollett, *The Expedition of Humphry Clinker*. All subsequent quotations from this text will be given in parentheses following the citation.

9. Bunn, 305.

10. The anthropologist Fernando Ortiz has labeled this process "transculturation." Transculturation, he argues, "does not consist merely in acquiring another culture, which is what the English word *acculturation* really implies, but the process also necessarily implies the loss or uprooting of a previous culture, which could be defined as a deculturation. In addition, it carries the idea of the consequent creation of new cultural phenomena, which could be called neoculturation" (102). The concept of transculturation can account for the way elements of a supposedly subjugated and disappearing culture might enter into the culture of its conquerors. In the process of transculturation, cultures work on one another to produce new social meanings. In eighteenth-century England, commercial exchange became a primary site of transculturation as trade goods were understood and desired through images of foreign cultures.

11. Montagu, 106–7.

12. Schumpeter, 11.

13. Ibid., 13.

14. For capital accumulation, see the fortunes described on 255 and 276. For entreprenuerial energy, see the story of Martin the Highwayman's "active and enterprizing disposition" (182).

15. Martz, 176–80; Preston, "Smollett Among the Indians."

16. Ortiz, 102.            17. Axtell, 4.

18. Ibid., 302–29.         19. Plummer, 14.

20. Colden, 5.

21. For similar accounts collected from French Jesuits among the Huron Indians, see Tooker.

22. Martz, 176.

23. Here, Colden describes the scene:

The Warriors think it for their Glory, to lead [the prisoners] through all the villages of the Nations subject to them, which lie near the Road; and these, to show their affection to the *Five Nations*, and their Abhorrence of their Enemies, draw up in two Lines, through which the poor Prisoners, stark naked, must run the Gauntlet; and on this occasion, it is always observed, the Women are much more cruel than the Men. The Prisoners meet the same sad Reception when they reach their Journey's End." (9)

24. Martz is even "tempted to assign either the compilation or the editorship of this history to Smollett himself" (180).

25. *British Magazine*, June 1760: 352.

26. Quoted in E. Richards, 107.

27. Crawford, 70.                28. Trumpener, 263.

29. Brown, *Alexander Pope*, 12.    30. Bunn, 303.

31. See Anstey, *The New Bath Guide* and "An Election Ball."

32. See Brewer, *The Sinews of Power*, 174–75.

33. Smollett says much the same thing in his medical treatise on the Bath waters: "some [women] may be apprehensive of being tainted with infectious distempers; or disgusted with the nauseating appearances of the filth, which, being washed from the bodies of the patients, is left sticking to the sides of the place." See Smollett, "Essay on the external use of water," 34.

34. Smollett, *The Adventures of Roderick Random*, 187. The disturbing resemblance between this description and descriptions of the middle passage of the slave trade is reinforced by Smollett's later assertion that "Such was the oeconomy in some ships, that, rather than be at the trouble of interring the dead, their commanders ordered their men to throw the bodies overboard, many without either ballast or winding-sheet; so that numbers of human carcasses floated in the harbour, until they were devoured by sharks and carrion crows; which afforded no agreeable spectacle to those who survived" (189).

35. This war began when "Jenkins's brig, *Rebecca*, returning from Jamaica to London, was boarded by the [Spanish] guarda-costa off Havana on April 9, 1731. The brig was plundered, and one of Jenkins's ears was cut off. This outrage caused considerable stir in London, where Jenkins finally arrived on the Thames, minus his ear. The affair died down, only to be revived in 1738, when Jenkins was examined before a committee of the House of Commons. The story lost nothing in the telling; the ear was even produced for the benefit of the committee. Public indignation was aroused, and the 'War of Jenkins' Ear' ensued." See McNeil, 231.

36. Giddings, 54. Giddings continues: "Smollett's associations with both are clear—he served in the West Indian campaign [to Cartagena in 1740] and it was at Jamaica that he met and fell in love with the handsome Creole Anne Lascelles, who became his wife in 1747. She was the heiress of an estate and

slaves valued then at 3,000 pounds. He was to experience great difficulties in laying hands on that wealth" (54).

37. Although he isn't concerned with colonialism, Rothstein also points out that "water, the most important element in the book, wells up in the spas and runs through the landscapes, for drinking, bathing . . . travel, irrigation, drowning and near drowning, eliciting a poem and so forth. . . . The internal or medical, the social and the scenes of physical nature are interconnected" (*Systems of Order and Inquiry*, 131–32).

38. For a similar reading of this episode, see Zomchick, 182.

39. The term is Rothstein's; see "Scotophilia and *Humphry Clinker*."

40. *The Briton* no. 4 (July 1762). See Smollett, *Poems, Plays and the Briton*, 258–59.

41. Gassman, 100.

42. Wilson, 282, 283.

43. Sancho, 234, 186, 198. Sancho explicitly modeled his style on Sterne's.

44. Equiano, 31.

## Chapter 4

1. For other recent discussions of women's role in the campaign against slave-grown sugar, see Coleman; M. Ferguson, 182–83; Kowaleski-Wallace, 41–51; and Midgley, "Slave Sugar Boycotts."

2. "Vindication of the use of sugar," 20; on the history of sugar in British culture, see Mintz.

3. "Strictures on an Address," 6.

4. Slare, 162. On the association, dating back to the seventeenth century, between sugar and women, see K. Hall.

5. See Trotter.

6. Hillier, 7.

7. For another representation of this scene, see William Cowper, "Sweet Meat has Sour Sauce, or, the Slave Trader in the Dumps." (1788):

> When a negro his head from his victuals withdraws,
> And clenches his teeth and thrusts out his paws,
> Here's a notable engine to open his jaws . . . (*Poems*, 15)

8. Ottabah Cugoano employs a similar image of cannibalistic false compassion in his condemnation of apologists for slavery; "the sneaking advocates for slavery, though a little ashamed of their craft . . . like the monstrous crocodile [weep] over their prey with fine concessions (while gorging their own rapacious appetite) to hope for universal freedom taking place over the globe" (19).

9. Douglas, 115.
10. Ibid., 121.
11. See Drescher, *Capitalism and Anti-Slavery.*
12. See Davidoff and Hall, and C. Hall, 1–43.
13. O. Smith, 57.    14. "Strictures on an Address," 2.
15. Fox, 2.    16. Ibid., 4.
17. Mosely, 166.    18. Malthus, 117–18.
19. Gallagher, "Body Versus the Social Body," 96.
20. See Gallagher, "The Bioeconomics of *Our Mutual Friend.*"
21. Hulme, 86.
22. See Hulme, 45–89. On allegations of cannibalism in Ireland, see chapter 2.
23. The British reading public was also familiar with accounts of cannibalism in West Africa during this period. See Hilliard.
24. Cowper, *Poems*, 14.
25. W. Allen, 22; *Manchester Herald*, April 24, 1792; "Considerations addressed to Professors of Christianity of every Denomination on the Impropriety of Consuming West-India Sugar and Rum as produced by the oppressive Labour of slaves"; Coleridge, *Lectures 1795*, 248.
26. Cowper, *Poems*, 183.
27. Spacks has remarked on a similar effect in Cowper's hymns: "Cowper's frequent references to the blood of Christ make it clear that he conceives it not as an image but as a symbol: what it stands for is of course immeasurably more important than what it *is*. Yet, since the poet insists on reminding us in some detail of what precisely it *is*, readers less tradition-steeped than he are likely to have difficulty making the transition from image to [metaphorical] meaning" (170).
28. *Gentleman's Magazine*, March 1792, 260.
29. "Second Address," 1, 6. (N.B.: The cataloger of the Friends House Library in London attributes this anonymous pamphlet to Andrew Burn).
30. Ibid., 2, 5, 6.    31. Ibid., 7.
32. Ibid., 9.    33. Fox, 11.
34. Coleridge, "On the Slave Trade," 139.
35. Southey, 35.
36. Quoted in "To Everyone who uses Sugar," 1.
37. "What does your sugar cost?" 6.
38. One might speculate that this opposition had a hidden analog in the fear that if humanitarian efforts to end slavery failed, British blood might be shed as the slaves took matters into their own hands. As Southey notes, in 1797:

"There are yet two other methods remaining [after Parliament's failure] by which this traffic will probably be abolished. By the introduction of East-Indian or Maple sugar, or by the just and general rebellion of the Negros: By the vindictive justice of the African, or by the civilized Christians finding it their interest to be humane" (32).

39. Armstrong, 3.

40. Davidoff and Hall, 170.

41. "Appeal to the Hearts," 3.

42. "Address to Her Royal Highness," 2.

43. "Strictures on an Address," 5.

44. Coleridge, *Collected Works*, 2: 139.

45. Ibid., 132.

46. Ibid., 140.

47. Wollstonecraft, *Vindication*, 257.

48. Allen, 22.

49. Ibid., 23.

50. Clarkson, 154. For instances of political messages appearing on pottery and other commodities earlier in the century, see Wilson, 50, 147.

51. See Chapter 1.

52. "Appeal to the Hearts," 6.

53. "To the Women of Great Britain and Ireland," 8.

## Chapter 5

1. Prince, 52. Page numbers from this text hereafter given in parentheses.

2. Sancho, 121–22.

3. Paquet, 138.

4. See O. Smith; Laqueur, "Towards a Cultural Ecology" and *Religion and Respectability*.

5. Zaret, 21. See also Keeble; MacLean.

6. See Mack.

7. Anderson, 36.

8. Turley, 50.

9. Coleridge, *Collected Works*, 2: 139.

10. See Mullan; also Taylor.

11. Gallagher, "Nobody's Story," 275.

12. See Lovell.

13. Habermas, 50–51. On women's contribution to early eighteenth-century ideas of the public sphere, see Klein, "Gender, Conversation, and the Public Sphere."

14. See Fraser; Landes; and Ryan.

15. Clarkson, 153.

16. Hobsbawm, 71.

17. O. Smith discusses the disruption of English class structure brought about by the growth of the reading public, explaining that "the problem that worried contemporaries of the 1790s and the post-Napoleonic War period, was not so much that the lower and middle classes were reading, but that they were reading unconventional material. A significant difference exists between reading chap-books, ballads and almanacs and reading pamphlets and newspapers that challenge one's social status or criticize the government" (161).

18. On women's political participation earlier in the eighteenth century, see Wilson, 50–53. Obviously, female participation was differentiated by class. On plebeian women, see Bohstedt.

19. Prochaska, 427.

20. Corfield, 41.

21. Billington and Billington, 82.

22. Midgley, *Women Against Slavery*, 202.

23. Billington and Billington, 83.

24. Quoted in Corfield, 49.

25. Vickery, 400. Lawrence Klein reminds us that "even when theory was against them, women in the eighteenth century had public dimensions to their lives. More over, engaging in those public practices involved a consciousness that they were behaving publicly and that their behavior implied its own sanction." See "Gender and the Public/Private Distinction," 102.

26. Vickery, 401.

27. "A dialogue between a well-wisher and a friend," 7.

28. Heyrick, 11.

29. "Appeal to the Hearts," 3.

30. Association for the Universal Abolition of Slavery, 9.

31. Birmingham Female Society for the Relief of British Negro Slaves, Seventh Report, 26.

32. "The Negro Mother's Petition."

33. Dublin Ladies' Anti-Slavery Society, "Rules and Resolutions."

34. Birmingham Female Society for the Relief of British Negro Slaves, First Report, 6.

35. Sheffield Female Anti-Slavery Society, a report on the proceedings of the first year of the society, 29.

36. Malmgreen, 106.

37. Association for the Universal Abolition of Slavery, 13.

38. "Picture of Colonial Slavery," 7.

39. Spivak, 311.

40. Sheffield Female Anti-Slavery Society, Report for 1827, 2.

41. "Ladies' Petition for the Abolition of Slavery."

42. Clarkson, 60.          43. Ellis, 67–71.

44. Sterne, 578.          45. "What does your sugar cost?" 12.

46. *Westminster Review*, April–December 1887, 168. For a critique of this simple connection between the anti-slavery movement and the struggle for women's suffrage see Midgley, *Women Against Slavery*, 203–5; Billington and Billington, 109. For corresponding accounts of the relations between female antislavery activism and the beginnings of feminism in the United States, see Yellin and Sanchez-Eppler.

47. Corfield, 52.

48. Billington and Billington, 109. See also Ware; and M. Ferguson.

49. Dublin Ladies' Anti-Slavery Society, 2.

50. "A dialogue between a well-wisher and a friend," 4.

51. Midgely, "Anti-Slavery and Feminism," 350.

52. On the ramifications of those differences, see Spillers; Nussbaum.

53. Cooper, 27.

54. Sanchez-Eppler, 20.

55. For the ways in which ladies' antislavery associations were even less open to women from the laboring classes—including black women resident in Britain, than they were to slave women, see Midgely, "Anti-Slavery and Feminism," 352.

56. On the shortage of biographical or autobiographical accounts of black women in Britain during the eighteenth and nineteenth centuries, see Alexander. She instructively concludes that the shortage of such accounts is due not so much to their nonexistence as to the way that "with very few exceptions, hardly any value has been placed on acquiring and exploiting relevant printed, manuscript and archival material" (25).

57. The woman was Susanna Strickland, a poet and (later) novelist herself, and a Methodist convert. For considerations of the effects of this transcription on the content and form of Prince's narrative, see M. Ferguson, and Sharpe.

58. Paquet identifies this as one of the "customary, poetic turns of phrase that are characteristic of West Indian speech" (137).

59. Sharpe notes that Prince here avoids mentioning the large number of slaves who ran away from Turks Island, and argues that "[her] statement conforms to a logic that locates the agency for social change in England" (40)—a logic that also elides any violent, or non-abolitionist, forms of resistance to slavery. Sharpe's argument seems to hold true for a number of abolitionist texts.

60. Midgley, "Anti-Slavery and Feminism," 351. She quotes from a "Petition of the Women of Spilsby in Lincolnshire to the House of Lords" (1833).

61. Midgley, "Anti-Slavery and Feminism," 353.

62. For an interesting discussion of the respectability that authorship offered female former slaves, see Newberry.

63. Quoted in M. Ferguson, 294.

64. Ibid., 295.

## Chapter 6

1. Sharpe demonstrates the effects these codes had on *The History of Mary Prince*. Moore and Nussbaum investigate the effects of colonial ideology on representations of sexuality among white women in Britain.

2. Stewart, 209.

3. Bush, "White 'Ladies,'" 257; Beckles, "White Women and Slavery."

4. The terms "black" and "white" had little to do with skin color; in Jamaica, anyone with at least one-quarter African blood was "black"—anyone with less was "white." Although, by using these terms, I am in some ways replicating the racist discourse of the eighteenth century, I intend them to refer explicitly to eighteenth-century constructions of racial difference. See Gates.

5. Edwards, 127–28. In eighteenth-century Jamaica, the term "Creole" referred to people of European descent born in the colonies.

6. Long, 2: 274. On Long, see Fryer, 157–60.

7. Mozly, 62.                     8. See Morrissey, 125–30.

9. M. Lewis, 125.                 10. Ibid., 82.

11. Morrissey, 117.               12. Edwards, 198.

13. For a detailed analysis of the myths and realities about reproduction in the slave populations of the West Indies, see Morrissey, particularly chapters 7 and 8.

14. Barbara Bush argues that polygamy among slaves was a way of preserving their African heritage. She relies, however, on a notion of "essential black womanhood" to ground this argument. While it is important to recognize that enslaved people resisted in unexpected ways, it is equally crucial to realize that their oppressors often preferred to project agency onto slaves rather than to acknowledge that their own cruelty penetrated even the most seemingly private areas of sexuality. See Bush, "The Family Tree is not Cut." See also Morrissey, 117; and Robertson.

15. For the advantages black and mulatto women derived from relationships with white men, see M. Campbell, 50–57. "Their preference for the white man was not only based on the obvious economic reason that white men could provide them with more material comforts, but also, sexual congress with whites was a means of blanching the color of the progeny in a society where whiteness and 'superiority' were identical" (51).

16. Long, 279–80.

17. Stewart, 303.

18. Ibid., 135. The anxiety over miscegenation was more intense in the colonial Caribbean than in the antebellum United States, because white men tended to both free and educate their "colored" children, creating a powerful and visible segment of the population. See Brathwaite, chapter 12. Also see Sio.

19. Long, 330.

20. Cundall, 117.

21. Doody, 559. Lee wrote other works of fiction and drama, but derived most of her income from a school she ran in Bath with her sister Harriet.

22. See Doody; also J. Lewis; Alliston, 150–86.

23. Since the novel takes place in the sixteenth century, Jamaica is ruled by the Spanish. Moira Ferguson connects the Maroons here with Mary Queen of Scots, arguing for the novel's tacit endorsement of both forms of rebelliousness (135).

24. Lee, 2: 134.

25. Ibid., 136.

26. Ibid., 138.

27. Ibid., 143–44.

28. Ibid., 147.

29. Sypher, 183.

30. Alliston points out that sentimental ties between women fail at other points in the novel, as its heroines' sympathy ultimately belongs to their male lovers, and the patriarchal systems for which they stand (178). My reading of this episode differs from M. Ferguson's (137).

31. See Barash. Barash treats texts from the beginning of the century, but she too concludes that "an ideology of passive womanhood often smooths over the radical disorder of economic and political activity" (410).

32. C. Smith, *Letters*, 2: 57.

33. Ibid., 58.

34. Ibid., *Desmond*. Desmond points out that "if the negro . . . is a monkey, let me hazard one remark—that their very near affinity to us, is too clearly ascertained by the alliances we have formed with them" (329).

35. Ibid., *Letters*, 2: 76–77. According to Ty, this recognition of women's status as "virtual commodities" shows up with some frequency in Smith's novels (138).

36. Ibid., 114.

37. Ibid., 309.

38. Ibid., 309.

39. Ibid., 314.

40. Conway argues that "for Jacobin feminist discourse, the transgressive [female] body, like revolution, generates a narrative of change by providing a disruptive force strong enough to crack the smooth surface of convention and history" (396). Smith seems to be using the same principle here, but for conservative ends.

41. Bohls, in relation to a slightly earlier, though certainly relevant, account of a white woman in Jamaica, Janet Schaw's *Journal of a Lady of Quality . . . 1774 to 1776*, demonstrates that aesthetic ideology also works to obscure the representation of slave labor in the Caribbean (58).

42. Cundall, 86.

43. See Beckles, "White Women and Slavery in the Caribbean," for the extent to which white women did own slaves, and contribute to the running of Caribbean slave economies.

44. Stewart, 160–62.

45. Ibid., 163.

46. Prince, 204.

47. "West-Indian Sketches," 49. The observations in this pamphlet are taken from the account of Dr. George Pinkard.

48. Poovey argues that this contradiction was inherent to eighteenth-century definitions of female subjectivity, and operated more generally within English society: "even though late eighteenth-century moralists described femininity as innate, they also insisted that feminine virtues needed constant cultivation" (*Proper Lady*, 15).

49. Riland, 2.

50. T. Cooper, 27.

51. Stewart, 162.

52. Wollstonecraft. "Vindication of the Rights of Men," 76.

53. Smith, *Wanderings*, 52. Franklin argues that much of the novel engages in a critique of sentimentality (xiii).

54. Smith, *Wanderings*, 53.

55. See Stanton.

56. One might even say that this relationship to the cruelty of slavery resembles the "epistemic violence of imperialism" Gayatri Spivak analyzes in *Jane Eyre*—"the construction of a self-immolating colonial subject for the glorification of the social mission of the colonizer" ("Three Women's Texts," 270). See also Sussman.

57. Smith, *Desmond*, 6. *Desmond*, Smith's most political novel, discusses the virtues of the French Revolution. Her apology, however, may be usefully examined in terms of the other political issues she illustrates, such as slavery. On Smith's conflicted expression of radical politics, see Ty.

58. Smith to Thomas Cadell Jr. and William Davies, September 16, 1794. Quoted in Blank and Todd, xix.

59. Cowper to William Hayley, January 29, 1793. In Cowper, *Letters and Prose Writings*, 4: 281.

60. It is worth noting in this context that because Smith was still married,

she did not officially own the profits of her own labor. Book contracts were actually made up in her husband's name, although he had deserted her (see Stanton, 376–77). Smith also on occasion compared herself to a slave (see Blank and Todd, xi, xv).

61. Long, 330.

## Conclusion

1. Kinsley, 6.
2. Bruland, 18.
3. See Mills.
4. See Meier and Rudwick.
5. Quoted in Weems, 73.
6. See Bayley. He also cites some interesting earlier examples of Indian refusal/boycott of British textiles.
7. McKillen, 48.
8. See Weems, 73.
9. Rose, 8–9.
10. Ibid., 17. Rose notes that this approach appealed to more traditional women, and did not forge an alliance with groups explicitly concerned with Women's Liberation.
11. Harvey, 159.
12. Ellison, 347.
13. Of course, for some social critics, mechanical reproduction and sensibility were inimical. Ruskin, for example, describing glass-factory workers, uses the language of earlier abstention movements to describe their plight: "neither they, nor the men who draw out the rods or fuse the fragments, have the smallest occasion for the use of any single human faculty; and every young lady, therefore, who buys glass beads is engaged in the slave trade, and in a much more cruel one than that which we have so long been endeavouring to put down" (200).
14. Popkin, 252.
15. Stepan, 4. For a discussion of how this change played out in Jamaica in particular, see C. Hall, 205–55.
16. On the Governor Eyre controversy, see C. Hall, 255–96. On Stowe, see Lorimer, 82–85.
17. Malik, 99.
18. Pick, 39.
19. For an overview of recent examinations of this very difficult economic transition, see Drescher, "*Capitalism and Slavery*."
20. Lorimer, 59.
21. Sancho, 138.
22. Equiano, 159.
23. Ibid., 234.

24. Set up in the late 1780s, the Sierra Leone experiment resettled impoverished people of African descent and "Black Loyalists" living in Canada after the American War of Independence on land purchased from chieftains on the West coast of Africa. It was intended to demonstrate that Africa could become prosperous without the slave trade. In 1813, a public inquiry revealed the corruption and abuses of labor policies carried out in the colony. See Fryer, 196–203; Aravamudan.

25. Paton, 179.

26. Quoted in Carby, 215.

27. Mohanty, 199.

28. Carby, 222.

29. See Parry, 115–16. I am grateful to Marjorie Stone for sharing with me her unpublished work on the poem's contexts and manuscript versions.

30. More, ll. 5–8.

31. ll. 49–52. Cowper, *Poems*, 14.

32. Blake, 125.

33. Stepan, 1.

34. For a recent examination of this claim, see Doyle, 161.

35. Lorimer, 113. A nonsectarian building for religious, scientific, and philanthropical meetings, Exeter Hall was used by the Anti-Slavery Society and the Temperance Society, among other groups. Weinreb and Hibbert cite the following poem in reference to its reputation:

> Mr. David has since had a "serious call"
> He never drinks ale, wine, or spirits at all,
> And they say he is going to Exeter Hall
> To make a grand speech,
> And to preach and to teach
> People that "they can't brew their malt liquor too small." (270)

36. For a history of the representation of maternity in eighteenth-century colonial discourse, see Nussbaum.

37. On infanticide in *Oroonoko*, see Sussman. In *Beloved*, Toni Morrison draws on the case of Margaret Garner, an escaped slave who tried to kill her four children in 1855 (see Clemons). See also Patterson, who cites the case of Sabina Park, a slave tried for the murder of her infant. She explained by saying "she had worked enough for buckra (master) already and that she would not be plagued to raise the child . . . to work for white people" (106).

38. Mohanty, 199.

39. Quoted in Mermin, 157. The possibility of Elizabeth Barrett Browning's own mixed-race ancestry has occasionally been raised, most recently by Markus. She quotes a letter to Robert Browning, in which the poet says she would "give ten towns in Norfolk (if I had them) to own some purer lineage than that of the blood of slave!—Cursed are we from generation to generation" (106). The letter to Ruskin suggests, however, that Barrett Browning felt that it

was the slave owners who were cursed, not slaves themselves, and that she refers to her inheritance of that guilt here. We shouldn't be surprised if Elizabeth and the other Barretts worried about their racial "purity" amid the evidence of so many acknowledged mixed-race Barretts in Jamaica, however, given the prevalence of just such anxiety in representations of the Caribbean, as discussed in chapter 6. For information about "concubinage" among the Barretts in Jamaica and about their relations with the offspring of such unions, see Marks. For illuminating extended discussion of the letter quoted above, see Stone.

40. Quoted in Leighton, 98.

41. H. Cooper also discusses the significance of the song, 120.

# Bibliography

"A vindication of the use of sugar and other products of the West India islands." London: for T. Boosey, 1792.

Advertisement for William Allen, "The duty of abstaining from the use of West India produce: a speech delivered at Coachmasters Hall, Jan. 12, 1792." London: T. W. Hawkins, 1792.

Agnew, Jean-Christophe. "Coming Up For Air: Consumer Culture in Historical Perspective." In *Consumption and the World of Goods*, eds. John Brewer and Roy Porter, pp. 19–39. London: Routledge, 1993.

Alexander, Ziggi. "Let it Lie Upon the Table: The Status of Black Women's Biography in the UK." *Gender and History* 2, no. 1 (spring 1990): 22–34.

Allen, William. "The duty of abstaining from the use of West India produce: a speech delivered at Coachmasters Hall, Jan. 12, 1792." London: T. W. Hawkins, 1792.

Alliston, April. *Virtue's Faults: Correspondences in Eighteenth-Century British and French Women's Fiction.* Stanford: Stanford University Press, 1996.

"An address to Her Royal Highness the Duchess of York, Against the Use of Sugar." London: 1792.

"An answer to a pamphlet entitled: An address to the people of England against the use of West India produce." London: for W. Moon, 1791.

Anderson, Benedict. *Imagined Communities: Reflections on the Origins and Spread of Nationalism.* London: Verso, 1991 (Revised Edition).

Anstey, Christopher. "An Election Ball: in poetical letters in the Zomersetshire Dialect, from Mr. Inkle, a Freeman on Bath, to his Wife at Gloucester." Dublin: 1776.

———. *The New Bath Guide.* London: 1766.

"Appeal to the Hearts and Consciences of British Women." Leicester: 1828.

Aravamudan, Srinivas. *Tropicopolitans: Colonialism and Agency, 1688–1804.* Durham, N.C.: Duke University Press, 1999.

Arens, W. *The Man-Eating Myth: Anthropology and Anthopophagy*. Oxford: Oxford University Press, 1979.

Armstrong, Nancy. *Desire and Domestic Fiction: A Political History of the Novel*. New York and Oxford: Oxford University Press, 1987.

Association for the Universal Abolition of Slavery. "Appeal to the Christian Women of Sheffield." Sheffield: 1837.

Axtell, James. *The Invasion Within: The Contest of Cultures in Colonial North America*. Oxford: Oxford University Press, 1985.

Barash, Carol. "The Character of Difference: The Creole Woman as Cultural Mediator in Narratives About Jamaica." *Eighteenth-Century Studies* 23, no. 4 (summer 1990): 407–24.

Bayley, C. A. "The Origins of Swadeshi (home industry): Cloth and Indian Society, 1700–1930." In Arjun Appadurai, ed., *The Social Life of Things: Commodities in Cultural Perspective*, pp. 285–323. Cambridge: Cambridge University Press, 1986.

Beckett, J. C. "Swift and the Anglo-Irish Tradition." In Claude Rawson, ed., *The Character of Swift's Satire: A Revised Focus*, pp. 151–66. Newark: University of Delaware Press, 1983.

Beckles, Hilary McD. *Natural Rebels: A Social History of Enslaved and Black Women in Barbados*. New Brunswick, N.J.: Rutgers University Press, 1989.

——. "White Women and Slavery in the Caribbean." *History Workshop* 36 (autumn 1993): 66–83.

Bender, Thomas, ed. *The Antislavery Debate: Capitalism and Abolitionism as a Problem in Historical Interpretation*. Berkeley: University of California Press, 1992.

Bhabha, Homi. "Signs Taken for Wonders: Questions of Ambivalence and Authority Under a Tree Outside Delhi, May 1817." In Henry Louis Gates Jr., ed., *"Race," Writing and Difference*, pp. 144–65. Chicago: University of Chicago Press, 1987.

Billington, Louis, and Rosamund Billington. "'A Burning Zeal for Righteousness': Women and the British Anti-Slavery Movement, 1820–1860." In Jane Rendall, ed., *Equal or Different: Women's Politics 1800–1914*, pp. 82–112. Oxford: Basil Blackwell, 1987.

Birmingham Female Society for the Relief of British Negro Slaves. First Report, for 1825. Birmingham: 1826.

——. Seventh Report, 1832. Birmingham: 1832.

Blackburn, Robin. *The Overthrow of Colonial Slavery 1776–1848*. London: Verso, 1988.

Blake, William. *Complete Writings*. Edited by Geoffrey Keynes. Oxford: Oxford University Press, 1966.

Blank, Antje, and Janet Todd. Introduction to *Desmond*, by Charlotte Smith. London: Pickering & Chatto, 1997.

Bohls, Elizabeth. *Women Travel Writers and the Language of Aesthetics, 1716–1818*. Cambridge: Cambridge University Press, 1995.

Bohstedt, John. "The Myth of the Feminine Food Riot: Women as Proto-Citizens in English Community Politics, 1790–1810." In *Women and Politics in the Age of the Democratic Revolution*, ed. Harriet B. Applewhite and Darline G. Levy, pp. 21–61. Ann Arbor, Mich.: University of Michigan Press, 1990.

Brathwaite, Edward. *The Development of Creole Society in Jamaica 1770–1820*. Oxford: Clarendon Press, 1971.

Breen, Tim. "Baubles of Britain: The American and Consumer Revolutions of the Eighteenth Century." *Past and Present* 119 (May 1988): 73–109.

Brewer, John. *The Sinews of Power: War, Money and the English State, 1688–1783*. London: Unwin Hyman, 1989.

*British Magazine*, June 1760.

Brown, Laura. *Alexander Pope*. Oxford: Basil Blackwell, 1985.

———. *Ends of Empire: Women and Ideology in Early Eighteenth-Century English Literature*. Ithaca, N.Y.: Cornell University Press, 1993.

Browning, Elizabeth Barrett. *Aurora Leigh and Other Poems*. Ed. John Robert Glorney Bolton and Julia Bolton Holloway. Harmondsworth, Middlesex, England: Penguin, 1995.

Bruland, Esther Byle. "Voting with Your Checkbook: What Every Christian Should Know About Boycotts." *Christianity Today*, August 19, 1991: 18–21.

Bunn, James. "The Aesthetics of British Mercantilism." *New Literary History* 11 (1980): 303–21.

Bush, Barbara. "The Family Tree is not Cut": Women and Cultural Resistance in the British Caribbean." In Gary Okihiro, ed., *In Resistance: Studies in African, Caribbean and Afro-American History*, 117–33. Amherst: University of Massachusetts Press, 1986.

———. *Slave Women in Caribbean Society, 1650–1838*. London: Currey, 1990.

———. "White 'Ladies,' Coloured 'Favourites' and Black 'Wenches': Some Considerations on Sex, Race and Class Factors in Social Relations in White Creole Society in the British Caribbean." *Slavery and Abolition* 2 (December 1981): 245–62.

Campbell, Colin. *The Romantic Ethic and the Spirit of Modern Consumption*. London: Basil Blackwell, 1987.

Campbell, Mavis Christine. *The Dynamics of Change in a Slave Society: A*

*Sociopolitical History of the Free Coloreds of Jamaica, 1800–1865.* Cranbury, N.J.: Associated University Presses, 1976.

Canny, Nicholas. "The Ideology of English Colonization: From Ireland to America." *William and Mary Quarterly* 30 (October 1973): 575–98.

———. *Kingdom and Colony: Ireland in the Atlantic World.* Baltimore, Md.: Johns Hopkins University Press, 1987.

Carby, Hazel V. "White Woman Listen! Black Feminism and the Boundaries of Sisterhood." In Centre for Contemporary Cultural Studies, *The Empire Strikes Back: Race and Racism in 70s Britain*, pp. 212–36. London: Hutchinson, 1982.

Carson, James. "Britons, 'Hottentots,' Plantation Slavery and Tobias Smollett." *Philological Quarterly* 75, no. 4 (1996): 471–99.

———. "Commodification and the Figure of the Castrato in Smollett's *Humphry Clinker.*" *The Eighteenth Century* 33, no. 1 (1992): 1–23.

Case, Arthur E. *Four Essays on Gulliver's Travels.* Princeton, N.J.: Princeton University Press, 1945.

Centre for Contemporary Cultural Studies. *The Empire Strikes Back: Race and Racism in 70s Britain.* London: Hutchinson, 1982.

Chaudhuri, K. N. *The Trading World of Asia and the East India Company 1660–1760.* Cambridge: Cambridge University Press, 1978.

Clarkson, Thomas. *The History of the Rise, Progress and Accomplishment of the Abolition of the African Slave Trade by the British Parliament.* Philadelphia: J. Parke, 1808.

Clemons, Walter. "A Gravestone of Memories." In Barbara H. Solomon, ed., *Critical Essays on Toni Morrison's Beloved*, pp. 43–46. New York: G. K. Hall, 1998.

Clifford, James. "Gulliver's Fourth Voyage: 'Hard' and 'Soft' Schools of Interpretation." In Larry S. Champion, ed., *Quick Springs of Sense: Studies in the Eighteenth Century*, pp. 33–51. Athens: University of Georgia Press, 1974.

Colden, Cadwallader. *History of the Five Nations.* London: 1757.

Coleman, Deirdre. "Conspicuous Consumption: White Abolitionism and English Women's Protest Writing in the 1790s." *ELH* 61 (1994): 341–62.

Coleridge, Samuel Taylor. *Collected Works.* Vol. 1, *Lectures 1795: On Politics and Religion.* Ed. Lewis Patton and Peter Mann. London: Routledge, 1969.

———. "On the Slave Trade." In *The Watchman*, no. 4. In Lewis Patton, ed., *Collected Works.* Vol. 2. London: Routledge and Keegan Paul, 1970.

Colley, Linda. *Britons: Forging the Nation 1708–1837.* New Haven, Conn.: Yale University Press, 1992.

"Considerations addressed to Professors of Christianity of every Denomination on the Impropriety of Consuming West-India Sugar and Rum as produced by the oppressive Labour of slaves." London: 1792.

"Considerations against laying any new duty upon sugar." London: 1747.

"Considerations on the slave trade; and the consumption of West India produce." London: for Darton and Harvey, 1791.

Conway, Alison. "Nationalism, Revolution and the Female Body: Charlotte Smith's *Desmond*." *Women's Studies* 24 (1995): 395–409.

Cooper, Helen. *Elizabeth Barrett Browning, Woman and Artist*. Chapel Hill: University of North Carolina Press, 1988.

Cooper, Thomas. "Facts Illustrative of the Condition of the Negro Slaves in Jamaica." London: 1824.

Copeland, Edward. "*Humphry Clinker*: A Comic Pastoral Poem in Prose?" *Texas Studies in Language and Literature* 16 (fall 1974): 493–501.

Corfield, Kenneth. "Elizabeth Heyrick: Radical Quaker." In Gail Malmgreen, ed., *Religion in the Lives of English Women, 1760–1930*, pp. 41–68. Bloomington: Indiana University Press, 1986.

Cowper, William. *The Letters and Prose Writings of William Cowper*. Vol. 4. Ed. James King and Charles Ryskamp. Oxford: Clarendon Press, 1984.

———. *The Poems of William Cowper*. Vol. 3. 1785–1800. Ed. John D. Baird and Charles Ryskamp. Oxford: Clarendon Press, 1995.

Crawford, Robert. *Devolving English Literature*. Oxford: Oxford University Press, 1992.

Cugoano, Ottabah. *Thoughts and Sentiments on the Evil of Slavery* (1787). Ed. and with an introduction by Paul Edwards. London: Dawsons of Pall Mall, 1969.

Cundall, Frank, ed. *Lady Nugent's Journal: Jamaica One Hundred Years Ago*. London: The Institute of Jamaica, 1907.

Curtin, Philip D. *The Atlantic Slave Trade: A Census*. Madison: University of Wisconsin Press, 1969.

Davidoff, Lenore, and Catherine Hall. *Family Fortunes: Men and Women of the English Middle Class, 1780–1850*. Chicago: University of Chicago Press, 1987.

Davis, David Brion. *The Problem of Slavery in the Age of Revolution*. Ithaca, N.Y.: Cornell University Press, 1975.

Davis, Ralph. "English Foreign Trade 1700–1774." In W. E. Minchinton, ed., *The Growth of English Overseas Trade in the Seventeenth and Eighteenth Centuries*, pp. 99–121. London: Methuen, 1969.

Day, Thomas. "The Dying Negro: a poetical epistle, supposed to be written by a Black (Who lately shot himself on board a vessel in the river Thames;) to his intended Wife." London: 1773.

Deane, Seamus. "Swift and the Anglo-Irish Intellect." *Eighteenth-Century Ireland* 1 (1986): 9–22.

Defoe, Daniel. *The Life and Surprizing Adventures of Robinson Crusoe.* Oxford: Oxford University Press, 1976.

"A dialogue between a well-wisher and a friend to the slaves in the British colonies, by a Lady." London: circa 1828.

Doody, Margaret Anne. "Deserts, Ruins and Troubled Waters: Female Dreams in Fiction and the Development of the Gothic Novel." *Genre* 10, no. 4 (winter 1977): 529–72.

Douglas, Mary. *Purity and Danger: An Analysis of Concepts of Pollution and Taboo.* New York: Frederick A. Praeger, 1966.

Doyle, Laura. "The Folk, The Nobles and the Novel: The Racial Subtext of Sentimentality." *Narrative* 3, no. 2 (May 1995): 161–87.

Drescher, Seymour. *Capitalism and Anti-Slavery: British Mobilization in Comparative Perspective.* New York: Macmillan, 1987.

———. "*Capitalism and Slavery* after Fifty Years." *Slavery and Abolition* 18, no. 3 (December 1997): 212–27.

———. *Econocide: British Slavery in the Era of Abolition.* Pittsburgh, Pa.: University of Pittsburgh Press, 1977.

Dublin Ladies' Anti-Slavery Society. "Rules and Resolutions." With Lists of district treasurers, committees and secretaries and of subscribers. Dublin: 1828. Quoted by permission of the John Rylands Library, Manchester.

Edwards, Bryan. *The History civil and commercial of the British Colonies in the West Indies.* London: 1798.

Ehrenpreis, Irvin. "Dr. S***t and the Hibernian Patriot." In Roger McHugh and Philip Edwards, eds., *Jonathan Swift: A Dublin Tercentenary Tribute,* pp. 24–27. Dublin: Dolman, 1967.

———. *Swift: The Man, His Works, and the Age.* 3 vols. Cambridge, Mass.: Harvard University Press, 1983.

Ellis, Markman. *The Politics of Sensibility: Race, Gender and Commerce in the Sentimental Novel.* Cambridge: Cambridge University Press, 1996.

Ellison, Julie. "A Short History of Liberal Guilt." *Critical Inquiry* 22 (winter 1996): 344–71.

Eltis, David. *Economic Growth and the Ending of the Transatlantic Slave Trade.* New York and London: Oxford University Press, 1989.

———, and James Walvin, eds. *The Abolition of the Atlantic Slave Trade:*

*Origins and Effects in Europe, Africa, and the Americas.* Madison: University of Wisconsin Press, 1981.

Emerson, Robin. *British Teapots and Tea-Drinking 1700–1850.* London: HMSO, 1992.

Equiano, Olaudah. *The Interesting Narrative of the Life of Olaudah Equiano, or Gustavus Vassa, the African, Written by Himself* (1789). Ed. Vincent Carretta. Harmondsworth: Penguin, 1995.

Ewald, Walter Bragg Jr. *The Masks of Jonathan Swift.* New York: Russell & Russell, 1954.

Fabricant, Carole. "Swift as Irish Historian." In Christopher Fox and Brenda Tooley, eds., *Walking Naboth's Vineyard: New Studies of Swift*, pp. 40–73. Notre Dame, Ind.: University of Notre Dame Press, 1995.

———. *Swift's Landscape.* Baltimore, Md.: Johns Hopkins University Press, 1982.

Ferguson, Moira. *Subject to Others: British Women Writers and Colonial Slavery, 1670–1834.* London: Routledge, 1992.

Ferguson, Oliver. *Jonathan Swift and Ireland.* Urbana: University of Illinois Press, 1962.

Ferris, Ina. *The Achievement of Literary Authority: Gender, History and the Waverley Novels.* Ithaca, N.Y.: Cornell University Press, 1991.

Firth, Sir Charles. *The Political Significance of Gulliver's Travels.* Oxford: Oxford University Press, 1919.

Foster, R. F. *Modern Ireland: 1600–1972.* London and New York: Penguin, 1989.

Foucault, Michel. *The History of Sexuality: An Introduction.* Trans. Robert Hurley. Harmondsworth, Middlesex: Penguin, 1984.

Fox, William. "An address to the People of Great Britain, on the utility of refraining from the use of West India Sugar and Rum." London: For M. Gurney, 1791.

Frank, Judith. *Common Ground: Eighteenth-Century Satiric Fiction and the Poor.* Stanford: Stanford University Press, 1997.

Frankenberg, Ruth. *White Women, Race Matters: The Social Construction of Whiteness.* Minneapolis: University of Minnesota Press, 1993.

Franklin, Caroline. Introduction to *The Wanderings of Warwick* by Charlotte Smith. London: Routledge/Thoemmes, 1992.

Fraser, Nancy. "Rethinking the Public Sphere: A Contribution to the Critique of Actually Existing Democracy." In Craig Calhoun, ed., *Habermas and the Public Sphere*, pp. 109–43. Cambridge, Mass.: MIT Press, 1992.

Fryer, Peter. *Staying Power: The History of Black People in Britain.* London: Pluto, 1984.

Gallagher, Catherine. "The Bioeconomics of *Our Mutual Friend*." In David Simpson, ed., *Subject to History: Ideology, Class and Gender*, pp. 47–65. Ithaca, N.Y.: Cornell University Press, 1991.

———. "The Body Versus the Social Body in the Works of Thomas Malthus and Henry Mayhew." *Representations* 14 (spring 1986): 83–106.

———. "Nobody's Story: Gender, Property and the Rise of the Novel." *Modern Language Quarterly* 53.3 (1992): 263–77.

Gassman, Byron. "*Humphry Clinker* and the Two Kingdoms of George III." *Criticism* 16 (1974): 95–108.

Gates, Henry Louis Jr. "Writing 'Race' and the Difference it Makes." In *"Race," Writing and Difference*, ed. Henry Louis Gates Jr., pp. 1–21. Chicago: University of Chicago Press, 1987.

*Gentleman's Magazine*, March 1792.

Giddings, Robert. "Matthew Bramble's Bath: Smollett and the West Indian Connection." In Alan Bold, ed. *Smollett: Author of the First Distinction*, pp. 47–64. London: Vision, 1982.

Goodwin, A. "Wood's Halfpence." *The English Historical Review* 51 (1936): 647–74.

Griffiths, Sir Percival. *The History of the Indian Tea Industry*. London: Weidenfeld and Nicolson, 1967.

Habermas, Jürgen. *The Structural Transformation of the Public Sphere: An Inquiry into a Category of Bourgeois Society*. Trans. Thomas Burger with the assistance of Frederick Lawrence. Cambridge, Mass.: MIT Press, 1995.

Hall, Catherine. *White, Male and Middle Class: Explorations in Feminism and History*. Cambridge: Polity Press, 1992.

Hall, Kim F. "Culinary Spaces, Colonial Spaces: The Gendering of Sugar in the Seventeenth Century." In Valerie Traub, M. Lindsay Kaplan, and Dympna Callaghan, eds., *Feminist Readings of Early Modern Culture: Emerging Subjects*, pp. 168–90. Cambridge: Cambridge University Press, 1996.

Hanway, Jonas. "An Essay on Tea: Considered as Pernicious to Health; Obstructing Industry; and Impoverishing the Nation: with a short account of its growth and great consumption in these kingdoms: with several political reflections in twenty-five letters addressed to two ladies." London: 1756.

Harth, Philip. "The Problem of Political Allegory in *Gulliver's Travels*." *Modern Philology* 73 (May 1976): S40–S47.

Harvey, David. *The Condition of Postmodernity: An Enquiry in the Origins of Cultural Change*. Oxford: Basil Blackwell, 1989.

Haskell, Thomas. "Capitalism and the Humanitarian Sensibility." *American Historical Review* 90 (April and June 1985): 339–62, 547–67.

Hawes, Clement. "Three Times Round the Globe: Gulliver and Colonial Discourse." *Cultural Critique* 18 (1991): 187–214.

Hechter, Michael. *Internal Colonialism: The Celtic Fringe in British National Development, 1536–1966.* Berkeley: University of California Press, 1975.

Heyrick, Elizabeth. "Apology for Ladies' Anti-Slavery Associations." London: 1828.

Hilliard, Raymond F. "*Clarissa* and Ritual Cannibalism." *PMLA* 105, no. 5 (October 1990): 1083–98.

Hillier, Richard. "A Vindication of the Address to the People of Great Britain, on the use of West India Produce: with some observations and facts relative to the situation of slaves: in a reply to a female apologist for slavery." London: 1791.

Hobsbawm, E. J. *Industry and Empire: An Economic History of Britain since 1750.* London: Weidenfeld and Nicolson, 1968.

Hulme, Peter. *Colonial Encounters: Europe's Experience of the Native Caribbean, 1492–1797.* London: Methuen, 1982.

Hunt, Lynn. "The Virtues of Disciplinarity." *Eighteenth-Century Studies* 28, no. 1 (fall 1994): 1–9.

Hunter, J. Paul. "*Gulliver's Travels* and the Novel." In Frederick N. Smith, ed., *The Genres of Gulliver's Travels*, pp. 56–75. Newark: University of Delaware Press, 1990.

Innes, William. "The Slave Trade Indispensable?" London: 1789.

Iser, Wolfgang. *The Implied Reader.* Baltimore: Johns Hopkins University Press, 1974.

Johnson, Claudia L. *Equivocal Beings: Politics, Gender and Sentimentality in the 1790s, Wollstonecraft, Radcliffe, Burney, Austen.* Chicago: The University of Chicago Press, 1995.

Kaul, Suvir. "Why Selima Drowns: Thomas Gray and the Domestication of the Imperial Ideal." *PMLA* 105, no. 2 (1990): 223–32.

Kearney, Hugh. *The British Isles: A History of Four Nations.* Cambridge: Cambridge University Press, 1989.

Keeble, N. H. *The Literary Culture of Nonconformity in Later Seventeenth-Century England.* Athens: University of Georgia Press, 1987.

Kelly, Ann Cline. "Swift's Explorations of Slavery in Houyhnhnmland and Ireland." *PMLA* 91 (1976): 846–55.

Kelly, P. "The Irish Woollen Export Prohibition Act of 1699: Kearney Re-visited." *Irish Economic and Social History* 7 (1980): 22–43.

Kemp, Martin. "'Wrought by No Artist's Hand': The Natural, The Artificial, the Exotic and the Scientific in Some Artifacts from the Renaissance." In *Reframing the Renaissance: Visual Culture in Europe and Latin America,*

1450–1650, ed. Claire Farago, pp. 177–97. New Haven, Conn.: Yale University Press, 1995.

Kinsley, Michael. "Sour Grapes." *The New Republic*, December 10, 1990: 6, 45.

Klein, Lawrence. "Gender, Conversation and the Public Sphere in Early Eighteenth-Century England." In Judith Still and Michael Worton, eds., *Textuality and Sexuality: Reading Theories and Practices*, pp. 100–16. New York: St. Martin's, 1993.

———. "Gender and the Public/Private Distinction in the Eighteenth Century: Some Questions About Evidence and Analytic Procedure." *Eighteenth-Century Studies* 29.1 (fall 1995): 97–111.

Kowaleski-Wallace, Elizabeth. *Consuming Subjects: Women, Shopping and Business in the Eighteenth Century*. New York: Columbia University Press, 1997.

Ladies' Negro's Friend Society of Birmingham Seventh Annual Report. Birmingham: 1832.

"Ladies' Petition for the Abolition of Slavery." London: 1838.

Landa, Louis. "A Modest Proposal and Populousness." *Modern Philology* 40 (1942): 161–70.

———. "Pope's Belinda, the General Emporie of the World, and the Wondrous Worm." *South Atlantic Quarterly* 70 (1971): 215–35.

———. "Swift's Economic Views and Mercantilism." *Journal of English Literary History* 10 (1943): 310–35.

Landes, Joan. "The Public and the Private Sphere: A Feminist Reconsideration." In *Feminists Read Habermas: Gendering the Subject of Discourse*, pp. 91–117. Ed. and with an introduction by Johanna Meehan. London: Routledge, 1995.

Laqueur, Thomas. *Religion and Respectability: Sunday Schools and Working Class Culture, 1780–1850*. New Haven, Conn.: Yale University Press, 1976.

———. "Towards a Cultural Ecology of Literacy in England, 1650–1850." In Daniel P. Resnick, ed., *Literacy in Historical Perspective*, Washington, D.C.: Library of Congress, 1983.

Lebow, Ned. "British Historians and Irish History." *Eire-Ireland* 8 (1973): 3–38.

Lee, Sophia. *The Recess: Or A Tale of Other Times*. 2 vols. London: 1785. Rpt. New York: Arno Press, 1972.

Leighton, Angela. *Victorian Women Poets: Writing Against the Heart*. Charlottesville and London: University Press of Virginia, 1992.

Lestringant, Frank. "Travels in Eucharistia: Formosa and Ireland from George Psalmanaazaar to Jonathan Swift." *Yale French Studies* 86 (1994): 109–25.

Lewis, Jayne Elizabeth. "'Ev'ry Lost Relation': Historical Fictions and

Sentimental Incidents in Sophia Lee's *The Recess.*" *Eighteenth-Century Fiction* 7, no. 2 (January 1995): 165–84.

Lewis, Matthew. *Journal of a West Indian Proprietor, kept during a residence on the island of Jamaica.* London: 1834.

Lock, F. P. *The Politics of Gulliver's Travels.* Oxford: Clarendon, 1980.

———. *Swift's Tory Politics.* Newark: University of Delaware Press, 1983.

Long, Edward. *The History of Jamaica.* 2 vols. London: 1774.

Lorimer, Douglas A. *Colour, Class and the Victorians: English Attitudes to the Negro in the Mid-Nineteenth Century.* Leicester: Leicester University Press, 1978.

Lovejoy, Paul E. "The Volume of the Atlantic Slave Trade: A Synthesis." *Journal of African History* 23 (1982): 474–500.

Lovell, Terry. *Consuming Fiction.* London: Verso, 1987.

Mack, Phyllis. *Visionary Women: Ecstatic Prophecy in Seventeenth-Century England.* Berkeley: University of California Press, 1992.

Maclean, Gerald. "Literacy, Class and Gender in Restoration England." *Text* 7 (1995): 307–35.

Malik, Kenan. *The Meaning of Race: Race, History and Culture in Western Society.* New York: New York University Press, 1996.

Malmgreen, Gail. "Anne Knight and the Radical Subculture." *Quaker History* (fall 1982): 106.

Malthus, Thomas. *An Essay on the Principle of Population.* Harmondsworth, Middlesex, England: Penguin, 1970.

*Manchester Herald*, April 24, 1792.

Mandell, Laura. "Bawds and Merchants: Engendering Capitalist Desires." *ELH* 59 (1992): 107–23.

Markley, Robert. "Sentimentality as Performance: Shaftesbury, Sterne and the Theatrics of Virtue." In *The New Eighteenth Century: Theory, Politics, English Literature*, ed. Felicity Nussbaum and Laura Brown, pp. 210–30. New York: Methuen, 1987.

Marks, Jeannette. *The Family of the Barrett.* New York: The Macmillan Company, 1938.

Markus, Julia. *Dared and Done: The Marriage of Elizabeth Barrett and Robert Browning.* New York: Alfred A. Knopf, 1995.

Martz, Louis. *The Later Career of Tobias Smollett.* London: Archon, 1967.

Marx, Karl. *Capital.* Trans. Eden Paul and Cedar Paul. London: Dent, Everyman's Library, 1930.

McKendrick, Neil. "Home Demand and Economic Growth: A New View of the Role of Women and Children in the Industrial Revolution." In

*Historical Perspectives: Studies in English Thought and Society*, pp. 152–211. London: Europa, 1974.

McKendrick, Neil, John Brewer, and J. H. Plumb. *The Birth of a Consumer Society: The Commercialization of Eighteenth-Century England*. London: Europa, 1982.

McKeon, Michael. *The Origins of the English Novel, 1600–1740*. Baltimore, Md.: The Johns Hopkins University Press, 1987.

McKillen, Elizabeth. "American Labor, the Irish Revolution, and the Campaign for a Boycott of British Goods: 1916–1924." *Radical History Review* 61 (winter 1995): 35–61.

McNeil, David. *The Grotesque Depiction of War and the Military in Eighteenth-Century English Fiction*. Cranbury, N.J.: Associated University Presses, 1990.

Meier, August, and Elliot Rudwick. "The Boycott Movement Against Jim Crow Streetcars in the South, 1900–1906." *Journal of American History* 55 (March 1969): 756–75.

Mermin, Dorothy. *Elizabeth Barrett Browning: The Origins of a New Poetry*. Chicago: University of Chicago Press, 1989.

Midgley, Clare. "Anti-Slavery and Feminism in Nineteenth-Century Britain." Gender and History 5.3 (autumn 1993): 343–63.

———. "Slave Sugar Boycotts, Female Activism and the Domestic Base of British Anti-Slavery Culture." *Slavery and Abolition* 17, no. 3 (December 1996): 137–62.

———. *Women Against Slavery: The British Campaigns, 1780–1870*. London: Routledge, 1992.

Mills, Claudia. "Should We Boycott Boycotts?" *Journal of Social Philosophy* 27, no. 3 (winter 1996): 136–48.

Mintz, Sidney. *Sweetness and Power: The Place of Sugar in Modern History*. New York: Viking, 1985.

Mohanty, Chandra Talpade. "Feminist Scholarship and Colonial Discourse." In Patrick Williams and Laura Chrisman, eds., *Colonial Discourse and Post-Colonial Theory: A Reader*, pp. 259–364. New York: Columbia University Press, 1994.

Montag, Warren. *The Unthinkable Swift: The Spontaneous Philosophy of a Church of England Man*. London: Verso, 1994.

Montagu, Lady Mary Wortley. *The Nonsense of Commonsense*, no. 1. In Robert Halsband and Isobel Grundy, eds., *Essays and Poems and Simplicity, a Comedy*, pp. 105–108. Oxford: Oxford University Press, 1993.

Moore, Lisa. *Dangerous Intimacies*. Durham, N.C.: Duke University Press, 1997.

More, Hannah. "Slavery, A Poem." (1788). In *Eighteenth-Century Women Poets*, ed. Roger Lonsdale, p. 330. Oxford: Oxford University Press, 1990.

Morrissey, Marietta. *Slave Women in the New World: Gender Stratification in the Caribbean.* Lawrence: University of Kansas Press, 1989.

Mosely, Benjamin. *A Treatise on Sugar.* London: 1800.

Mozly, Geraldine, ed. *Letters to Jane from Jamaica 1788–1796.* London: The Institute of Jamaica, 1938.

Mullan, John. *Sentiment and Sociability: The Language of Feeling in the Eighteenth Century.* Oxford: Clarendon Press, 1988.

"The Negro Mother's petition to the Ladies of Bristol; That in Pity to the Poor Slaves, They would entreat their Fathers, Husbands, Brothers and Sons to vote for Edward Protheroe, Esq." Handbill in the Bristol University Library, Pinney Collection.

Newberry, Michael. "Eaten Alive: Slavery and Celebrity in Antebellum America." *ELH* 61, no. 1 (spring 1994): 159–89.

Nokes, David. "The Radical Conservatism of Swift's Irish Pamphlets." *The British Journal for Eighteenth-Century Studies* 7 (1984): 170–76.

"No rum!—No sugar! or, the voice of blood; being half an hour's conversation between a Negro and an English gentleman, showing the horrible nature of the slave trade and pointing out an easy, effectual method of terminating it, by an act of the people." London: for L. Wayland, 1792.

*Northampton Mercury.* December 24, 1791.

Nuermberger, Ruth Kettring. *The Free Produce Movement: A Quaker Protest Against Slavery.* Durham, N.C.: Duke University Press, 1942.

Nussbaum, Felicity A. *Torrid Zones: Maternity, Sexuality and Empire in Eighteenth-Century English Narratives.* Baltimore, Md.: Johns Hopkins University Press, 1995.

"On sophistical arguments against a conscientious disuse of sugar produced by slave labour." Dublin: n.d. (1790s).

Ortiz, Fernando. *Cuban Counterpoint: Tobacco and Sugar.* New York: Alfred A. Knopf, 1947.

Paquet, Sandra Pouchet. "The Heartbeat of a West Indian Slave: *The History of Mary Prince.*" *African American Review* 26, no. 1 (1992): 131–46.

Parry, Ann. "Sexual Exploitation and Freedom: Religion, Race and Gender in Elizabeth Barrett Browning's 'The Runaway Slave at Pilgrim's Point.'" *Studies in Browning and His Circle* 16 (1988): 114–28.

Parry, Benita. "Problems in Current Theories of Colonial Discourse." *The Oxford Literary Review* 9, nos. 1–2 (1987): 27–58.

Paton, Diana. "Decency, Dependence, and the Lash: Gender and the British

Debate over Slave Emancipation, 1830–1834." *Slavery and Abolition*, 17, no. 3 (December 1996): 163–84.

Patterson, Orlando. *The Sociology of Slavery*. Rutherford, Madison, Teaneck, N.J.: Farleigh Dickinson University Press, 1967.

Petty, William. *The Political Anatomy of Ireland*. In *The Economic Writings of Sir William Petty*. Vol. 1. Ed. Charles Henry Hull. Cambridge: Cambridge University Press, 1899.

Pick, Daniel. *Faces of Degeneration: A European Disorder, c. 1848–1918*. Cambridge: Cambridge University Press, 1989.

"Picture of Colonial Slavery in the Year 1828, Addressed especially to the Ladies of Great Britain." London: 1828.

Pietz, William. "The Problem of the Fetish, I." *Res* 9 (spring 1985): 5–17.

———. "The Problem of the Fetish, II." *Res* 13 (spring 1987): 23–45.

Plummer, Rachel. *The Narrative of the Capture and Subsequent Sufferings of Mrs. Rachel Plummer: During a Captivity of Twenty-one Months among the Comanche Indians; With a Sketch of Their Manners, Customs, Laws, &c., &.* (1839); Waco, Tex.: Texian Press, 1968.

Pollak, Ellen. *The Poetics of Sexual Myth: Gender and Ideology in Swift and Pope*. Chicago: University of Chicago Press, 1985.

Poovey, Mary. *The Proper Lady and the Woman Writer: Ideology as Style in the Works of Mary Wollstonecraft, Mary Shelley and Jane Austen*. Chicago: University of Chicago Press, 1984.

———. "The Social Constitution of 'Class': Toward a History of Classificatory Thinking." In Wai Chee Dimock and Michael T. Gilmore, eds., *Rethinking Class: Literary Studies and Social Formations*, 15–56. New York: Columbia University Press, 1994.

Pope, Alexander. *The Poetry and Prose of Alexander Pope*. Ed. Aubrey Williams. Boston: Houghton Mifflin, 1969.

Popkin, Richard. "The Philosophical Basis of Eighteenth-Century Racism." *Studies in Eighteenth-Century Culture* 3 (1973): 245–62.

Porter, Roy. *English Society in the Eighteenth Century*. Harmondsworth, Middlesex: Penguin, 1990.

Preston, Thomas. Introduction to *The Expedition of Humphry Clinker* by Tobias Smollett. Athens: University of Georgia Press, 1990.

———. "Smollett Among the Indians." *Philological Quarterly* 61 (summer 1982): 231–41.

Prince, Mary. *The History of Mary Prince, A West Indian Slave, Related by Herself*. Ed. Moira Ferguson. London: Pandora, 1987.

Prochaska, F. K. *Women and Philanthropy in Nineteenth-Century England*. Oxford: Oxford University Press, 1980.

Rawson, Claude. "Gulliver, Marlow and the Flat-Nosed People: Colonial Oppression and Race in Satire and Fiction." *Dutch Quarterly Review of Anglo-American Letters* 13, nos. 3 and 4 (1983): 162–78; 282–99.

———. "'Indians' and Irish: Montaigne, Swift, and the Cannibal Question." *MLQ* 53, no. 3 (1992): 263–99.

———. "The Injured Lady and the Drapier: A Reading of Swift's Irish Tracts," *Prose Studies* 3 (1980): 15–43.

———. "A Reading of 'A Modest Proposal.'" In *Order from Confusion Sprung: Studies in Eighteenth-Century Literature from Swift to Cowper*, pp. 121–47. London: Allen & Unwin, 1985.

Richards, Eric. "Scotland and the Uses of the Atlantic Empire." In *Strangers Within the Realm: Cultural Margins of the First British Empire*, ed. Bernard Bailyn and Philip D. Morgan, pp. 67–115. Chapel Hill, N.C.: University of North Carolina Press, 1991.

Richardson, David. "The Slave Trade, Sugar, and British Economic Growth, 1748–1776." In *British Capitalism and Caribbean Slavery: The Legacy of Eric Williams*, ed. Barbara Solow and Stanley Engerman, pp. 103–35. Cambridge: Cambridge University Press, 1987.

Richardson, Samuel. *Pamela.* New York: W. W. Norton, 1958.

Richetti, John. "Representing an Under Class: Servants and Proletarians in Fielding and Smollett." In *The New Eighteenth Century: Theory, Politics, English Literature*, ed. Felicity A. Nussbaum and Laura Brown, pp. 84–98. New York: Methuen, 1987.

Riland, Rev. John. *Memoirs of a West-India Planter.* London: Hamilton, Adams, 1827.

Robertson, Claire. "The Perils of Autonomy." *Gender and History* 3, no. 1 (spring 1991): 91–98.

Rose, Margaret. "From the Fields to the Picket Line." *Labor History* 31, no. 3 (1990): 271–93.

Rothstein, Eric. "Scotophilia and *Humphry Clinker*: The Politics of Beggary, Bugs and Buttocks." *University of Toronto Quarterly* 52, no. 1 (fall 1982): 63–78.

———. *Systems of Order and Inquiry in Later Eighteenth-Century Fiction.* Berkeley: University of California Press, 1975.

Ruskin, John. *The Stones of Venice.* In *Selected Writings*, ed. Philip Davis, pp. 171–258. London: Everyman, 1995.

Ryan, Mary. "Gender and Public Access: Women's Politics in Nineteenth-Century America." In *Habermas and the Public Sphere*, ed. Craig Calhoun, pp. 259–89. Cambridge, Mass.: MIT Press, 1992.

Said, Edward. *Orientalism.* Harmondsworth, Middlesex: Penguin, 1985.

———. *The World, The Text, and the Critic.* Cambridge: Harvard University Press, 1983.

Sanchez-Eppler, Karen. *Touching Liberty: Abolition, Feminism, and the Politics of the Body.* Berkeley: University of California Press, 1993.

Sancho, Ignatius. *The Letters of Ignatius Sancho.* Ed. Paul Edwards and Polly Rewt. Edinburgh: Edinburgh University Press, 1994.

Schellenberg, Betty. *The Conversational Circle: Rereading the British Novel, 1740–1775.* Lexington: The University Press of Kentucky, 1996.

Schumpeter, Elizabeth B. *English Overseas Trade Statistics 1697–1808.* Oxford: Oxford University Press, 1960.

*Scots Magazine* (April 1788).

"A Second Address to the People of Great Britain: containing a new and most powerful argument to abstain from the use of West Indian Sugar, by an Eye Witness to the facts related." Rochester: 1792.

Sekora, John. *Luxury: The Concept in British Thought, Eden to Smollett.* Baltimore, Md.: Johns Hopkins University Press, 1977.

Shammas, Carole. *The Pre-industrial Consumer in England and America.* Oxford: Clarendon, 1990.

Shapiro, Susan C. "'Yon Plumed Dandebrat': Male 'Effeminancy' in English Satire and Criticism." *Review of English Studies* (new series) 39 (1988): 400–12.

Sharpe, Jenny. "'Something Akin to Freedom': The Case of Mary Prince." *Differences* 8, no. 1 (1996): 31–55.

Sheffield Female Anti-Slavery Society. A report on the proceedings of the first year of the society. Sheffield: 1825.

———. Report for 1827. Sheffield: 1827.

Shyllon, Folarin. *Black People in Britain, 1555–1833.* London: Oxford University Press, 1977.

Sio, Arnold. "Race, Class and Miscegenation: The Free Coloured of Jamaica and Barbados." *Caribbean Studies* 16, no. 1 (April 1976): 5–22.

Slare, Frederick. *A Vindication of Sugars against the Charge of Dr. Willis, other Physicians and common Prejudices. Dedicated to the Ladies.* London: 1715.

Smith, Adam. *An Inquiry into the Nature and Causes of the Wealth of Nations.* 2 vols. Oxford: Clarendon, 1976.

Smith, Charlotte. *Desmond.* Ed. and with an introduction by Antje Blank and Janet Todd. London: Pickering & Chatto, 1997.

———. *Letters of a Solitary Wanderer.* 2 vols. London: 1800.

———. *The Wanderings of Warwick.* London: J. Bell, 1794.

Smith, Olivia. *The Politics of Language, 1791–1819.* Oxford: Clarendon, 1984.

Smollett, Tobias. *The Adventures of Roderick Random*. Oxford: Oxford University Press, 1979.

————. "An essay on the external use of water, in a letter to Dr. \* \* \* \*." London: 1767.

———. *The Expedition of Humphry Clinker*. Ed. Thomas Preston and O. M. Brack Jr. Athens: The University of Georgia Press, 1990.

———. *Poems, Plays and the Briton*. Ed. O. M. Brack Jr. Athens: University of Georgia Press, 1993.

Solow, Barbara, and Stanley Engerman, eds. *British Capitalism and Caribbean Slavery: The Legacy of Eric Williams*. Cambridge: Cambridge University Press, 1987.

Sorensen, Janet. "Women, Celts and Hollow Voices: Tobias Smollett as Broker of Anglo-British Linguistic Identities." Manuscript.

Southey, Robert. Sonnet III in "Poems on the Slave Trade." In *Poems*. London: 1797. Rpt. Woodstock Books: Oxford, New matter copyright, 1989.

Spacks, Patricia Meyer. *The Poetry of Vision: Five Eighteenth-Century Poets*. Cambridge, Mass: Harvard University Press, 1967.

Spillers, Hortense J. "Mama's Baby, Papa's Maybe: An American Grammar Book." *diacritics* 17.2 (summer 1987): 65–73.

Spivak, Gayatri Chakravorty. "Can the Subaltern Speak?" In *Marxism and the Interpretation of Culture*, ed. Cary Nelson and Lawrence Grossberg, pp. 271–313. Chicago: University of Illinois Press, 1988.

———. "Three Women's Texts and a Critique of Imperialism." In Henry Louis Gates Jr., ed., *"Race," Writing and Difference*, pp. 262–81. Chicago: University of Chicago Press, 1986.

Stanton, Judith Phillips. "Charlotte Smith's 'Literary Business': Income, Patronage and Indigence." *The Age of Johnson* 1 (1987): 375–401.

Staves, Susan. "A Few Kind Words for the Fop." *Studies in English Literature* 22 (summer 1982): 413–28.

Stepan, Nancy. *The Idea of Race in Science: Great Britain 1800–1960*. Hamden, Conn.: Archon, 1982.

Sterne, Lawrence. *The Life and Opinions of Tristram Shandy*. London: Penguin, 1967.

Stewart, John. *An Account of Jamaica and its Inhabitants*. London: 1808.

Stone, Marjorie. "Tracking Elizabeth Barrett Browning's 'Slave': Manuscripts, Contexts and Contemporary Feminist Praxis." Manuscript.

"Strictures on an Address to the People of Great Britain, on the propriety of abstaining from West India sugar and rum." London: For T. Boosey, 1792.

Sussman, Charlotte. "The Other Problem with Women: Reproduction and

Slave Culture in Aphra Behn's *Oroonoko*." In *Rereading Aphra Behn: History, Theory and Criticism*, ed. Heidi Hutner, pp. 212–34. Charlottesville: University of Virginia Press, 1993.

Swift, Jonathan. *The Drapier's Letters and Other Works: 1724–25*. Ed. Herbert Davis. Oxford: Basil Blackwell, 1966.

———. *Gulliver's Travels and Other Writings*. Ed. Louis Landa. Boston: Houghton Mifflin, 1960.

———. *Irish Tracts 1720–1723 and Sermons*. Ed. Herbert Davis and Louis Landa. Oxford: Basil Blackwell, 1968.

———. *Irish Tracts 1728–1733*. Ed. Herbert Davis. Oxford: Basil Blackwell, 1955.

———, and Thomas Sheridan. *The Intelligencer*. Ed. James Wooley. Oxford: Clarendon, 1992.

Sypher, Wylie. *Guinea's Captive Kings: British Anti-Slavery Literature in the Eighteenth Century*. Chapel Hill: University of North Carolina Press, 1942.

Taatgen, H. A. "The Boycott in the Irish Civilizing Process." *Anthropological Quarterly* (1992): 163–76.

Taylor, Aline MacKenzie. "Sights and Monsters and Gulliver's Voyage to Brobdingnag." *Tulane Studies in English* 7 (1957): 29–82.

Taylor, John Tinnon. *Early Opposition to the English Novel: The Popular Reaction for 1760–1830*. New York: King's Crown Press, 1943.

Thomas, Nicholas. *Entangled Objects: Exchange, Material Culture and Colonialism in the Pacific*. Cambridge, Mass.: Harvard University Press, 1991.

Thompson, E. P. *The Making of the English Working Class*. New York: Vintage Books, 1966.

"To Everyone who uses Sugar." London: n.d. Quoted by permission of the John Rylands University Library, Manchester.

"To the Women of Great Britain and Ireland, on the Disuse of Slave Produce." London: circa 1828.

Todd, Dennis. "The Hairy Maid at the Harpsichord: Some Speculations on the Meaning of *Gulliver's Travels*." *Texas Studies in Literature and Language* 34, no. 2 (summer 1992): 239–83.

Tooker, Elizabeth. *An Ethnology of the Huron Indians, 1615–1649*. American Ethnology Bulletin 190 (1964). Washington, D.C.: Smithsonian Institution, 1964.

Torchiana, Donald. "Jonathan Swift, The Irish and the Yahoos: The Case Reconsidered." *Philological Quarterly* 54 (1975).

Trotter, David. *Circulation: Defoe, Dickens and the Economics of the Novel*. London: Macmillan, 1988.

Trumpener, Katie. *Bardic Nationalism: The Romantic Novel and the British Empire.* Princeton: Princeton University Press, 1997.

Turley, David. *The Culture of English Antislavery.* London: Routledge, 1991.

Ty, Eleanor. *Unsex'd Revolutionaries: Five Women Novelists of the 1790s.* Toronto: University of Toronto Press, 1993.

Uphaus, Robert W. "Jane Austen and Female Reading." *Studies in the Novel* 19, no. 3 (fall 1987): 334–45.

Vickery, Amanda. "Golden Age to Separate Spheres? A Review of the Categories and Chronology of English Women's History." *Historical Journal* 36 (1993): 383–414.

Wallerstein, Immanuel. *The Modern World System (I): Capitalist Agriculture and the Origins of the World Economy in the Sixteenth Century.* New York: The Academic Press, 1974.

Walvin, James. *Black Ivory: A History of British Slavery.* London: Fontana, 1992.

———. "The Rise of British Popular Sentiment for Abolition." In *Anti-Slavery, Religion and Reform: Essays in Memory of Roger Anstey,* ed. Christine Bolt and Seymour Drescher, pp. 149–63. Folkestone, Kent, England: Wm. Dawson & Sons, 1980.

Ware, Vron. *Beyond the Pale: White Women, Racism and History.* London: Verso, 1992.

Weatherill, Lorna. "A Possession of One's Own: Women and Consumer Behavior, 1660–1740." *Journal of British Studies* 25, no. 2 (1986): 131–57.

Weems, Robert E. Jr. "African-American Consumer Boycotts During the Civil Rights Era." *The Western Journal of Black Studies* 19, no. 1 (spring 1995): 72–79.

Weinreb, Ben, and Hibbert, Charles, eds. *The London Encyclopaedia.* Bethesda, Md.: Adler and Adler, 1983.

Wesley, John. "A Letter to a Friend, Concerning Tea." London: 1758.

"West-Indian Sketches, drawn from authentic sources." No. V: "Anecdotes, tending to elucidate the nature of our colonial bondage." Section III: "The effects produced by slavery on the character of white women." London: 1816.

*Westminster Review* (April–December 1887). Volume 128.

"What does your sugar cost?: A cottage conversation on the subject of British negro slavery." London: 1826. Quoted by permission of the John Rylands University Library, Manchester.

Williams, Eric. *Capitalism and Slavery.* Chapel Hill: University of North Carolina Press, 1944.

Williams, Raymond. *Keywords: A Vocabulary of Culture and Society.* Glasgow: Fontana, 1976.

Wilson, Kathleen. *The Sense of the People: Politics, Culture and Imperialism in England, 1715–1785.* Cambridge: Cambridge University Press, 1995.

Wittkowsky, George. "Swift's Modest Proposal: The Biography of an Early Georgian Pamphlet." *Journal of the History of Ideas* 4, no. 4 (January 1943): 75–104.

Wollstonecraft, Mary. "A Vindication of the Rights of Men" (1792). In Janet Todd, ed., *A Wollstonecraft Anthology,* pp. 64–84. Cambridge: Polity, 1989.

———. *Vindication of the Rights of Woman.* Harmondsworth, Middlesex: Penguin Books, 1975: Rpt. 1985.

Yellin, Jean Fagan. *Women and Sisters: The Antislavery Feminists in American Culture.* New Haven, Conn.: Yale University Press, 1989.

Young, Alfred F. "The Women of Boston: 'Persons of Consequence' in the Making of the American Revolution, 1765–76." In *Women and Politics in the Age of the Democratic Revolution,* ed. Harriet B. Applewhite and Darline G. Levy, pp. 181–227. Ann Arbor: The University of Michigan Press, 1990.

Zaret, David. "Religion, Science and Printing in the Public Sphere in Seventeenth-Century England." In *Habermas and the Public Sphere,* ed. Craig Calhoun, pp. 212–36. Cambridge, Mass.: MIT Press, 1992.

Zomchick, John P. "Social Class, Character and Narrative Strategy in *Humphry Clinker." Eighteenth-Century Life* 10, no. 3 (October 1986): 172–85.

# Index

Abolition movement. *See* Antislavery movement

Abstention movements: and cannibalism affect, 14–15; colonialism/consumerism connection of, 1–2, 8–9, 13–16, 23, 47–48; ethical dimension of, 35–37, 41–42, 114–15; free-market dependency of, 18, 42–43, 212nn62,63; individual consumer focus of, 23, 37, 39, 189; political efficacy of, 32–34, 45–46, 127–28, 210n29; politically excluded participants in, 3–4, 44; public sphere of, 2–3, 207n3; racialized discourse of, 16–17, 23–24; sentimentalism of, 10–11, 34–35, 124–27, 159, 188–89; against sugar, 37–39, 111–13, 210–11n43, 211n48; against tea, 25–28, 32–34, 35–36, 210n29; twentieth century, 189–92, 229n10. *See also* Consumer choice

Act of Explanation (1665), 53, 213n10

"An Address to her Royal Highness the Duchess of York, against the use of sugar" (pamphlet), 38, 124

"An address to the People of Great Britain, on the utility of refraining from the use of West India Sugar and Rum" (Fox), 38, 114

*The Adventures of Roderick Random* (Smollett), 97–98, 220n34

African American abstention movements, 189

Agnew, Jean-Christophe, 210n29

Alexander, Ziggi, 225n56

Algonquin torture ritual, 86–87

Allen, William, 126, 211n55

Alliston, April, 227n30

American colonies. *See* North American colonies

American Revolution, 13, 107

Anderson, Benedict, 132, 135

Anglo-Irish: as cannibalistic consumers, 75–77, 78; as invisible, 79; status concerns of, 65, 71, 215n38

Anne, Queen, 54

Anstey, Christopher, 95

"An Answer to the Craftsman" (Swift), 72, 74, 218n80

Antislavery discourse: anonymous female authors of, 157; bodily pollution fears of, 113, 118–21, 122, 161; circumscribed domesticity of, 113–14, 149–51; on degraded female character, 177–78, 179, 228n48; ethical concerns of, 36–37, 41–42, 114–15; of female slave Prince, 152–55, 157–58, 225nn56–59; feminine moral authority of, 7, 19–20, 123–24, 138–40; of former slaves, 108–9; ladies' dissemination of, 130–31, 135, 141–43, 148–49; literalized images of, 16, 17–18, 119–21, 128–29; literary devices used in, 145–47; metaphorical urgings of, 121–22, 222–23n38; printing's impact on, 132, 192–93; privileging of consumer in, 22–23, 40–41, 42–44, 209n2; on production/consumption linkage, 37–38, 40–41, 114–15; racialized rendering of, 16–17, 23–24, 198–200, 201–2; sentimental reading in, 130–31, 132–34, 143–45; of transgressive female writers, 182–84, 228–29n60. *See also* Reading practices

Antislavery movement: cultural racism of, 193; female virtue's role in, 19–20, 110, 123–27, 128–29; feminist intersection with, 5–6, 147–49, 151; and free-market capitalism, 42–43, 46–47, 113–14, 195–96, 212nn62,63, 230n24; laboring classes in, 47, 151; literary/political juxtaposition in, 3–4, 131–35, 141–44; politically excluded participants in, 3–4, 44; reconfigured domestic boundaries of, 113–14, 120–21, 129, 148–49; scholarship on, 5–7, 46–47; sugar-abstention campaign of, 37–39, 111–13, 210–11n43. *See also* Antislavery discourse; Ladies' antislavery societies

"Apology for Ladies' Anti-Slavery Associations" (Heyrick), 138

"Appeal to the Christian Women of Sheffield," 139, 143

"Appeal to the Hearts and Consciences of British Women," 128, 138–39

Armstrong, Nancy, 7, 123

Assam (British colonial territory), 29

Atlantic Ocean (image), 12–13

Austen, Jane, 167

Axtell, James, 85–86

Barash, Carol, 227n31

Bath (*Humphry Clinker*): commercial metaphor of, 93; corporeal contamination at, 95–97, 98, 101–2, 220n33; randomness at, 94–95

"Baubles of Britain: The American and Consumer Revolutions of the Eighteenth Century" (Breen), 9

Beckett, J. C., 216n57

*Beloved* (Morrison), 201, 230n37

Billington, Louis, 148

Billington, Rosamund, 148

Biological determinism, 193–94

Birmingham Female Society for the Relief of British Negro Slaves, 141

Birmingham Ladies' Society for the Relief of Negro Slaves, 158

*The Birth of a Consumer Society: The Commercialization of Eighteenth-Century England* (McKendrick, Brewer, and Plumb), 8, 24

Blackburn, Robin, 212n63

Blake, William, 199

Blood: commercial metaphor of, 93, 112; of slaves, contamination from, 118–21, 122, 161; sugar's association with, 117–18

Bodily fluids. *See* Fluidity images

Bohls, Elizabeth, 228n41

96–98, 220nn33–35; domestic site
of, 26; emulations's impact on,
24–25, 44–45; luxury's destabiliza-
tion of, 92–96, 98–99; reading's
impact on, 224n17; role of, for
female abolitionists, 6; as scientifi-
cally determined, 194
Colden, Cadwallader, 85, 87,
219–20n23
Coleridge, Samuel Taylor, 118, 121,
124–25, 132–33
Colley, Linda, 13
Colonial capital: and class destabi-
lization, 92–95, 98–99; corporeal
contamination from, 96–98; fluidity images of, 93
Colonial commodities: fetishization
of, 47–48, 54–55; mass consumption of, 8, 29–31, 209n22; mutation
of objects into, 55–56; naturalized
reactions to, 14–15; physical alter-
ation from, 27–28, 209n12; pro-
ducer-consumer connection of,
15–17, 24, 25; as threat to national
identity, 12–14, 82, 83–85. See also
Commodified human bodies
Colonialism: and cannibalism, 14–15,
78, 222n23; and commodification
of bodies, 57–59, 61–63; consumerism's connection to, 1–2,
8–9, 13–16, 23, 47–48; female sub-
ject/objects of, 105–6;
femininity/consumption linkage
in, 9–10; and racism, 64, 214n30;
reconfigured as dangerous, 12–13;
social disruption tied to, 97–98;
transculturation process of, 219n10
Commodified human bodies: corporeal contamination from, 97–98,

117–22; cultural exchange of, 56,
57–60; feminized as disgusting,
60–61, 214n27; mercantilist ideal
of, 73–75, 217n74, 218n80; portabil-
ity of, 90; racial difference of, 64,
214n30; of Scottish, 100–101; Swift's
consumerist solution to, 75–78,
218n84; as useful objects, 63
Commodities. See Colonial commodities
Consumer choice: abstention's negative manifestation of, 18, 23, 43–44,
45, 65–68; aligned with sentimentalism, 10–11, 34–35, 126–27, 159,
188–89; commodity culture's
reliance on, 93, 100, 106–7; ethical
dimension of, 35–37, 41–42, 114–15,
188–90; in globalized economy,
191–92; and individual identity,
34–35; political dimension of, 22,
31–32, 43–44, 127–28; production
subordinated to, 22–23, 40–41,
42–43; Swift's formulation of,
31–32, 75–77. See also Abstention
movements; Individual consumers
Consumerism: and class destabiliza-
tion, 25–27, 44–45, 82, 83–84,
101–2, 209n6; colonialism's connection to, 1–2, 8–9, 13–16, 47–48;
emulation element of, 24–25; and
oral consumption, 28, 76, 84–85,
100; reconfigured female practices
of, 9–11, 19–20, 127, 133, 135, 147.
See also Consumer choice;
Individual consumers
Contaminated food: from blood of
slaves, 118–21, 122, 161; female
responsibility for, 103–5; nutritional ideal versus, 102–3; Scottish

defined, 219n10; of former slaves,
107–9; and oral consumption anxi-
eties, 84–85, 106–7; survival-suffer-
ing contradiction of, 86–87
Treaty of Utrecht (1713), 4, 11, 80
*Tristram Shandy* (Sterne), 3
Trumpener, Katie, 91, 100
Truth, Sojourner, 196–97
Turley, David, 132
Ty, Eleanor, 227n35
Tyrone's Rebellion, 77

Ulster rebellions, 49

Value: colonial power's imposition
of, 66–68; of commodified bodies,
73–75, 217n74, 218n80; food/labor
gauge of, 115–16; intercultural
inequities of, 19, 51–52, 54–55,
57–58, 62–63; mutation of, into
commodity status, 55–56
Vickery, Amanda, 137
Victoria, Queen, 148, 149
"Village Politics" (More), 212n56
"Vindication of the Rights of Men"
(Wollstonecraft), 179
*Vindication of the Rights of Woman*
(Wollstonecraft), 125
"A vindication of the use of sugar and
other products of the West India
islands" (pamphlet), 38–39
"Voting With Your Checkbook: What
Every Christian Should Know
About Boycotts" (Bruland), 189

Walpole, Sir Robert, 54
Walvin, James, 210–11n43
*Wanderings of Warwick* (Smith), 160,
180–81
War of Jenkins' Ear, 98, 220n35

War of Spanish Succession, 4
*The Wealth of Nations* (Smith), 22–23
Wedgwood's ceramics, 127
Weinreb, Ben, 230n35
Wesley, John, 35–36
West India Company, 29
West Indian slaves. *See* Slaves
*Westminster Review*, 148, 149
"What does your sugar cost" (pam-
phlet), 122
Wheatley, Phillis, 152, 199
Wilberforce, William, 137, 211nn48,55
William of Orange, 65
Williams, Eric, 5, 46, 212n62
Williams, Raymond, 209n2
Wilson, Kathleen, 107, 209n12
"Windsor Forest" (Pope), 12
Wittkowsky, George, 73, 74
Wollstonecraft, Mary, 125–26, 179
Women. *See* Middle-class women
*Women Against Slavery: The British
Campaigns* (Midgley), 5
Women slaves. *See* Slave women
Wood, William, 66
Wood's halfpence: consumer strategy
against, 66–68, 200; patent for,
65–66; repeal of, 70, 76; and
Swift's writings, 53, 212–13n5,
213n7, 215n31
Woolen manufacture, 55–56, 65
Woolman, John, 36–37, 42

Yahoos (*Gulliver's Travels*), 52, 62, 63,
64, 71, 72, 75, 76, 80, 214n30

Sophia Lee's The Recess.

Matilda kidnapped to Jamaica where she and Anana
a black woman, cooperate in the nurture of her child
170   Mary. Anana the wealthy mistress of the governor, who
has died, kills herself and leaves all her wealth to Matilda
So instead of traditional domesticity we get an allegory
of exploited black bodies and white independence if
women.

Charlotte Smith Letter of a Solitary Wanderer
171   describing the characteristics of a creole face: small
eye, prominent brow, and something particular in
the tone of the cheek.
forced marriage = chattel slavery — a novel, however,
that establishes segregated domesticity.

John Stanart talking of the metamorphosis of white
women under the influence of slavery.
176   An Account of Jamaica and its Inhabitants 160-2
                    1808
they "contract harsh and domineering ideas with respect
to slaves — ideas ill-suited to the softness and humanity
of the female mind" "the tender heart of a lovely woman
should weep at a tale of distress, rather than inflict pain."
as Sussman points out, the tale, not the scene the tale is based on
She takes another example from Mary
Wollstonecraft in the V. of the R. of Men : the female
Sulla. + Charlotte S's
The Wanderings of Warwick (1794) 52.

180   tender heroine found supervising the torture of a 10 yr
old girl
the qu. is whether this is a discontinuity between sympathy
and cruelty, or only its other side.

183   C. Smith deprived of a Barbadian inheritance takes to her pen
to give the executors of her father-in-law "a public flogging.
chained to her desk like a slave to her oar" — Cowper

186   the absence of the abolitionist sympathiser from the scene
she observed was crucial. — what about the
male counterpart?

14 national identity compromised by the ingestion of colonial material within domestic space, so that a feeling for the victims of colonial oppression coincides with the elaboration of domestic ideology.

30 The role of sympathy — Ignatius Sancho

33 opp. of Client: That the private element of the public sphere is consolidated in the latter [so as the privacy of the sentimental female reader — with the exception of abolitionist who "construct there foundational relationships between private and public, sentiment and reason."

36 citing Clare Midgely to the effect that this was "the first large-scale political campaign by middle-class women," demonstrating "interconnection between domestic and political life, and between public and private activities."
See also Amanda Vickery.

39 an anon. pamphleteer on the qualification of women for anti-slavery agitation:
"their strong feelings and quick sensibilities, especially qualify her, not only to sympathize with suffering, but also to plead for the oppressed."

47 how Sterne's voyeurism of slavery provides the basis of an active female role of standing up for slaves

53 salt in Mary Prince: what she is born to produce, what comes into her eyes as she remembers she described that labour; mirrored in the tears of the dryer of her readers.

64 pro- and anti-abolitionists both extending an ideal of sympathetic womanhood: the woman freed by freedom, the woman who must be protected from and black life, whose virtue is exemplary of the order of settler/creole life acting as a barrier to interracial sex and forcing to separate and unequal communities.

1: the crucial role of commodity fetishism in colonial ideology: there is a mixture,

2 private issues becoming public issues misunderstands Habermas,

3 Laurence Sterne

6 How feminism cuts across class + racial lines by grouping women with other oppression: however, the aspect of "good causes" int. abolition such as missionary work which provides the ideological vehicle of colonised middle and upper middle women are to the fore — so class level re-form,

7 and is this domestic sphere a public sphere?

9 women central to the consumer revolution, but also the objects of violence and ?? — Laura Brown,

13 doubts about slavery may have intersected with doubts about luxury, but tobacco (N. Amer) and sugar (Caribbean) scarcely constitute a tide of luxury — indeed the Navigation Acts prevented items of luxury from being exported from the colonies. Soon tea from Tobacco and sugar as the dregs of a working class. Mintz and Dunn need more attention, SEE 30

17 acquired moral conscience of consumer nevertheless dehumanises slave labour!
— identifying disquiet and sentiment as the surplus affect by which this is accomplished
in utopian vision / racist revulsion
(I wonder whether this is not a problem of sympathy in general
18 these are the limits of discourse at the colonial periphery

20 female anti-slavery societies aiming to realign sentiment and politics

23 abstention provides a possibility of social act to the nonfrench
40 also makes consumer the master spring of world trade
42 the fetishistic side of abstention — alter your relation to a commodity and then you alter your relation to the human producer
c56 Gulliver brings home sorrow that he converts into canned
—7 to himself a curiosity for sale.
61 you can't have it both ways: the goblet made of a coin is either pure currency or (to a sign of) something else: but
63 it can't be both
64 he uses human but to leave a place he would rather remain in; not to develop new markets. there are some useful distinction